CAMBRIDGE LIBRARY COLLECTION

Books of enduring scholarly value

Classics

From the Renaissance to the nineteenth century, Latin and Greek were
compulsory subjects in almost all European universities, and most early
modern scholars published their research and conducted international
correspondence in Latin. Latin had continued in use in Western Europe long
after the fall of the Roman empire as the lingua franca of the educated classes
and of law, diplomacy, religion and university teaching. The flight of Greek
scholars to the West after the fall of Constantinople in 1453 gave impetus
to the study of ancient Greek literature and the Greek New Testament.
Eventually, just as nineteenth-century reforms of university curricula were
beginning to erode this ascendancy, developments in textual criticism and
linguistic analysis, and new ways of studying ancient societies, especially
archaeology, led to renewed enthusiasm for the Classics. This collection
offers works of criticism, interpretation and synthesis by the outstanding
scholars of the nineteenth century.

Practical Introduction to Greek Prose Composition

Thomas Kerchever Arnold's *Practical Introduction to Greek Prose Composition*
first appeared in 1838 and was reprinted in several editions due to popular
demand, being adopted as a textbook in leading public schools. Ordained as
a priest in 1827 after graduating from Trinity College, Cambridge in 1821,
Arnold had studied both theology and classics, and wrote prolifically on both
subjects. His first school textbook was published in 1836 and others followed
steadily until his death in 1853. One of the chief merits of Arnold's classical
publications was his use of contemporary works German scholarship, to
which he readily acknowledged his debt. He produced, alongside Latin
and Greek textbooks, grammars of English, French, German, Italian, and
Hebrew, and editions of many Greek and Latin authors. This introduction
was designed to provide students with the basic tools with which to construct
sentences and includes exercises on syntax and a vocabulary index.

Cambridge University Press has long been a pioneer in the reissuing of out-of-print titles from its own backlist, producing digital reprints of books that are still sought after by scholars and students but could not be reprinted economically using traditional technology. The Cambridge Library Collection extends this activity to a wider range of books which are still of importance to researchers and professionals, either for the source material they contain, or as landmarks in the history of their academic discipline.

Drawing from the world-renowned collections in the Cambridge University Library, and guided by the advice of experts in each subject area, Cambridge University Press is using state-of-the-art scanning machines in its own Printing House to capture the content of each book selected for inclusion. The files are processed to give a consistently clear, crisp image, and the books finished to the high quality standard for which the Press is recognised around the world. The latest print-on-demand technology ensures that the books will remain available indefinitely, and that orders for single or multiple copies can quickly be supplied.

The Cambridge Library Collection will bring back to life books of enduring scholarly value (including out-of-copyright works originally issued by other publishers) across a wide range of disciplines in the humanities and social sciences and in science and technology.

Practical Introduction
to Greek Prose
Composition

THOMAS KERCHEVER ARNOLD

CAMBRIDGE
UNIVERSITY PRESS

CAMBRIDGE UNIVERSITY PRESS

Cambridge, New York, Melbourne, Madrid, Cape Town, Singapore,
São Paolo, Delhi, Dubai, Tokyo

Published in the United States of America by Cambridge University Press, New York

www.cambridge.org
Information on this title: www.cambridge.org/9781108011426

© in this compilation Cambridge University Press 2009

This edition first published 1843
This digitally printed version 2009

ISBN 978-1-108-01142-6 Paperback

A

PRACTICAL INTRODUCTION

TO

GREEK PROSE COMPOSITION.

BY

THOMAS KERCHEVER ARNOLD, M.A.

RECTOR OF LYNDON,

AND LATE FELLOW OF TRINITY COLLEGE, CAMBRIDGE.

FIFTH EDITION.

LONDON:

PRINTED FOR J. G. F. & J. RIVINGTON,

ST. PAUL'S CHURCH YARD,

AND WATERLOO PLACE, PALL MALL.

1843.

PREFACE

(TO THE

FIRST EDITION).

THE plan of this Introduction requires some explanation. Its object is to enable the student, as soon as he can decline and conjugate with tolerable facility, to translate simple sentences after given examples and with given words; the principles trusted to being those of *imitation* and *very frequent repetition*. It is at once a Syntax, a Vocabulary, and an Exercise-book; the Syntax being in *substance* that of *Buttmann's* excellent School Grammar.

One object I have steadily kept in view, that of making the *general construction of sentences* of more importance than the *mere government of cases*, which is nearly all that most Exercise-books * pretend to teach. The Exercises are adapted for *vivâ voce* practice; but if the book is so used, they should by all means be written down afterwards. The Vocabularies, if possible, but at all events the Examples, should be committed to memory and carefully kept up.

---

* I beg to except Mr. Kenrick's Exercises, which, however, in my opinion, should be used *after* some work like the present.

It is due to Mr. *Ollendorff*, whose Introduction to German is, I see, about to appear* in English, to state that the publication of a work like the present was suggested to me by the advantage I myself derived from the use of his book. I had originally drawn it up *exactly* on his plan; but the probable expense of publication has deterred me, for the present, from publishing it in that shape †. The present work differs therefore from his, in requiring from the pupil a general acquaintance with the Accidence.

For the convenience of those who may wish to use the Syntax *as such*, I have added a complete set of Questions to the work.

T. K. A.

Lyndon,
May 24, 1838.

---

* The work alluded to is now published.

† The very great success of this work, and the similar one on " *Latin Prose Composition,*"—which are now used at all, or nearly all, our public schools,—has encouraged the author to send to press the more elementary Exercises here alluded to, under the title of a " Practical Introduction to Greek Accidence." T. K. A. [*Lyndon*, 1841.]

CONTENTS.

viii   CONTENTS.

EXPLANATION OF ABBREVIATIONS, &c.

B., K., M., R., T., denotes respectively the Greek Grammars of *Buttmann, Kühner, Matthiä, Rost,* and *Thiersch.* Kr. stands for *Krüger.*

But B., when followed by a *numerical* reference, refers to *Bishop Blomfield's Abridgment of Matthiä* (fifth edit.).

E. refers to the *Eton* Greek Grammar.

R., after a declinable word, stands for *root.* Thus, γόνυ, R. γόνατ, means, that the *regular* terminations are to be added to γόνατ.

V. refers to Vömel's Synonymisches Wörterbuch.

A Greek letter added after a verb, shows that the *simpler root* (as it appears, for instance, in *aor.* 2.) ends in that letter.

The *superior* references are to the Table of Differences.

GREEK EXERCISES.

§ 1. *On the Tenses.—The Article.*

1. THE Imperfect, besides the usual meaning of that tense, is used to express *continued* or *repeated actions*, taking place in past time.

    2. The Aorists express actions *completed* in past time.

> Hence the Aorist is used of *momentary* and *single* actions ; the Imperfect, of *continued* and *repeated* ones.
>
> The dog *bit* him (*aor.*) : the dog *howled* all night (*imperf.*).
>
> Obs. The Imperfect (of *habitual* actions) is often construed by ' *used to,*' &c.

    3. The Perfect expresses actions *continued* or *remaining in their effects* up to the present time.

    a) Hence the *aor.* is nearly our *perfect indefinite* (the perf. formed by *inflection*) : the *perf.* our *perfect definite* (or perfect with ' *have* ').

    b) But when the connexion of the past with the present is obvious from the context, the aorist may be used for the perfect ; or, in a narrative, for the pluperfect.

    c) It is only when a particular stress is to be laid on the time of the occurrence, that the perfect or pluperf. *must* be used. All this is, however, greatly influenced by euphony.

    4. It is taken for granted that the pupil knows

> (1) That the verb agrees with its nominative case.
>
> (2) That every *adjective* word—whether adjective, participle, pronoun, or article—must agree with its substantive in *gender*, *number*, and *case*.
>
> (3) That the transitive verb is followed by the accusative, &c. &c.

5. *a.* τὸ τῆς ἀρετῆς κάλλος, *the beauty of virtue.*

   b. ὁ τὰ τῆς πόλεως πράγματα πράττων, he who transacts (*or*, manages) *the affairs of the state.*

6. (*a*) A governed genitive is often placed between an article and its noun.

In this way *two* and even *three* articles stand together.

7. (*b*) ὁ πράττων, (*the* person *doing* =) *he who does.*

Hence the *artic.* with a *participle* is equivalent to a personal or demonstrative pronoun with a relative sentence.

Thus,

   ὁ πράττων, *he who does.*
   τοῦ πράττοντος, *of him who does.*
   &c.

Pl. οἱ πράττοντες, *those who do.*
   τῶν πραττόντων, *of those who do.*
   &c.

8. VOCABULARY 1.

Virtue (ἀρετή). *Beauty* (κάλλος, n.). *City, state* (πόλις). *Thing,* or *affair* (πρᾶγμα [a]). *To do, transact, manage* (πράττω).
Wonder or *am surprised at, admire* (θαυμάζω, with *fut. mid.*—but aor. 1. *act.*). *Well* (εὖ). *Ill* (κακῶς). *Often, frequently* (πολλάκις). *Citizen* (πολίτης, ῐ,[b]). *Judge* (κριτής).
πράττω, *do,* has also the *intransit.* meaning of our *to be doing well* or *ill :* i. e. to be *prosperous* or *unfortunate.* In this sense it has the *perf.* 2. πέπραγα. The α is long throughout.

Exercise 1.

9. I admire the beauty of the city. The citizens are doing well. I have often admired the beauty of the cities. The Judge often admired the beauty of virtue. I admire those who transact (7) the affairs of the state. He transacts the affairs

Nouns in μα from *verbs* generally denote the *thing produced by the act.* They may be compared with the *pass.* participle (τὸ πεπραγμένον).

[b] Nouns in της of the first *decl.* from *verbs,* denote the *male doer of the action :* those from *substantives* denote a *person* standing in any near relation to what is denoted by the substantive : as πολίτης from πόλις. Those in ιτης from *subst.* have the ι long. Κριτής is from κρίνω.

of the state ill. The citizens are doing ill. I have often admired the virtue of the citizen. The citizens admire the virtue of the Judge.

---

§ 2. *The Article continued.*

10. *a.* ὁ Σωκράτης, *Socrates;* αἱ ᾿Αθῆναι, *Athens.*

    b. Σωκράτης ὁ φιλόσοφος, *Socrates the Philosopher.*

    c. ἵππος ἔτεκε λαγών, *a mare brought forth a hare.*

    d. γυνή τις ὄρνιν εἶχεν, *a woman* (or, *a certain woman*) *had a hen.*

    e. ἡ κόρη ἐγένετο ἀσκός* [c], *the girl became* (or, *was turned into*) *a leather bottle.*

11. (*a*) Proper names often take the article, if they are the names of persons *well known.*

> Hence the names of *Deities, Heroes,* &c. generally take the article; and the names of persons *recently mentioned.*

12. (*b*) But if the proper name is followed by a *description* which has the article, the proper name is without the article, unless it is to be expressed *emphatically,* as being *well-known,* or as having been *previously mentioned* [d].

13 (*c*) The Greek has no indefinite article (our '*a*').

(*d*) Our '*a*' should be translated by τίς, when a *particular* person or thing is meant, though not named : in other words, wherever we might substitute '*a certain*' for '*a.*'

---

[c] Or, ἀσκὸς ἐγένετο ἡ κόρη. So, Θεὸς ἦν ὁ Λόγος, *the Word was God.* This arises from the nature of a proposition. We usually assert of a particular thing that it is *included*, as *an* individual, in a particular class ; not that it is the *whole* of that class.

[d] Kr. who quotes *Bacch.* 1314 : νῦν ἐκ δόμων ἄτιμος ἐκβεβλήσομαι | ὁ Κάδμος ὁ μέγας.

14. (e) The *subject* ᵉ generally has the article, the *predicate* not.

15. VOCABULARY 2.

Socrates (Σωκράτης ᶠ). *Athens* ('Αθῆναι). *Philosopher* (φιλόσοφος). *Horse, mare* (ἵππος). *Hare* (λᾰγώς, acc. λαγών and λαγώ). *Woman* (γύνη. R. γυναικ. V. γύναι). *Hen* (ὄρνις ᵍ). *Water* (ὕδωρ, n. R. ὕδατ). *Wine* (οἶνος ʰ). *Boy, son* (παῖς, G. παιδός). *To have* (ἔχω ⁱ). *To bring forth,* or, of birds, *to lay* (τίκτω ᵏ, τεκ). *Damsel* or *maiden* (κόρη). *Leather bottle* (ἀσκός). *Become* (γίγνομαι ˡ, γεν). *An egg* (ὠόν). *Three* (τρεῖς, τρία, B. 34. E. 30).

Exercise 2.

16. I admire the beauty of the hen. *A* (*d*) boy had a hare. The water was turned into wine (*e*). The hen laid three eggs. A certain damsel had three hens. I admire the virtue of the maiden. The hare was turned into a horse. The boy admires the beauty of Athens. The citizens admire the beauty of the woman. I admire *those who transact* ¹ the affairs of Athens. I have often admired the virtue of Socrates. I admire Socrates the philosopher. The woman shall have a hen. The water has been turned into wine. A certain judge has three hens.

ᵉ That is, the *nominative before the verb.* See note ᶜ, page 3.

ᶠ Σωκράτης, G. ους, D. ει, &c. A. Σωκράτη (Plato), Σωκράτην (Xenoph.), V. Σώκρατες.

ᵍ ' *Bird,*' but in *Att.* generally *cock, hen ;* just as we use *fowl.* G. ὄρνιθος, &c. A. α and ν. *Plur.* reg., but also ὄρνεις, G. ὀρνέων, D. ὄρνῑσι(ν) only, Acc. ὄρνεις (ὄρνῑς).

ʰ οἶνος, with the *digamma* Fοῖνος, *vinum.* So ὠόν, ὠϜόν, *ovum.*

ⁱ ἔχω, ἕξω and σχήσω, ἔσχηκα. Imperf. εἶχον: aor. ἔσχον, ἐσχέθην. [ἔσχον, σχές (σχέ in compounds), σχοίην, σχῶ, σχεῖν, σχών.]

ᵏ τίκτω, (τέξω) τέξομαι, τέτοκα, ἔτεκον, ἐτεκόμην.

ˡ γίγνομαι, γενήσομαι, γεγένημαι and γέγονα, ἐγενόμην. All *intrans.* for am born ; become. ἐγενόμην and γέγονα also serve for preterites of the verb ' *to be.*' When γέγονα may be construed ' *I am,*' it means, ' *I am by birth,*' or ' *have become.*' B.

γείνομαι, *am born,* poet.: aor. ἐγεινάμην, *begot, bore* (in *prose* as well as *poetry*).

§ 3. Article continued.

17. *a.* ὁ σὸς δοῦλος, *your slave.* *b.* ἀλγῶ τὴν κεφαλήν (I am pained as to *the* head =) *I have a pain in* my *head.* *c.* ἥδετο ἐπὶ πλουσίοις τοῖς πολίταις, *he rejoiced* (or *was glad*) *when the citizens were wealthy* (or, *that the citizens were wealthy*). *d.* ὁ ἐμὸς πατὴρ καὶ ὁ τοῦ φίλου, *my father and my friend's* (literally, *my father and the of my friend*).

18. (*b*) *My, your, his,* &c. are to be translated by the article, when it is quite obvious *whose* the thing in question is.

Whenever there is any opposition (as, when *mine* is opposed to *yours* or any other person's) the pronouns must be used.

19. (*c*) When an *adj. without the article* stands *before* the article of the substantive, the thing spoken of is not distinguished from any thing else, but *from itself* under other circumstances [m].

20. VOCABULARY 3.

Slave (δοῦλος). *To feel* or *suffer pain; to be pained* at (ἀλγέω). *Head* (κεφαλή). *To rejoice, be glad,* or *take pleasure in* (ἥδομαι, dat.). *Wealthy, rich* (πλούσιος [n]). *Father* (πατήρ [o]). *Friend* (φίλος). *Thine, thy* (σός). *Mine, my* (ἐμός). *Jaw* (γνάθος, f.). *Tooth* (ὀδούς, G. ὀδόντος, m.). *Ear* (οὖς, ὠτός, n.). *Foot* (πούς, ποδός, m.). *Hand* (χείρ, χειρός, f. but R. χερ for G. D. *dual*, and D. *plur.*). *Knee* (γόνυ, n. R. γόνατ). *Brother* (ἀδελφός). *Daughter* (θυγάτηρ [o]). *Mother* (μήτηρ [o]). *Wise, clever* (σοφός). *Happy* (εὐδαίμων). *To love* (φιλέω). *To be vexed at* (ἄχθομαι, ἔσομαι, ἠχθέσθην, dat.). *Beautiful* (καλός). *Bad* (κακός).

---

[m] Thus in the example it is not, ' *rich citizens*,' as opposed to *other* citizens ; but ' he rejoiced in *their being rich* ; or in *the wealth of* . . .' &c.

[n] Adjectives in ιος denote what *belongs to, concerns,* or *comes from* what the root expresses. They are formed from *substantives,* and sometimes from other adjectives in ος. When the root ends in τ it is sometimes changed into σ: πλοῦτος, *wealth,* πλούσιος.

[o] Πατήρ, μήτηρ, θυγάτηρ, γαστήρ, throw away ε in G. and D. *sing.* and D. *pl.* They have V. ερ, and insert ά before σι in D. *pl.*

Obs. 1. *ἥδεσθαι and ἄχθεσθαι are more commonly followed by the* dat.[p] (without a prepos.) *except in the construction explained in* 19, *c.*

Obs. 2. '*That*,' when it stands for a subst. before expressed, is to be translated by the article. (See 17, *d.*)

Exercise 3.

21. The mother of the beautiful daughter has a pain in her jaws. I am glad that my brothers are happy[5]. The father rejoiced in his son's being wise (*c*). My friend and my brother's (*d*). I often have a pain in my foot. My mother was suffering from a pain in her hands (*b*). I am vexed that the bad are wealthy (*c*). The daughter loves *her* mother. My slave loves my brother's. I admire your virtue and *that* of your friend. The beautiful damsel shall be turned into a horse. I am pleased with *those who transact*[1] the affairs of the state. He was vexed that the citizens were rich. I take pleasure in my daughter's being beautiful (*c*).

---

§ 4. *Article continued.*

22. *a.* ἡ τοῦ ποιητοῦ σοφία[q], or ἡ σοφία ἡ τοῦ ποιητοῦ, *the wisdom* (cleverness, &c.) *of the poet.* ἡ καλὴ κεφαλή, or ἡ κεφαλὴ ἡ καλή[r], *the beautiful head.* *b.* Ἀλέξανδρος ὁ Φιλίππου, *Alexander the son of* Philip (υἱός, *son*, understood). ὁ Σωφρονίσκου, *the son of Sophroniscus.* *c.* εἰς τὴν Φιλίππου, *into Philip's* country (χώραν, *country*, understood). *d.*

---

[p] Ἄχθομαι, and in the poets ἥδομαι, are also followed by the *acc.*, especially of neut. pronouns.

[q] Substantives in ῐᾰ are derived from *adj.*, and express the *abstract* notion of the *adj.*

The other positions of the *gen.* are frequently met with: Μηδείης τὴν ἁρπαγήν. Herod. i. 3. ἡ ἀναχώρησις τῶν Ἀθηναίων. Thuc. i. 12. For a *partitive* gen. these are the only correct positions.

[r] The latter position gives emphasis to the adjective or dependent gen.

τὰ τῆς πόλεως, the affairs *of the state* (πράγματα understood). τὰ ἐμά, *my* affairs, *my* property. οἱ ἐν ἄστει, the people *in the city*, those *in the city*. οἱ σὺν τῷ βασιλεῖ, those *with the king*. 23. (*d*) A *noun* or *participle* is often understood, so that the *article* stands alone.

24. VOCABULARY 4.

Poet (ποιητής). Wisdom, cleverness (σοφία). Alexander ('Αλέξανδρος). Philip (Φίλιππος). Sophroniscus (Σωφρονίσκος). Son (υἱός). Country (χώρα). Our (ἡμέτερος). Yours (ὑμέτερος). March an army, when spoken of its general (ἐλαύνω [s]). March of the army, and of a person *undertaking an expedition ;* also *journey, set out, &c.* (πορεύομαι, with *aor.* 1. *pass.* ; ἐπί τινα, against a person). Persian (Πέρσης, ου). Scythian (Σκύθης, ου). Cyrus (Κῦρος). King (βασιλεύς). Madness (μανία [t]). People (δῆμος). Army (στράτευμα [u], n.). Geometer (γεωμέτρης, ου). With (σύν, dat.). City, town (ἄστυ [v], n.).

Exercise 4.

25. I admire the wisdom of the geometer. *The people in the city* admire the beautiful mother of the damsel. The people in the city admire the very beautiful daughter of the very beautiful mother. The king marches *into the country* of the Scythians. The army of the Persians marches into the country of the Scythians. Cyrus marches against the king of the Persians. The son of Sophroniscus is astonished at the madness of the people. The poet admires *those who manage* [1] the affairs of the state. I rejoice in the king's being wealthy [5]. I

---

[s] ἐλαύνω, ἐλάσω (ἄ), ἐλήλακα, ἐλήλαμαι, ἠλάθην. Att. fut. ἐλῶ, ᾷς, ᾷ, &c. infin. ἐλᾷν. It is *trans.* (*drive, urge on*), but used as *intrans.* (*march, ride*), by omission of *acc.*

[t] This word was formed from an *adj.* μανός, *mad*, which is quoted by Suidas. See 22, q.

[u] στρατός, στρατιά, *army ;* στρατεία, *expedition.* στράτευμα has both meanings; the latter often in Herodotus.

[v] ἄστυ never means *the state*, as πόλις does. It is often used of an *old* or *sacred* part of a πόλις, as *we* speak of ' *the City*,' as a part of London.

am vexed when the bad are wealthy. The people in the
city (d) admire the son of Philip. The king has the tooth-
ache (*i. e.* suffers pain in his teeth⁴). The clever geometer has
a pain in his knees. A certain poet had a very beautiful horse.
Those with the king will march against *the son of Philip.*

§ 5. *Article continued.*

26. οἱ πάλαιᵂ, the *long ago* men = *the men of old.* ὁ
μεταξὺ χρόνος, the *between* time = *the intermediate time.*
ἡ αὔριον, adv. (ἡμέρα, *day,* understood), *the morrow, the next
day.*

27. An adverb with the Article is equivalent to an adjective.

28. VOCABULARY 5.

> *Long ago* (πάλαι). *Man* (ἄνθρωπος, *homo*). *Between* (μεταξύ). *To-
> morrow* (αὔριον, adv.). *Time* (χρόνος). *Near* (πέλας—πλησίον). *One's
> neighbour* (ὁ πλησίον). *Then* (τότε). *Now* (νῦν). *Here* (ἐνθάδε).
> *There* (ἐκεῖ). *Up, upwards* (ἄνωˣ). *Down, downwards* (κάτω). *Move*
> (κῑνέω). *Crocodile* (ὁ κροκόδειλος). *Both* (ἄμφω, ἀμφότερος; the latter
> often in the *plural; ἀμφότερα τὰ ὦτα, both his ears,* Xen.). *Life* (βίος).
> *This* (οὗτος, B. 38. W. 33).

Exercise 5.

[In doing the exercise, consider which of the adverbs *comes nearest* to
the meaning of the adjective or equivalent phrase.]

29. The men *of old* did this. They did this the next day
(*dat.*). The crocodile moves its *upper* jaw. The son of Sophroniscus has a pain ⁴ in both his ears. I am surprised at the
madness of the *Persians of old times.* I wonder at *the men of*

ᵂ So in English ' the *then* Mayor.'

ˣ Of countries, ἄνω is used of marching into the *interior ;* κάτω, of marching
down to the coast.

the present day ᵞ. I admire *the wise men of old.* They love *the present life.* We wonder at the madness of our neighbours. *The people there* ᶻ are astonished at the madness of those with the king. I am astonished at the cleverness of those who manage my affairs.

Exercise 6.

30. He had a pain (*imperf.*) in both his knees. The people here admire the son of Sophroniscus. The crocodile was turned into a hare (10, *e*). The people here admire my daughter and my brother's. The people there are doing well. I have often wondered at the wisdom of our *present* geometers. The crocodile lays eggs. The king of the Scythians has a pain in ᵗ his *lower* jaw.

§ 6.   *Article continued.*

31. *a.* ὁ ῥινόκερως τὴν δορὰν ἰσχυροτάτην ἔχει, *the rhino-
        ceros has a very strong hide.*

   b. φεύγωμεν τὰ αἰσχρά· διώκωμεν τὰ καλά, *let us fly
        from* what is base; *let us pursue* what is honorable.

   c. μὴ διώκωμεν τὰ αἰσχρά, *let us not pursue* what is base.

   d. τὸ ταχὺ λαλεῖν, talking *fast;* τοῦ ταχὺ λαλεῖν, *of*
        talking *fast,* &c.; τὸ πάντας κακῶς λέγειν, the
        speaking ill *of every body.*

   e. ἡ ἀρετή, *virtue;* ὁ χρυσός, *gold;* οἱ ἀγαθοί, *the good;*
        οἱ ἀετοί, *eagles.*

   f. τὸ τελευταῖον, *at last ;* τὸ ἀπὸ τοῦδε ᵃ, *henceforth.*

ᵞ The *now* men.

ᶻ People = *persons* must not be translated by δῆμος. *The people there,* οἱ ἐκεῖ.

ᵃ Literally, '*the from this*' (time).

31*. (*a*) To express that a person 'has *a* very beautiful head,' the Greeks said: 'has *the* head very beautiful ᵇ.'

32. (*b*) τὸ καλόν, is: '*the beautiful*ᶜ,' '*the honorable*,' in the *abstract ; beauty.* τὰ καλά, are: *beautiful* (or *honorable*) *things ; whatever things are beautiful ; what is beautiful ;* or simply, *beautiful things.*

[*Obs.* We learn from *b*, that the *first person plur.* of the *pres. subj.* is used in exhortations; and from *c*, that μή is used with it for '*not.*' See 108, 1.]

33. (*d*) The infinitive with the article becomes a substantive declinable throughout, and answering to the English '*participial substantive*' in —*ing*.

34. (*e*) *Abstract* nouns, and the *names of materials*, generally take the article. When a *whole class*, or *any* individual of that class, is meant, the noun, whether singular or plural, takes the article.

35. Vocabulary 6.

Rhinoceros (ῥινόκερως, G. ωτος). *Nose* (ῥίς, G. ῥινός, f. : plur. *nostrils*). *Horn* (κέρας, n. W. 20. B. p. 20). *Hide* (δορά ᵈ). *Strong* (ἰσχῦρός). *To fly from* (φεύγω). *Base, disgraceful* (αἰσχρός—αἰσχίων, αἴσχιστος). *To pursue* (διώκω *). *Fast, quick* (ταχύς ᵉ, neut. adj. = adv.). *Talk* (λαλέω). *Speak, say* (λέγω). *Speak ill of* (κακῶς λέγειν, acc.). *Speak well of* (εὖ λέγειν, acc.). *Treat ill, behave ill to* (κακῶς ποιεῖν, acc.). *Treat well, do kind offices to, confer benefits on* (εὖ ποιεῖν, acc.). *Elephant* (ἐλέφας, ντος, m.). *Stag* (ἔλαφος, m.). *Gold* (χρῦσός). *Good* (ἀγαθός—ἀμείνων, ἄριστος). *Eagle* (ἀετός).

διώκειν is also, *to prosecute ;* φεύγειν, *to be prosecuted :* διώκειν τινὰ φόνου, *to prosecute a man on a charge of murder ;* φεύγειν φόνου (understand δίκην, *cause, trial*), *to be tried for murder.*

ᵇ The article must not be used, unless it is *assumed* that the thing in question *has* the property, the object being only to describe of *what kind* it is. If the writer wished to *inform* us that the rhinoceros *had a hide*, which was moreover a *strong* one, he would *not* use the article. Thus of the crocodile : ἔχει δὲ καὶ ὄνυχας καρτερούς, *it also has* strong claws.

ᶜ Thus in English, "Burke on *the* Sublime and Beautiful."

ᵈ Nouns in α and η, from verbal roots, are generally oxytone. The abstract notion predominates in them (B.) ; the vowel of the root is often changed into *o*, as in perf. 2. (mid.) δέρω, *flay ;* δορά.

* The *fut. mid.* is the more common in Attic Greek.   ᵉ B. 33.

Exercise 7.

36. The elephant has *a* strong hide. The maiden has very beautiful hands. The stag has very beautiful horns [12]. The Persian's boys pursue *what is honorable.* Let us fly from those who pursue [1] *what is disgraceful.* Do not let us fly from *what is honorable.* Let us avoid (*fly from*) talking fast. Let us fly from the madness *of speaking ill of every body.* Let us do kind offices to our friends. The citizens *prosecute Philip on a charge of murder* [17]. Sophroniscus *was tried for murder* [17]. Let us henceforth pursue *the honorable.* Let us not treat our (18) slaves ill. He took pleasure in doing kind offices to the good (*Obs.* 1. *p.* 6). The Scythians admire the beauty of gold. The boy wonders at the horn of the rhinoceros.

---

§ 7.　*Article as demonstrative pronoun.　Pronouns.*

37. *a.* τὰ αὐτὰ τοὺς μὲν λυπεῖ, τοὺς δὲ τέρπει, *the same things pain* some *persons, but delight* others.

    b. λύκος ἀμνὸν ἐδίωκεν· ὁ δὲ εἰς ναὸν κατέφυγε [f], *a wolf was pursuing a lamb; and* (or *but* [g]) *it fled for refuge into a temple.*

    c. καὶ ὃς ἐξαπατηθεὶς διώκει ἀνὰ κράτος, *and he, being deceived, pursues at full speed* (literally, ' *at* or *with force* or *strength*').

    d. αὐτὸς ἔφη, *he* himself *said* (*it*). αὐτὸς ὁ δοῦλος, *or,* ὁ δοῦλος αὐτός, *the slave* himself: ὁ αὐτὸς

---

[f] καταφεύγω.

[g] δέ is not only *but,* but also *and,* and in Homer *for.* It is used where no other particle is required, to avoid having a proposition in the middle of a discourse *unconnected* with what goes before. It is often, therefore, omitted in translating into English.

δοῦλος, the same *slave*. μᾶλλον τοῦτο φοβοῦμαι ἢ τὸν θάνατον αὐτόν, *I fear this more than death itself.* ἔδωκεν αὐτοῖς τὸ πῦρ, *he gave* them *the fire.* αὐτὸν γὰρ εἶδον, *for I saw the man himself*: εἶδον γὰρ αὐτόν, *for I saw* him.

38. (*a*) ὁ μέν—ὁ δέ[h], *this—that ; the one—the other*, &c. οἱ μέν—οἱ δέ, *these—those; some—others.* (More than one ὁ δέ may follow.)

39. (*b*) In a narrative ὁ δέ stands (once) in reference to an object already named. So καὶ ὅς, when the reference is to a *person*.

40. (*d*) 1) αὐτός is '*self*,' when it stands in the *nom. without a substantive*, or, in *any case with one*.

2) αὐτός is *him, her, it*, &c. in an oblique case without a substantive.

3) ὁ αὐτός is '*the same*.'

4) αὐτός standing alone in an oblique case, is never '*self*,' except when it is *the first word* of the sentence.

41. VOCABULARY 7.

Same (ὁ αὐτός). *Some—others* (οἱ μέν— οἱ δέ). *To pain, annoy* (λυπέω). *Delight* (τέρπω). *Wolf* (λύκος). *Lamb* (ἀμνός). *Fly for refuge* (κατα-φεύγω). *Temple* (ναός [i]). *More—than* (μᾶλλον—ἤ). *To fear* (φοβέομαι [k]). *Death* (θάνατος). *Fire* (πῦρ, n.). *Say* (φημί, B. p. 114. W. 86). *Give* (δίδωμι, W. 84. B. p. 102). *Sheep* (ὄϊς, οἶς [l]). *Dog* (κύων, m. if the *sex* is not to be specified. R. κυν. V. κύον). *House*

---

[h] μέν, *indeed ;—*δέ, *but.* Often, however, there is no considerable opposition between words so connected, the use of μέν being principally to prepare us for a coming δέ. It need not be translated, except when the context plainly requires an *indeed.*

In translating from English into Greek, whenever the *second* of two connected clauses has a *but*, the first should have a μέν.

[i] νεώς, *Att.*

[k] In act. *frighten.* It has *f.* mid. and *pass.* ; aor. *pass.*

[l] The forms in Attic Greek are : *S.* οἶς, οἱός, οἶϊ, ὄϊν,—*D.* οἶε, οἰοῖν.

P. οἶες, οἰῶν, οἰσί, οἶας and οἶς. (It is *m.* and *f.*)

(οἶκος). *Deceive* (ἀπατάω, ἐξαπατάω, the latter being stronger, *to deceive thoroughly*). *At full speed* (ἀνὰ κράτος, *at force*). *Force, strength* (κράτος, n.). *Ride* (ἐλαύνειν, *to drive on*—ἵππον understood). *For* (γάρ). Can γάρ begin the sentence? (*No.*) Can δέ? (*No.*) Can μέν? (*No.*)

Exercise 8.

42. A dog was pursuing a sheep, *and it* fled-for-refuge into a house. *Some* admire the mother; *others* the daughter. Cyrus rides at full speed. I [m] *myself* say it. I admire the mother more than the daughter *herself.* They will give *him* the gold. I will give the gold to (the man) *himself* (40, 4). I deceived the slave *himself. And they* (c), being deceived, fly-for-refuge into a temple. *And he,* riding at full speed, flies from those who [1] are pursuing him [n]. The wolves fly at full speed. Let us pursue the wolves at full speed. *The same* dogs are pursuing the hares. Let us pursue them [n] *ourselves.* Let us not deceive our neighbour. *The Persians of those days* [11] pursued honorable things [13]. Speak well of those who [1] have done you kind offices [16].

§ 8. *Pronouns continued.*

43. *a.* ἄλλοι, *others;* οἱ ἄλλοι, *the others;* οἱ ἕτεροι, *the others* (with a stronger opposition), *the other party.*

b. ἡ ἄλλη χώρα, *the rest of the country.*

c. πολλοί, *many;* οἱ πολλοί, *the many, the* multitude, most *people.*

---

[m] The nom. of the *personal* pron. is not to be expressed.

[n] The *acc.* of the pronoun is seldom expressed when the person meant is quite obvious.

d. πᾶσα πόλις, every *city ;* πᾶσα ἡ πόλις, *the* whole *city,* all *the city.*

e. οὗτος ὁ ἀνήρ, *or* ὁ ἀνὴρ οὗτος [*not* ὁ οὗτος ἀνήρ], *this man.* ἐκεῖνος ὁ ἀνήρ, *or* ὁ ἀνὴρ ἐκεῖνος, *that man.* αὐτὸς ὁ βασιλεύς, *or* ὁ βασιλεὺς αὐτός, *the king himself.*

44. The noun with οὗτος, ὅδε (*this*), ἐκεῖνος (*that*), takes the article ; the pronoun standing *before* the article, or *after* the noun.

45. πᾶς in the sing.[o] *without* the article (= ἕκαστος), 'each,' ' every ;' with the article, ' *the whole,*' ' *all.*'

46. VOCABULARY 8.

Others (ἄλλοι). *The others* (οἱ ἄλλοι). *The other party* (οἱ ἕτεροι). *The rest of* — (ὁ ἄλλος agreeing with its *subst.*). *Many, much* [P] (πολύς). *Great* (μέγας—μείζων, μέγιστος). *The many, the multitude, most people* (οἱ πολλοί). *Every, each* (πᾶς in the sing. without the *art.*). *The whole, all* (πᾶς ὁ, or ὁ πᾶς, in the sing. *Pl.* πάντες: see note on 45). *This* (οὗτος, ὅδε). *That* (ἐκεῖνος). *Man* (ἀνήρ, ἄνθρωπος). *Cut* (τέμνω [q] ; of a country, *to ravage* or *lay waste,* by cutting down its trees, crops, &c.). *The enemy* (οἱ πολέμιοι, *adj.*).

Obs. ἀνήρ [r] (*vir*), *man* as opposed to *woman,* and used in a good sense. ἄνθρωπος (*homo*), *man* as a *human being,* opposed to other animals ; and often used, like *homo,* when *contempt* is to be expressed.

Exercise 9.

[*Obs.* With ' *this,*' ' *that,*' the order is,

Pron.	Art.	Noun.
(or,) Art.	Noun,	Pron.]

47. The enemy laid waste *the whole* country. The other party are laying waste *the rest* of the country. My brother is

---

[o] In the plur. πάντες must have the article, when there is reference to *particular* objects : when not, the usage is variable.

[P] W. 24. B. p. 29, 30.

[q] τέμνω, τεμῶ, τέτμηκα, ἔτεμον, ἐτμήθην. (Roots; τεμ, τμε.)

[r] W. 15, Obs. 3. B. p. 15.

pursuing the same Persians. I admire *this* city. I often admired *that* city. The many do not (οὐ) admire the beauty of wisdom. The king *himself* is laying waste *the rest* of the country. A certain man was pursuing his slave; *but he* fled for refuge into the upper [11] city. The others were turned into eagles. I will give *the whole egg* to my brother. He gave *all the water* to his (18) horses. I feel pain [4] in every part of my head (*in my whole head*). *Most people* rejoice when [5] their friends are wealthy. *The other party* manage the affairs of the city.

---

§ 9. *Pronouns continued.*

48. *a.* ἔθιζε σαυτόν, *accustom yourself.*

    b. ἔφη πάντας τοὺς ἀνθρώπους τὰ ἑαυτῶν ἀγαπᾷν, he said that all men loved [s] their own *things.*

    c. νομίζει τοὺς πολίτας ὑπηρετεῖν ἑαυτῷ, *he thinks that the citizens serve him.*

    d. στρατηγὸς [t] ἦν Ξενοκλείδης, πέμπτος αὐτός, *Xenoclides was their general* (*himself the fifth* =) with four others.

49. (*a*) In the reflexive pronouns (ἐμαυτοῦ, &c.[u]) the αὐτός is not *emphatic.* To express '*self*' emphatically, αὐτός must precede the pronoun, αὐτὸν σέ, &c.

50. (*b*) '*Own*' is translated by the *gen.* of the reflexive pronoun (ἑαυτοῦ). '*His*' by the *gen.* of αὐτός. (So '*their*' by *gen. plur.*)

---

[s] It is an idiom of our language to use a *past* tense in a sentence beginning with '*that*' (and other dependent sentences), when the verb on which they depend is in a *past* tense. The *pres.* infin. must be used in Greek, whenever the action to be expressed by it did not *precede* the time spoken of.

[t] From στρατός *army,* ἄγω *lead.*

[u] W. 34, g. B. p. 43.

51. (*c*) ἑαυτοῦ is often used (like *sui*) in a dependent sentence, or in a clause having *acc.* and *infin.*, for the *subject* of the principal sentence ᵛ.

But the simple αὐτόν is often used, or ἕ (οὗ, οἷ, &c. σφεῖς, σφᾶς, &c.). οὗ is never *simply* reflexive in Attic prose, but is confined to *this kind* of reflexive meaning. B.ʷ The forms οὗ, ἕ, occur in *Plato*, but not in the other great Attic prose-writers. Kr.

52. VOCABULARY 9.

Accustom (ἐθίζω ˣ). *I am accustomed* (εἴθισμαι or εἴωθα, a *perf.* 2. from ἔθω : κατὰ τὸ εἰωθός, neut. part., *according to my, his,* &c. *custom ; as my, his,* &c. *custom was*). *Love, like, am fond of* (ἀγαπάω : also, with *acc.* or *dat., I am contented with*). *Think, am of opinion* (νομίζω). *Serve, perform service* (ὑπηρετέω ʸ). *General* (στρατηγός). *To command* an army (στρατηγέω). *Third* (τρίτος). *Fourth* (τέταρτος). *Every body* (πᾶς τις). *I am present, am here,* &c. (πάρ-ειμι. τὰ παρόντα, *present things, circumstances,* or *condition*).

To perform this service, ὑπηρετεῖν τοῦτο.
————— these services, ὑπηρετεῖν ταῦτα.

Exercise 10.

53. Accustom yourself to confer benefits upon [16] the good. Every body loves *his own* things. I accustom myself to serve the state. Cyrus, as his custom was, was riding at full speed. I will give the gold to you yourself (49). Philip was their general *with two others*. He thinks that the citizens have conferred benefits upon him. Accustom yourself to be contented with your (18) present condition. Let us not treat those ill who [1] have done good to us. He accustomed himself (*imperf.*) to perform these services for the good. I will perform this service for you. He has a [12] large head. I am accustomed to perform you these services.

ᵛ Of course only when it *cannot* be mistaken for the subject of the *infin.* or dependent verb.

ʷ This passage is misconstrued, and so made incorrect, by the Eng. Translator of Buttmann, p. 325.

ˣ Aug. ι. εἴθιζον, εἴθισμαι. It is used in *pass.*

ʸ ὑπό, ἐρέτης, *rower,* properly, *to row for a person,* or *at his command.*

§ 10. *Of the Neut. Adjective.*

54. *a.* εἶπε ταῦτα, *he said* this. *b.* τὰ τῶν θεῶν φέρειν δεῖ, *we should bear* what comes from the gods. *c.* σοφώτερον ποιεῖς, *you act more wisely.* αἴσχιστα διετέλεσεν, *he lived in a most disgraceful way.* *d.* ἡ ἀρετή ἐστιν ἐπαινετόν, *virtue is* praiseworthy. *e.* ἡ πολλὴ τῆς χώρας, *the greater part of the country.* ὁ ἥμισυς τοῦ χρόνου, *half the time.*

55. (*a*) In Greek, as in Latin, the *neut. plur.* of an adjective is used without a substantive, where *we* should rather use the *singular.*

56. (*b*) The *neut. article* with a *gen.* case, is used in an indefinite way for any thing that *relates to*, or *proceeds from*, what the *gen.* expresses.

57. (*c*) Neuter adjectives are used *adverbially;* and generally,

The neuter *sing.* of the *comparative*⎫ serve also for the *comp.*
The neuter *plural* of the *superlative*⎭ and *superl.* of the adv.

58. (*d*) When an adjective is the *predicate*, it is often in the *neut. singular*, when that is not the gender, or even number, of the *subject.*

> This can only be, when the assertion is made of a class or general notion; not of a particular thing. It may be supposed to agree with *thing* understood.

59. (*e*) πολύς (πλέων or πλείων, πλεῖστος), superlatives, and the *adj.* ἥμισυς [z] stand in the gender of the *gen.* that follows them, when we might have expected the *neut. adj.* (Not τὸ πολὺ τῆς γῆς, but ἡ πολλή.)

60. VOCABULARY 10.

> *We ought, should* or *must* (δεῖ [a], oportet). *Bear* (φέρω [b]). *Said*

---

[z] *Acc. plur.* εἴς and εας. G. ους in later writers.
[a] δεῖ (—δέοι, δέῃ, δεῖν, δέον), δεήσει. *Imperf.* ἔδει.
[b] φέρω, οἴσω, ἐνήνοχα: aor. 1. ἤνεγκα.
  Pass. ἐνεχθήσομαι and οἰσθήσομαι, ἐνήνεγμαι, ἠνέχθην.

C

(εἶπον c). *Live* (διατελέω, ἐσω, properly *finish, go through ;* βίον or χρόνον understood). *Praiseworthy* (ἐπαινετός). *To praise* (ἐπαινέω d). *To act* (ποιέω). *Forwardness, zeal* (τὸ πρόθυμον, adj. for ἡ προθυμία). *Peloponnesus* (Πελοπόννησος, f.).

Exercise 11.

61. The others laid waste *half* the country. The other party [19] act more wisely. The rest [19] of the Scythians act more wisely. He spent half his life in a most disgraceful way. The others are doing better e. The *rest* of the citizens are doing very well e. The king of the Persians has ravaged the greater part of the Peloponnesus. Wisdom is praiseworthy (*d*). The son of Sophroniscus [9] said *this* (*a*). Let us bear *what comes from the gods.* The son of Philip will command (the army) *with three others* [21]. Accustom yourself to bear what comes from the gods. One ought to like one's own things. A certain man had a hen. Eagles [15] have a [12] very beautiful head.

---

§ 11. *Subject and Predicate.*

62. *a.* τὰ ζῶα τρέχει, *the animals run.* τῶν ὄντων τὰ μέν ἐστιν ἐφ' ἡμῖν, τὰ δ' οὐκ ἐφ' ἡμῖν, *of existing things some are in our power, and others are not in our power.* *b.* τοσάδε ἔθνη ἐστράτευον, *so many nations* went on the expedition. *c.* τὰ τῶν φίλων κοινά, *the property of friends is common.*

63. (*a*) The *nom. neut. plur.* generally has the verb in the *singular ;* but often not (*b*) when *persons* or *living creatures* are spoken of.

64. (*c*) The verb ' *to be* ' is often omitted.

---

c εἶπον (εἶπέ, &c.) an aor. 2. Also εἶπα aor. 1., of which εἴπατε, εἰπάτω, and also εἶπας, are used by *Attic* writers.

d —ἐσω (Xen. but generally ἐσομαι), ἤνεσα, ἤνεκα, ἠνέθην : but ἤνημαι.

e By 57 the compar. and superl. of good must here be used.

65. VOCABULARY 11.

Animal (ζῶον). *Run* [f] (τρέχω· δραμ). *In a person's power* (ἐπί with the *dat*. of the *person* ; ἐπ' ἐμοί, *in my power* ; ἐπ' ἐμοῦ, *in my time* ; ἐπι τοῦ πατρός, *in my father's time*). *So many* (τόσος, τοσόσδε, τοσοῦτος). *Nation* (ἔθνος, n.). *Go on an expedition* (στρατεύω). *Existing things, things that are*, or (55, *a*.) *what is* (τὰ ὄντα, part. from εἰμί, B. p. 117. W. 95. τῷ ὄντι, *in reality, really*). *To go away* (ἀπ-ειμι [g]. W. 96. B. p. 118). *Now* (= *already, at once*, without waiting any longer—ἤδη). [Words after which the omission of the *copula* (' *is*,' ' *are*,' &c.) is very common.]

Ready (ἐτοῖμος [h]). *Disappeared, vanished* (φροῦδος [i]). (*It is*) *time* (ὥρα). *Easy* (ῥᾴδιον, n.). *Hard, difficult* (χαλεπόν, n.). *Worthy* (ἄξιος). *Possible* (δυνατός). *Impossible* (ἀδύνατος). *Necessity* (ἀνάγκη = *it is necessary*). *Lawful, fas* (θέμις), &c.

Exercise 12.

66. These things were not in my power. These things took place in our fathers' times. This (*plur.*) is good. It *is* now time to go away. They *are* ready to do this. The judge *is* worthy of death (*gen.*). The boys have disappeared [k]; the father has disappeared. Many nations will go on the expedition. It is easy to the wise, to bear *what comes from the gods* [25]. It is necessary to bear what comes from the gods. Let us go away at once. Socrates, the son [9] of Sophroniscus, was really wise. For it is not lawful to speak ill of the gods. It is hard to deceive the wise.

---

[f] τρέχω, δραμοῦμαι, δεδράμηκα, ἔδραμον.

[g] εἰμι has a *fut*. meaning, and is more common in this sense than ἐλεύσομαι, *fut*. of ἔρχομαι. In the *moods* it is used as *pres*. or *fut*. B.

[h] Afterwards ἕτοιμος.

[i] From πρό, ὁδός : only found in *nom*. of all numbers.

[k] Begin with *adj*. *Have, has*, are not to be translated.

§ 12. *On the Moods.*

67. *a.* μὴ κλέπτε, do not steal (forbids stealing *generally*).

μὴ κλέψῃς, do not steal (forbids stealing in a *particular* instance).

b. {πάρειμι, ἵνα ἴδω, I am *here* to see.

{παρῆν, ἵνα ἴδοιμι, I was *there* to see.

{οὐκ ἔχω (or οὐκ οἶδα), ὅποι¹ τράπωμαι, *I don't know which way to turn myself.*

{οὐκ εἶχον (or οὐκ ᾔδειν), ὅποι¹ τραποίμην, *I did not know which way to turn myself.*

c. ἤρετο, εἰ οὕτως ἔχοι, he asked if it were so.

ἔλεξέ μοι, ὅτι ἡ ὁδὸς φέροι εἰς τὴν πόλιν, ἥνπερ ὁρῴην, he told me that the road led to the city which I saw.

68. (*a*) 1) *The moods of the* aorist *do not refer to past time,* and are therefore construed by the *present* in English.

2) The moods of the aorist express *momentary* ᵐ actions; those of the present, *continued* ones.

3) But the *participle* of the aorist *does* refer to past time. πεσών, *having fallen.*

69. (*a*) μή, when it *forbids*, takes the imperative of the present, the subjunctive of the aorist ⁿ.

---

¹ In *dependent* (or *indirect*) questions, the *regular* rule is to use,

not πόσος ;	ποῖος ;	πηλίκος ;
(*quantus ?*)	(*qualis ?*)	how old or big ?
but ὁπόσος,	ὁποῖος,	ὁπηλίκος.

So not πότε ;	ποῖ ;	ποῦ ;	πῶς ;	πόθεν ;	πῇ ;
when ?	whither ?	where ?	how ?	whence ?	how ? whither ?
but ὁπότε,	ὅποι,	ὅπου,	ὅπως,	ὁπόθεν,	ὅπη.

So, also, not τίς, but ὅστις. But the *direct* interrogatives are very often used in *indirect* questions, as: ἠρώτα με τίς εἴην, he asked me who I was.

ᵐ Momentary is here used in a somewhat loose way, to express *single definite* actions, not contemplated as *continuing.*

ⁿ μή with *imperative present* tells a man to *leave off* what he has already begun :

[In doing the exercises, consider (1) whether a *single definite action* is spoken of; or a *continued* action, or *habit*. Having thus determined whether the aorist should be used, or the present, (2) *if* you use the *present*, you must also use the *imperative;* if the *aorist*, the *subjunctive*.]

> Of course the *subj.* of the *present* must be used for the *first person* (when the present is to be used), as the *imperat.* has no first person.

70. ☞ The optative *is the regular attendant of the historical tenses.* Hence,

71. (*b*) The *relatives* and *particles* (except the compounds of ἄν; see 77, 90), which take the *subjunctive* after the *present* and *future*, take the *optative* after the *historical*[o] tenses.

> The *optative* is thus, in fact, the *subjunctive* of the *historical* tenses, answering to the *imperfect* and *pluperfect* of the Latin subjunctive.

72. (*c*) So the particles and pronouns, which go with the indicative *in direct*[p], take the optative *in oblique*[p] narration.

73. VOCABULARY 12.

> *Steal* (κλέπτω, with fut. mid.). *Theft* (κλοπή). *Know* (οἶδα[q]).
> *Whither* (ποῖ;—in dependent questions, ὅποι). *Turn* (τρέπω. Mid. *turn myself*). *To ask* (ἠρόμην aor. 2: ἐρωτάω used for the other

---

μή with *aor. subj.*, tells him *not to begin* the action. (H.) This is a *consequence* of the distinction pointed out, not a *new* distinction.

o i. e. *Imperf.*, *aorists*, and *pluperf.*

p *Oblique* narration (*sermo obliquus*) is when the *opinions*, *assertions*, &c., of *another* are related in the *third person*. " He said that *he thought*, &c."—" He said, ' *I think*,' &c." would be in *direct* narration (*sermo rectus*).

q Properly a *perf.* from εἴδω, *see*. *I have perceived = I know*.

> οἶδα, ἴσθι, εἰδείην, εἰδῶ, εἰδέναι, εἰδώς.
> Plup. ᾔδειν. Fut. εἴσομαι (εἰδήσω).
> Perf. οἶδα, οἶσθα, οἶδε | ἴστον, ἴστον | ἴσμεν, ἴστε, ἴσασι.
> Plup. S. ᾔδειν, Att. ᾔδη (from ᾔδεα).
> ᾔδεις, commonly ᾔδεισθα, Att. ᾔδησθα.
> ᾔδει, Att. ᾔδειν, and ᾔδη.
> P. ᾔδειμεν and ᾖσμεν.
> ᾔδειτε, ᾖστε.
> ᾔδεσαν, ᾖσαν.

tenses). *Road* (ὁδός, f.). *Lead*, of a road (φέρω). *See* (ὁράω ʳ). *To be so* (οὕτως ἔχειν, to have *themselves* so). To be *found* or *brought in guilty* (ἁλῶναι ˢ with *gen.*). *Battle* (μάχη). *Fight* (μάχομαι, ἔσομαι, οὖμαι, ημαι). *That* = in order that, *ut* (ἵνα). *That*, after verbs of *telling*, &c., for Latin *acc.* with *infin.* (ὅτι, with *indic.* unless the *optative* is required by 72.—The *acc.* with *infin.* also occurs. See 89, *b.*) For what is ἔχω sometimes used? (*to know :* so '*non habeo quo me vertam.*') What are *strengthening* particles, and with what words are they often used? (γέ, *at least ;* πέρ, *very ;* δή, *now.* They are frequently used with *relatives.*)

Exercise 13.

74. I am here *to see* the battle. I was there *to see* the battle. Do not pursue *what is disgraceful* [13]. The road leads to Athens. The boy says that the road leads to Athens. The boy told me that the road led ᵗ to Athens. Do not deceive your father (Of a *particular* instance of deceit). The Persian was found guilty of murder. I asked him what he was doing. He asked me who I was. Who are you (*plur.*)? I asked them who they were. He told me that Xenoclides commanded them *with two others* [21]. Do not steal these things. Do not accustom yourself to deceive your mother. I was there to fight. He asked me whether (εἰ) these things were so.

---

§ 13.   *The Moods continued.*

On εἰ and ἄν.   *Conditional Propositions.*

(Introductory remarks on ἄν.)

75.   This particle (of which Hermann considers the real meaning to be *by*

ʳ The tenses supplied from the roots ὀπ, εἰδ :
  ὁράω, ὄψομαι, ἑώρᾱκα, ἑώρᾱμαι (ὦμμαι), ὤφθην. *Imp.* ἑώρων.
  For *aor.* εἶδον, ἰδέ, &c. and εἰδόμην, ἰδοῦ, &c.
ˢ ἁλίσκομαι (*am taken* or *caught*), ἁλώσομαι, ἑάλωκα.
  Aor. ἑάλων (ἥλων), ἁλοίην, ἁλῶ (φῶς, &c.), ἁλῶναι, ἁλούς.
The *a* is *long* in the augmented, *short* in the unaugmented forms.
ᵗ See note on 48, *b.*

chance, perhaps ; but Hartung, *else, otherwise*) gives an expression of *contingency* and *mere possibility* to the assertion.

76.   Its *principal* use is in the *conclusion* of a hypothetical sentence ; and when it stands in other sentences, it often refers to an *implied condition.*

77.   It coalesces with several particles, so as to form one word with them.

        Thus with εἰ,   ὅτε,   ἐπειδή,

        it forms ἐάν, ἤν, ἄν,   ὅταν,   ἐπειδάν.

78.   The ἄν = ἐάν, εἰ ἄν, *regularly* begins the sentence, and is thus distinguished from the simple ἄν, which *must have some words* before it.

---

79. *a.* ⎧ εἰ ἐβρόντησε καὶ ἤστραψεν, *if it has thundered, it*
       ⎨   *has also lightened.*
       ⎩ εἴ τι ἔχεις, δός, *if you have anything, give it.*

    b. ἐάν τι ἔχωμεν, δώσομεν, *if we have anything, we will give it.*

    c. εἰ τις ταῦτα πράττοι, μέγα μ' ἂν ὠφελήσειε, *if any one should do this, he would do me a great service.*

    d. εἴ τι εἶχεν, ἐδίδου ἄν, *if he had any thing* ᵘ*, he would give it.*

        εἴ τι ἔσχεν, ἔδωκεν ἄν, *if he had had any thing, he would have given it.*

80. εἰ (like our '*if*') has the two meanings of *if* * and *whether :* it goes with the *indic.* or *optative ;* but not, in good writers, with the subjunctive.—(See example in 67, *c.*)

81. *a.* *Possibility* without any expression of *uncertainty :* εἰ with *indic.* in both clauses.

    b. *Uncertainty* with the *prospect of decision ;* ἐάν with *subjunctive* in the conditional, and the *indic.* (generally the *future*) in the consequent clause.

    c. *Uncertainty* without any such accessary notion : εἰ

ᵘ It is implied, that he *has not* any thing.   * See 335.

with the *optative* in the conditional clause, and ἄν
with the optative in the consequent clause.

d. Impossibility, or belief that the thing is *not* so: εἰ
with *imperfect* or *aorist indic.* in the conditional
clause; ἄν with *imperf.* or *aorist indic.* in the consequent clause.

(1) The imperfect is used for *present* time, or when the time is quite
indefinite.

(2) If both condition and consequence refer to *past* time, the *aorist*
must be used, at least in the *consequent* clause; unless the consequence
is to be represented as *continuing.*

(3) The condition may refer to past, and the consequence to *present*
time.

εἰ ἐπείσθην, οὐκ ἂν ἠρρώστουν, *if I had* (then) *been persuaded,* I
should not (now) *be out of health.*

82. VOCABULARY 13.

To benefit, to do a service (ὠφελέω). *Hurt, injure* (βλάπτω). *Kill,
put to death* (ἀπο-κτείνω). *Speak the truth* (ἀληθεύω). *Mina* (μνᾶ).
Talent (τάλαντον). *Not only—but also* (οὐχ ὅτι ᵛ—ἀλλὰ καί). *Even*
(καί). *Not even* (οὐδέ).

[*Obs.* ὠφελεῖν, βλάπτειν, &c. take besides *acc.* of *person,* an *adj.* in
the *acc. neut. plur.*, where *we* should use adverbs; *very, more,* &c. μεγάλα,
μικρά, μείζω, τὰ μέγιστα.]

Exercise 14.

83. If I have any thing [36], I will give it. If you were to do
this, you would confer the greatest benefit upon me (c). If any
one should do this, he would greatly injure me. If I had a
mina, I would give it to the slave. If he had had even three
talents, he would have given them to his brother. If any one
were to do (c) this, he would do the greatest [28] injury to the
state. If you speak the truth (i. e. *if what you say should prove
true*), I will give you three talents. If the wise were to manage
the affairs of the state, they would confer a great benefit [28]
upon all the citizens. If this be so [27], I will go away at once.

ᵛ Such a verb as '*I do not say*' is understood: I saw, *not that* my son, *but also*
&c. = I saw (*I do not say*) that (*I saw*) my son, but also, &c.

If you were really wise, you would admire the beauty of virtue. I am here to see *not only* the city, *but also* the whole [20] country. If the citizens were wise, they would have killed not only Xenoclides, but also Philip. If you *should be found guilty* [27] of murder, the citizens will put you to death.

----

§ 14. *The Moods continued.*

84. *a.* ἡδέως ἂν θεασαίμην ταῦτα, I would *gladly* see *this*, or, *I should like to see this.* ἄνθρωπον ἀναιδέστερον οὐκ ἄν τις εὕροι, a man (or, *one*) could not find *a more shameless fellow.*

b. οὐκ ἂν φεύγοις, *you* will *not* escape.

c. πόσον ἂν οἴει εὑρεῖν τὰ σὰ κτήματα πωλούμενα; how much do you think that your possessions would fetch (literally, *find*) *if they were sold?*

d. οὐκ ἔστιν ἕνα ἄνδρα ἂν δυνηθῆναί ποτε ἅπαντα ταῦτα πρᾶξαι, it is not possible that one man should *ever* be able *to do all this.*

e. τἆλλα[w] σιωπῶ, πόλλ᾽ ἂν ἔχων εἰπεῖν, I hold my tongue about the rest, though *I* should have *much* to say. αἰτεῖ μισθὸν, ὡς οὕτως περιγενόμενος ἂν [*] τῶν πολεμίων, he asks for pay on the plea that he could then conquer *his enemies.*

84*. *a.* The optative with ἄν is equivalent to our *may, might, would, should,* &c.

It properly refers (as our *would,* &c.) to a condition supposed. Thus in (*a*), ‘*I would gladly see it,*’ *if* it were possible; in (*b*) ‘ *one could not,*’ &c. *if* one were to look.

85. (*b*) The optative with ἄν is often translated by the *future.*

----

* Literally ‘ *as thus being-likely-to-conquer.*’

The Attics were peculiarly fond of expressing themselves in a doubtful way; of avoiding all *positiveness* in their assertions; and hence the optative with ἄν is used of the most positive assertions.

86. (*c. d. e.*) ἄν gives to the *infinitive* and the *participle* the same force that it gives to the *optative*.

Thus (as in *d.*) the *infin.* gets the force of an *infin. future* ˣ.

This is the common way of expressing the future after verbs of *hoping, thinking, trusting, praying, knowing, confessing,* &c., when it is dependent on a *condition expressed or implied.*

Of a *positive unconditional* expectation, &c. the infinitive without ἄν is to be used; the *future,* if future time is to be strongly marked; if not, the *aor.* or *present,* according as the action is *momentary* or *continued.* (K.)

87. VOCABULARY 14.

How is ' *would* (or *should*) *like to* . . .' translated? (By ἡδέως ʸ, *gladly.* ἥδιστ' ἄν . . . . *should like extremely;* ἥδιον ἄν . . . . ἤ, I *would rather—than*). *See, behold* (θεάομαι). *Shameless* (ἀναιδής). *Shamelessness, impudence* (ἀναίδεια ᶻ). *Find;* of things sold, *fetch* (εὑρίσκω ᵃ) *Possession* (κτῆμα, n. ᵇ). *Acquire, get* (κτάομαι, perf. κέκτημαι = I *possess*). *Sell* (πωλέω). *Can, am able* (δύναμαι ᶜ). What does ἔστιν sometimes mean? (*It is possible.*) *One* (εἷς, μία, ἕν). *Hold my tongue about* (σιωπάω, with *fut. mid.*). *Ask for;* in mid. *ask for myself* (αἰτέω). *Pay* (μισθός). *Conquer, get the better of* (περιγίγνομαι with *gen.*—15, 1).

ˣ γράφειν ἄν = *scripturum esse.*
  γεγραφέναι ἄν = *scripturum fuisse.*
  γράψαι ἄν = (*a*) *scripturum fuisse,* or
    as *pres.* (*b*) *scripturum esse.*
  γράψειν ἄν = *scripturum fore.* (K.)

(γράψειν ἄν is proved, I think, to be correct by *Hartung,* against *Porson, Hermann,* &c. *Kühner* and *Rost* both agree with *Hartung.*)

ʸ From ἡδύς, *sweet.* Adverbs in ως are formed by adding ως to the root; καλ-ός, καλῶς· ταχύς, ταχέ-ος, ταχέ-ως.

ᶻ The termination ια becomes εια when derived from adjectives in ης, by contraction with the ε of the root; ἀναιδής, ἀναιδέ-ος, ἀναίδειᾰ. The α is then shortened, and the accent thrown back to the *last syllable but two.*

ᵃ is an inseparable particle, meaning '*not*' in compound words. It generally takes ν before a vowel: α *not,* αἰδ, the root of words denoting *reverence, respect, shame,* &c.

ᵃ εὑρίσκω, εὑρήσω, εὕρηκα, εὕρημαι. εὗρον, εὑρόμην, εὑρέθην.
ᵇ See 8, *a.*
ᶜ δύναμαι, δυνήσομαι, δεδύνημαι, ἠδυνήθην. (2 sing. δύνασαι.)

Escape from (φεύγω, acc. *fut. mid.*).   *Black* (μέλας).   *Flatterer* (κόλαξ).
Flatter (κολακεύω).   *Ever, at any time* (ποτέ ᵈ).   *Just* (δίκαιος).
Faithful (πιστός).   *How much* (πόσον, n.).   *Think* (οἴομαι ᵉ).   *Hope*
(ἐλπίζω).

Exercise 15.

88. One cannot find a more shameless flatterer.   One
cannot find a blacker dog.   You will not escape from those
who are pursuing you.   If I possessed a talent, I would not ask
you ᶠ for pay.   It is not possible that you, being a man, should
be able to deceive the gods.   You will not deceive God, the
judge of all.   I should like to find these things.   I should like
to see the old geometers.   Let us fly from the shamelessness
of wicked men.   You will not find a juster judge.   Do not
steal the poet's gold.   Do not flatter.   If you do this, you
will conquer your enemies.   How much do you think the
eagle will fetch, if offered for sale ?   I asked him how much
(67, ¹) his possessions would fetch, if sold ?   I will ask for
three talents, *on the plea that I shall then conquer* (e) all my
enemies.   I hope that you will be able to do all this (d).

---

§ 15.   *The Moods continued.*

89. *a.* παρέσομαι ἐάν τι δέῃ ᵍ (60, ᵃ), *I will come to you* (or,
be with you), *if I am wanted.*

b. ἔφη παρέσεσθαι, εἴ τι δέοι or δεήσοι, *he said that he
would come, if we were wanted.*

ᵈ πότε; *interrog. when ?*
ᵉ οἴομαι and οἶμαι (2 sing. οἴει), οἰήσομαι, ᾠήθην. *Imperf.* ᾠόμην, ᾤμην.
ᶠ See 123, *a*, and 124.
ᵍ τί = *at all.* ἐάν τι δέῃ, *if it should be at all necessary.*

c. τότε δὴ[h], ὅταν ἃ χρὴ[i] ποιῇς, εὐτυχεῖς, *then only are
you prosperous, when you do what you ought.* τότε
δὴ, ὅταν ἃ χρὴ ποιήσῃς, εὐτυχήσεις, *then only will
you be prosperous, when you* have done[k] *what you
ought* (tum demum, quum officia tua *expleveris,*
felix eris).

d. ἐπειδὰν ἅπαντα ἀκούσητε, κρίνατε, *when* (or *after*)
you have heard *all, decide.*

e. διαφθερεῖ ὅ,τι ἂν λάβῃ, *he will destroy whatever he*
takes or *lays hold of* (ceperit).

90. (*a*) The compounds of ἄν (ἐάν, ὅταν, ἐπειδάν, &c. 77)
regularly take the *subjunctive.* The same rule
applies to *relatives* with ἄν.

91. (*b*) When they come into connexion with *past time*
or the *oblique narration,* they either remain unchanged, or the
simple words (εἰ, ὅτε, ἐπειδή—ὅς, ὅστις, ὅσος, &c.) take their
place with the *optative* (70).

91*. (*c. d. e.*) When these compounds of ἄν, and relatives
with ἄν, go with the *subjunctive of the aorist,* they answer to
the Latin *future perfect* (*futurum exactum*).

92. VOCABULARY 15.

> At all (τί, neut. of τίς). *Also* (καί). *One ought* (χρή). *If there is any
> need,* or *occasion* (ἐάν τι δέῃ, or εἴ τι δέοι). *Am prosperous* or *fortunate,
> prosper* (εὐτυχέω). *Fortune* (τύχη). *Hear* (ἀκούω[l]). *Judge, decide*
> (κρίνω). *When* (ὅτε[m]). *Then* (τότε). *When?* (πότε;) *Destroy* (δια-

---

[h] *Then truly* (and not before) = *then only.*

[i] χρή (oportet)—χρείη, χρῇ, χρῆναι, *part. neut.* (τὸ) χρεών. Imperf. ἐχρῆν or
χρῆν (not, ἔχρη) : *fut.* χρήσει.

[k] Properly, ' *when you shall have done :*' but in English a *future* action, that is to
precede another *future* action, is generally put in the *present* or *perfect* tense. We
do not, that is, mark that it is *now* future, but consider ourselves as removed by the
' *when,*' &c. to the time of its happening.

[l] *Fut.* ἀκούσομαι (but *aor.* 1. ἤκουσα), ἀκήκοα, ἤκουσμαι.

[m] ὅταν when the subj. should be used with ἄν.

φθείρω ⁿ). *Take* (λαμβάνω ^o). *Whosoever, whatsoever* (ὅστις ^p). *When, after* (ἐπειδή, or with ἄν, ἐπειδάν).

[παρεῖναι, *to be present* (*here* or *there*), is often used of *being present to assist;* where we should use ' *come to you,*' or ' *be with you.*']

Exercise 16.

[When the consequent verb is in the *fut.*, how is '*if*' translated? with what mood ?—79, *b.*]

93. He says that he will come, if he is wanted (*b*). If we do what we ought, we shall be happy. If the citizens were to do ³⁶ what they ought, they would be prosperous. If the citizens had done what they ought (*imperf.*), they would be prosperous (*now*). When I have any thing, I will give it. When they see this, they will fear. When you have managed the affairs of the state well, you shall manage mine also. He hopes that he shall (*thus*) be able to deceive the gods also. I am glad that the enemy are destroyed ^s. If the enemy had done this, they would have been destroyed. The judge said, that he would come, if he were wanted.

---

§ 16.   *The Moods continued.*

94. *a.* ὑπερῷον ^q εἶχεν ὁπότ᾽ ἐν ἄστει ^r διατρίβοι ^s, he had an upper chamber whenever he stayed in town.

b. ἔπραττεν ἃ δόξειεν αὐτῷ, he did what (in each case) seemed good to him.

ⁿ B. p. 63, 7. and 66, 3. W. 74. Obs. 2.

^o λαμβάνω, λήψομαι, εἴληφα. ἔλαβον.

^p The neut. of ὅστις (W. 33. Obs. *d.f.* B. 41.) has generally a mark like a *comma* (called *diastole* or *hypodiastole*) after the *o*, to distinguish it from ὅτι, *that.*

^q ὑπερῷον, adj. understand οἴκημα. ὑπερῷιος, ῷος from ὑπέρ, as πατρώϊος, —ῷος from πατήρ. P.

^r ἄστυ is used of *Athens* as we use ' *town*' of London.

^s διατρίβειν, *to rub* (or *wear*) *away*, χρόνον, βίον (*conterere* tempus, *terere* vitam). Without *acc.* to *linger, stay*, &c.

c. οὓς (μὲν) ἴδοι εὐτάκτως καὶ σιωπῇ ἰόντας, ἐπῄνει [t],
he used to praise those whom (at any time) *he saw
marching in good order and in silence.*

95. (*a*) The *optative* is used of what *happened often*, when
the time spoken of is *past.*

(1) For *pres.* or future *time,* the relatives with ἄν and compounds of ἄν
would be used.

(2) To relatives ἄν gives in this way the force of our *ever.* ὃς ἄν (=
quicumque, siquis) *whoever, any man who ;* in plur. *all who.*

96. VOCABULARY 16.

Upper chamber (ὑπερῷον). *Whenever* (ὁπότε). *Stay* (in a town)
(διατρίβω, ī). *It seems good* (δοκεῖ [u] = videtur, videntur ; ἃ δοκεῖ μοι,
what seems good to me, what I please or *choose to do*). *In good order*
(εὐτάκτως). *Rank* (τάξις, f.[v]). *Order, arrange* (τάσσω, ξω). *Dining-
room* (ἀνώγεων, n.[w]). *March* of a single soldier (εἶμι [x]). *Silence* (σιωπή).
Horse-soldier (ἱππεύς, plur. *cavalry*). *To charge an enemy* (ἐλαύνειν εἰς
with *acc.*, sometimes ἐπί).

Exercise 17.

[What is the *fut.* of ἐπαινέω ?—p. 18. note d.]

97. He had a dining-room whenever he stayed in town.
The judge had an upper chamber whenever he stayed in town.
I praise all whom I see (95, 1.) acting well. The judge praised
all whom he saw acting well. I will do whatever (95, 1.) I
please [33]. Whenever he took any city, he used to kill all the
citizens. When I have taken [32] the city, I will kill all the citizens. When you have taken the city, do not kill the citizens.
I praise those who march in silence. If you march in good
order, I will praise you. Who would not admire cavalry

---

[t] The imperfect of an habitual action ; translated by ' used to,' &c. See 2, *Obs.*

[u] δοκέω (*seem* and also *think*), δόξω, δέδογμαι (*visus sum*), aor. 1. ἔδοξα. (The
3 sing. δοκεῖ, imperf. ἐδόκει, δόξει, ἔδοξε(ν), δέδοκται.)

[v] τάσσω, real root ταγ. Hence ταγ-σις = τάξις. Nouns in σις, σια, from
verbs, denote regularly the *abstract* notion of the verb. Hence τάξις = the *putting
in order ;* but also, *order, a place assigned,* &c.

[w] = ἀνώγαιον from ἄνω, γαῖα, *earth, ground.*

[x] εἶμι, *ibo.* See W. 96. B. p. 118.

marching (*riding*) in order? The cavalry of the Persians charge the ranks of the enemy. *I should like to see* [29] cavalry charging the enemy.

---

§ 17. *On the Moods.*

98. *a.* βούλει[y] οὖν σκοπῶμεν; *do you wish, then, that we should consider* (the question)?

    b. πόθεν βούλει ἄρξωμαι; *what do you wish me to begin with?*

    c. τί ποιῶ; *what shall I do? what am I to do?* ποῖ τράπωμαι; *whither shall I turn myself?*

    d. εἴπω οὖν σοι τὸ αἴτιον; *shall I then tell you the cause?*

    e. νῦν ἀκούσω[z] αὖθις—; *shall I now hear again—?*

99. The subjunctive is used in *doubting* questions either alone, or after βούλει, θέλεις (*do you wish?*).

So also after οὐκ ἔχω (or οἶδα: 67, *b.*), and ἀπορῶ(έω) *I am at a loss*, ἐρωτῶ(άω) *ask*, ζητῶ(έω) *seek.* (Optat. after the historical tenses, 67, *b.*)

100. VOCABULARY17.

Wish (βούλομαι, θέλω or ἐθέλω[a]). *Consider, examine* (σκοπέω). *Whence* (πόθεν). *Begin* (ἄρχομαι). *Cause* (αἴτιον[b]). *Again* (αὖθις). *Then* (of inference: οὖν). *Am at a loss* (ἀπορέω[c]). *Seek* (ζητέω).

[ἀφ᾽ ὑμῶν, ἀπὸ σοῦ, &c. ἀρξάμενος[d] (*having begun with you* =) *and you among the first; and you as much as any body.*]

---

z The subjunctive used in this way (subjunctivus *dubitativus* or *deliberativus*) must not be mistaken for the *future.*

a ἐθέλω (the most general expression for *wishing*) denotes particularly that kind of wish in which there lies a *purpose* or *design;* consequently the desire of something, the execution of which *is,* or *appears to be,* in *one's own* power. Βούλομαι, on the other hand, is confined to that kind of *willingness* or *wishing,* in which the *wish* and *inclination towards* a thing are either the only thing contained in the expression, or are at least intended to be marked particularly. Hence it expresses a *readiness* and *willingness to submit to* what does not exactly depend upon oneself. —(*B. Lexilogus,* Eng. Trans. 194.)

b Properly *adj.*   c From *a* not, πόρος, *passage, outlet.*

d The ἀρξάμενος must be in the case of whatever it refers to.

Exercise 18.

[After what tenses must the *opt.* be used in dependent sentences?]

101. What shall I say? Do you wish, then, (that) we should go away? What shall we do? Do you wish, then, that we should tell you the cause? Do you wish that I should hold-my-tongue-about this? Do you wish, then, that I should begin? All men, *and you as much as any body,* praise this man. This eagle has a [12] black head. They praise *not only* [28] the mother, *but also* the daughter. Not only you, but also your friends, will prosper, if you do this. We must bear what fortune sends (*what comes from fortune* [25]). You yourself shall hear. I am at a loss what (67, 1) to do. They are at a loss which way to turn themselves. They did not know which way to turn themselves.

---

§ 18. *The Moods continued.*

102. *a.* εἴ τι ἔχοι (or ἔχει), ἔφη δώσειν [e].
   b. εἴ τι ἔχοι, ἔφη δοῦναι ἄν.   ⎫ Compare examples
   c. εἴ τι εἶχεν, ἔφη δοῦναι ἄν. ⎬ in 79.

103. *a.* When conditional propositions become dependent on another verb, the *consequent clause* is in the *infinitive.*

   b. Instead, therefore, of the *optative with* ἄν (in 79, *c.*) we shall have the *infin. with* ἄν.

   c. Instead of the *imperfect* or *aorist* with ἄν (79, *d.*) we shall have the *present* or *aorist infin.* with ἄν.

104. *a.* Instead of the *indic. future* (79, *b.*) we shall have the *infin. future;* and εἰ *with optative* instead of ἐάν *with subj.*, if in connexion with *past time.*

---

e Also εἴ τι ἔχει (or ἔχοι), ἔφη δώσειν ἄν. See 86, x.

105. Thus where we should have had in the *consequent clause*,

$$\pi οιήσω, \begin{cases} \pi οιοῖμ' \ ἄν, \\ ἐπ οίουν \ ἄν, \end{cases} \begin{cases} \pi οιήσαιμ' \ ἄν, \\ ἐπ οίησα \ ἄν, \end{cases} \begin{cases} \pi επ οιήκοιμ' \ ἄν, \\ ἐπ επ οιήκειν \ ἄν, \end{cases}$$

we shall have,

$$\pi οιήσειν, \quad \pi οιεῖν \ ἄν, \quad \pi οιῆσαι \ ἄν, \quad \pi επ οιηκέναι \ ἄν.$$

Exercise 19.

106. He said that, if you were to do this, you would do him the greatest service [28]. I said that, if any one should do this, he would greatly injure me. He said that, if he had a mina, he would give it to the slave. He said that, if any one were to do this, he would do the greatest injury [28] to the state. He said that he was there to see the battle. How much do you think that your horses would fetch, if they were sold (84, c)? Who would not wonder at the shamelessness of this basest flatterer? He told me, that his daughter had very beautiful hands [12]. I *should extremely like to see* [29] the wise men *of old* [11]. If the Persians *of the present day* [11] were wise, they would be doing better. I should wish to be contented with what comes from the gods [25].

---

§ 19. οὐ and μή.

107. *a.* Οὐκ ἐθέλειν [f] φησίν, *he says that he does not choose.*

b. Νομίζει οὐ καλὸν εἶναι, *he thinks that it is not honorable.*

c. οὐ δύναται οὔτ' εὖ λέγειν, οὔτ' εὖ ποιεῖν τοὺς φίλους, *he* cannot either *speak well of his friends,* or *treat them well.*

d. οὐκ ἐξῆν εἰσελθεῖν παρὰ τὸν στρατηγόν, ὁπότε μὴ

---

[f] Of ἐθέλω, θέλω (see 100, a), the former is the common prose form: ἐθέλω —ήσω, —ηκα.

σχολάζοι, *persons were not allowed to go in to the general, when he was not at leisure.* (Here a condition is implied: *if* he was not at leisure at that time.)

107*. 1) Οὐ denies *independently* and *directly.*

2) Μή does not deny independently and directly, but *in reference to something else;* to some *supposed case, condition,* or *purpose;* or in the expression of some *fear, solicitude,* or *care.*

108. 1) Μή is used in all *prohibitions* (see 32).

2) With all *conditional* particles, εἰ, ἐάν (ἤν, ἄν), ὅταν, ἐπειδάν, &c., and with ὅτε, ὁπότε, '*when*,' if a condition is implied (*d.*).

3) With all particles expressing *intention* or *purpose;* ἵνα, ὅπως, ὡς, &c.

Note.—In the same cases the compounds of μή will be used when required.

109. But οὐ is used with ὅτι, ὡς (*that*): and also with ἐπεί, ἐπειδή (*when, after,* and as *causal* conjunctions, *as, since*), because they relate to *actual facts.*

110. (*a. b.*) Οὐ is also (*generally*) used when the *opinions,* &c. of another person are stated in *oblique narration.*

> For though these seem to be dependent, they are only distinguished from direct assertions in *form.*

111. (*c.*) In *negative* propositions, positive pronouns and adverbs should be translated into Greek by the corresponding *negative* forms.

> Hence the particles for *neither—nor* are to be used for *either—or* after a negative; and *no, nobody, nowhere,* for *any, anybody, anywhere,* &c. (See note † p. 145.)

112. VOCABULARY 18.

> Nobody (οὐδείς, μηδείς). Not a single person (οὐδὲ εἷς, μηδὲ εἷς). No longer (οὐκέτι, μηκέτι ᵍ). Not even (οὐδέ, μηδέ). Neither—nor (οὔτε—οὔτε; μήτε—μήτε). Neither—nor yet (οὔτε—οὐδέ; μήτε—μηδέ).

ᵍ ἔτι is *yet, still;* with negatives, *any longer.*

Both—and (καί—καί, or τέ—καί).   *Unless* (εἰ μή).   *Go into* (εἰσέρχομαι).   *Go away* (ἀπέρχομαι[h]).   *Company* (= intercourse with; ὁμιλία).
Bid, order (κελεύω).   *One is allowed, licet* (ἔξεστι).   *To be at leisure*
(σχολάζω).   *Leisure* (σχολή.   σχολῇ, *slowly :* with a verb = *am slow to
do a thing,* &c.).

Obs. τέ—καί is very often used, where *we* should only use '*and*.'—The
notions are thus brought into closer connexion, and the τέ prepares us
for the coming καί.

Exercise 20.

[When should μὴ κλέπτε be used? when μὴ κλέψῃς? 67.]

113. I will go away (65, g), that I may not see the battle.
Let us no longer pursue *what is disgraceful*[13].   He told me,
that the road did not lead to Athens (109).   Do not think,
that the citizens serve you.   If you do not do what you ought
(89, *c*), you will not prosper.   No longer accustom yourself
to deceive your father.   I will not take it, unless you bid
(me).   Let no one steal this.   Let not a single person go
away.   He says that the boys do not wish to go away.   Let
us not fly-from the company of the good.   He said that, unless
the citizens performed him this service[22], he would lay waste
the rest[19] of the country.   I shall be slow to do that[35].

---

§ 20.   *Verbals in* τέος.

114. *a.* G. ἐπιθυμητέον ἐστὶ τῆς ἀρετῆς, *we, you,* &c.
should desire *virtue.*

D. ἐπιχειρητέον ἐστὶ τῷ ἔργῳ, *we, you,* &c.
should set about *the work.*

A. κολαστέον ἐστὶ τὸν παῖδα, *we, you,* &c. should
punish *the boy.*

b. ἀσκητέον ἐστί σοι τὴν ἀρετήν,⎫ *you should cultivate*
ἀσκητέα ἐστί σοι ἡ ἀρετή,   ⎭   *virtue.*

c. πειστέον ἐστὶν αὐτόν, *we must persuade him.*
πειστέον ἐστὶν αὐτῷ, *we must obey him.*

---

[h] ἔρχομαι, ἐλεύσομαι, ἐλήλυθα, (ἤλυθον) ἦλθον.   See 65, g.

N.B. These examples may all be translated *passively*. *Virtue should be cultivated*, &c.

---

115. These verbals are formed both from *trans.* and *intrans.* verbs; and also from *mid.* (*deponent*) verbs, since they are sometimes used in a passive meaning.

116. (*a*) They are *passive*, and take the agent in the *dative;* but they *also* govern the object in the same case as the verbs from which they come.

117. (*a*) When used in the *neuter* (with the agent in the *dat.* omitted), they are equivalent to the participle in *dus* used in the same way, and express: ‘ *one must, ought,*’ &c. ; ‘ *we, you,* &c. *must, ought,*’ &c. ; or, ‘ *is to be,*’ &c.

118. (*b*) When formed from transitive verbs, they may also be used in *agreement with* the object, the agent being still in the dative.

Here, too, they exactly agree with the participle in *dus.*

119. Two peculiarities in Attic Greek deserve notice :
  1. The *neut. plur.* is used as well as the *neut. sing.*
  2. The *agent* is sometimes put in the accus. as well as the object.

120. (*c*) When a verb has two constructions with different meanings, the verbal adjective sometimes has both : thus πειστέον with *accus.* has the meaning of *persuade* (πείθειν τινά); with the *dat.* that of to *obey* (πείθεσθαί[i] τινι).

121. VOCABULARY 19.

To practise, exercise, cultivate (ἀσκέω). *Desire* (ἐπι-θυμέω gen., from ἐπί on, θυμός mind, passion). *Set about, take in hand* (ἐπι-χειρέω dat. from ἐπί, χείρ). *Work, task, production* (ἔργον). *Parent* (γονεύς). *Attempt, endeavour, try* (πειράομαι, v. adj. πειρᾱτέος). *Permit, suffer* (ἐάω[k], v. adj. ἐατέος). *Restrain by punishment, punish, chastise* (κολάζω, fut. —άσομαι). *Run, or fly, to the assistance of, assist in the defence of* (βοηθέω, dat.[l]).

Obs. These verbals should be formed from aor. 1. pass.[m] by rejecting

---

[i] Perf. 2. (or *mid.*) πέποιθα, *I trust*, or *feel sure* ; *I am persuaded.*

[k] Augment ι.

[l] From βοή *cry*, θέω *run.*

[m] For if the *aor.* 1. has a different vowel, &c. from *perf. pass.*, the *verbal adj.* follows *it*, and not the *perf.*

the *augment*, turning θην into τέος, and *therefore* the preceding *aspirate* (if there is one) into its *mute* (*i. e.* πτ, κτ, for φθ, χθ).

Form verbals from διώκω *pursue*, φεύγω *fly from*, ὠφελέω *benefit*.

Exercise 21.

122. The great work must be set about. We must not shun the labour. All the citizens should confer benefits on the state. He said that all the citizens ought to confer benefits on their country (*state*), when there is any occasion. We must fly-to-the-assistance of our country. We must set about the task of chastising [14] the boy. If the slave had done this, it would [26] be necessary to punish him. If the boy should do this, it would be necessary to punish him. He told us, that if this were so [27], we ought to set about the task. We must punish *not only* [28] my boy, *but also* my brother's [6]. Parents [15] and poets [n] love their own productions. He said that virtue should be cultivated by all. Whoever (ὅστις ἄν. 95, 2) *is* [32] caught, shall be punished. We must not *be slow* [35] to obey our parents.

§ 21. *Double Accusative.*

123. *a.* Θηβαίους χρήματα [o] ᾔτησαν [p], *they asked the Thebans for money.* *b.* οὔ σε ἀποκρύψω ταῦτα, *I will not hide this from you.* *c.* τοὺς πολεμίους τὴν ναῦν ἀπεστερήκαμεν, *we have deprived the enemy of their ship.* *d.* διδά-

[n] The *art.* must be repeated before '*poets*,' or the meaning would be '*those who are parents and poets :*' in other words, *both* attributes would be spoken of the *same subject.*

[o] From χράομαι (see 8, a). It is only in the *plur.* that it means *money*, &c. Properly, *a thing used.*

[p] αἰτεῖσθαι in the *mid.* (*sibi aliquid expetere*) does *not* take two accusatives, but one acc. and παρά; or one noun and an *infin.* *Poppo.*

σκουσι τοὺς παῖδας σωφροσύνην, *they teach the boys modesty* (*moderation* or *self-restraint*). *e.* τὸν παῖδα ἐξέδυσε τὸν χιτῶνα, *he stript the boy of his tunic.*

124. Verbs of *taking away from, teaching, concealing, asking, putting on* or *off,* take two accusatives.

125. VOCABULARY 20.

Thebans (Θηβαῖοι). *Money* (χρήματα). *Hide* (κρύπτω q, ἀπο-κρύπτω). *Ship* (ναῦς r). *Deprive of* (ἀποστερέω). *Take away from* (ἀφ-αιρέω s). *Teach* (διδάσκω t). *Modesty, moderation, self-restraint* (σωφροσύνη u). *To be wise* (i. e. *prudent*) or *in one's right mind* (σω-φρονέω). *To be mad* (μαίνομαι v). *Die* (θνήσκω w, ἀποθνήσκω). *Mortal* (θνητός). *Immortal* (ἀθάνατος). *Strip* or *take off* (ἐκδύω x). *Put on* (ἐνδύω x, in mid. *on* or *off myself*). *Tunic* (χιτών y). *Misfortune* (δυσπραγία, ā).

PHRASES.

But for (εἰ μὴ διά, acc.). *All but* (ὅσον οὐ, i. e. *just as much as not*). *Outside, without* (ἔξω, gen., τὰ ἔξω, external, outward things). *External* (ὁ ἔξω, 26). *Within* (ἔνδον, also *in doors, at home*; ἔνδον καταλαβεῖν, *to find* a man *in* or *at home*).

---

q In *aor.* 2. this verb has β for charact.

r ναῦς, νεώς, νηΐ, ναῦν, — νῆες, νεῶν, ναυσί, ναῦς. These are the forms as used in Attic Greek.

s αἱρέω (ἥσω, &c.), εἷλον, ᾑρέθην.

t διδάσκω, διδάξω -ομαι, δεδίδαχα.
   Act. *I teach.*   Mid. *I have* (them) *taught.*

u Σωφροσύνην .... quam soleo equidem quum *temperantiam* tum *moderationem* appellare, nonnunquam etiam *modestiam.* CIC. —σύνη, abstract nouns from adj. in ων (especially) and others.   σώφρων (from σῶς salvus, φρήν mens), *moderate, temperate,—prudent.*

v μαίνομαι, μανοῦμαι, μέμηνα (with meaning of *pres.*), aor. ἐμάνην.

w θνήσκω, θανοῦμαι, τέθνηκα, ἔθανον. The *perf.* and *aor.* = *I am dead.*

x δύω, *go into,* and also *make to go into,—sink, enclose.* Act. *fut.* and *aor.* with the trans. meaning. *Mid.* δύομαι, (δύσομαι, ἐδυσάμην) *enclose myself* = *put on* (a garment). ἔδυν (δῦθι—δῦναι, δύς) has also this meaning. Hence ἐνδύω, *put on:* ἐκδύω, *put off, strip* (with *fut.* and *aor.*); both of *another:* mid. *of myself.*

y An under-garment with sleeves, over which a mantle was worn out of doors.

Exercise 22.

[What is the *literal* English of εἰ μὴ διά?]

126. I will put on my tunic. Do not hide your misfortunes
from me. We will teach our daughters modesty. O mother,
do not teach your daughter impudence. We will take away
this from the woman. Let us not teach these most disgraceful
things to our boys. The rest of the Thebans were there to
see the battle. He would have died [37] *but for* the dog. Let us
not fly from the *all but present* war. I will put his tunic on
the boy. If the enemy do this [36], we will deprive them of their
ship. I should have died [37] *but for* my faithful slave. This
man has stript me of my tunic. If you do not perform me this
service [22], I will deprive you of your pay. If we find him at
home, we will kill him. He killed all who were within. Let
us love the company of the temperate. Let us not fear
external evils.

---

§ 22.   *The Accusative after Passive and Neuter Verbs.*

127. *a.* ἀφαιρεθεὶς [z] τὴν ἀρχήν, *having had his government
taken from him.*   *b.* ὁ Σωκράτης ἐπιτρέπεται τὴν δίαιταν,
Socrates is entrusted with the arbitration ; πεπίστευμαι [a] τοῦτο,
this is entrusted to me, or *I am entrusted with this.*   *c.* ἐκκοπεὶς
τοὺς ὀφθαλμούς, *having had his eyes knocked out.*   *d.* ῥεῖν
γάλα, *to flow with milk ;* ζῆν [b] βίον, *to live a life ;* κινδυνεύειν
κίνδυνον, *to brave a danger ;* πόλεμον πολεμεῖν, *to wage a war ;*
ὕπνον κοιμᾶσθαι, *to sleep a sleep.*   *e.* ἐνίκησε τοὺς βαρβά-
ρους τὴν ἐν Μαραθῶνι μάχην, *he conquered the barbarians
in the battle of Marathon.*

---

z 125, s.

a ἐγὼ πιστεύομαι (ὑπό τινος), *I am trusted, confided in,* or *believed.*

b ζάω, χράομαι, πεινάω, διψάω (*live, use, hunger, thirst*), contract αε into η
(not a). ζῶ, ζῇς, &c.

128. The *accus.* of the *active* becomes the *nom.* of the *pass.*

129. (*a*) If the verb governs two accusatives, that of the *person* becomes the *nominative;* that of the *thing* continues to be the object of the passive verb, as in Latin.   But also,

130. (*b*) The *dat.* of the active sometimes becomes the *nom.* of the passive ; the object of the active continuing to be the object of the passive in the accusative (ἐπιτρέπειν, πιστεύειν τινί τι).

131. (*d*) Intransitive verbs take an *acc.* of a noun of *kindred meaning;* and (as in ῥεῖν γάλα) of one that *restricts* the general notion of the verb to a particular instance.

(*e*) Here the ordinary *accus.* of the object is found together with this *limiting accusative.*

132. VOCABULARY 21.

To *commit, confide* or *entrust to* (ἐπιτρέπω *).   *Entrust to* (πιστεύω * ; also with *dat.* only, *to trust a person*).   *Arbitration* (δίαιτα).   *Faith* (πίστις, f.).   *Disbelieve, disobey* a person or law (ἀπιστέω, *dat.*).   *Law* (νόμος).   *Cut out, knock out* (ἐκ-κόπτω).   *Cut to pieces* (κατα-κόπτω).   *Government, magistracy* (ἀρχή, also *beginning:* acc. ἀρχήν, or τὴν ἀρχήν, used adverbially for '*at all*' or '*ever*' after negatives, when an *action* is spoken of).   *Danger* (κίνδυνος).   *Brave, incur, expose* oneself *to, a danger* (κινδυνεύειν κίνδυνον).   *Eye* (ὀφθαλμός).   *To sleep* (κοιμάομαι, aor. θην).   *Sleep* (ὕπνος).   *Fountain* (πηγή).   *Flow* (ῥέω [c]).   *Flows with a full* or *strong stream* (πολὺς ῥεῖ, the *adj.* being in the case and gender of its noun).   *Honey* (μέλι, ιτος, n.).   *Conquer* (νικάω).   *Victory* (νίκη).   *Barbarian,* i. e. *one who is not a Greek* (βάρβαρος).   *To hold a magistracy* or *office* (ἄρχειν ἀρχήν).   *Milk* (γάλα, n. R. γαλακτ).   *River* (ποταμός).

Exercise 23.

133. I have had the arbitration entrusted to me.   He said, that he had had the arbitration entrusted to him (67, *c*).   The eagle has had its eyes knocked out.   The fountains flow with milk and honey.   If the fountains flow with both milk and

---

* For the distinction between these words, see Index under '*entrust to.*'

[c] ῥέω, ῥυήσομαι, ἐρρύηκα; aor. ἐρρύην (*flowed*); (ἔρρευσα and ῥεύσομαι, not Attic.)

honey, we shall become rich [36]. If the rivers had flowed with
wine, the citizens would have become rich. If the citizens are
wise, they will put him to death. If the citizens are mad (*aor*.),
they will put you to death. You will not be able (84, *b*) to
disbelieve your mother. The rivers are flowing with a strong
stream. The thing has *all but* [40] been done. I should have
killed you, *but for* [39] your father. Sophroniscus had his government taken away from him. He has had his government taken
away from him. Hares have large eyes [12]. Let us try to bear
what comes from the gods [25]. We must try [38] to bear *what fortune
sends* [25]. He conquered the Persians in the battle that took
place there (*in the there battle*). I will not expose myself to
this danger. The people outside were cut to pieces. I asked
the boy himself, whether (67, *c*) the river was flowing with a
strong stream. I asked Sophroniscus what magistracy he held.

---

§ 23.　*The Accusative continued.*

134. *a.* καλὸς τὸ σῶμα, *beautiful in person.* Σωκράτης τοὔ-
νομα[d], *Socrates by name.* πλήττομαι τὴν κεφαλήν,
I am struck on the head. πάντα εὐδαιμονεῖ, *he is
happy in all respects.*

b. τί χρῶμαι αὐτῷ; *what use shall I make of it? what
am I* [e] *to do with it?* οὐκ οἶδα ὅ,τι σοι χρῶμαι,
*I don't know what use to make of you; I don't
know what to do with you.*

c. πολὺν χρόνον, *a long time.* τρεῖς ὅλους μῆνας, *three
whole months.* τὰ πολλά, *mostly,* (for) *most of
his time.* ἀπέχει δέκα σταδίους, *it is ten stadia*

---

[d] = τὸ ὄνομα.

[e] The *subj.* used as in 98, *c.* expresses more *doubt* as to what *is to be done* than
the *fut.*

off. d. τοὐναντίον [f], *on the contrary.* τὸ λεγόμενον, *as the saying is.*

135. (*a*) The accus. is used after nouns and adjectives where
κατά, *as to*, might be *supposed* understood.

It thus *limits* the preceding word to a particular *part, circumstance, &c.*

136. (*b*) The accus. of a *neut. pronoun* or any general expression, is often used in this way after verbs that would govern
a *substantive* in another case.

137. (*c*) The accusative is used to express *duration of time*,
and the *distance* of one place from another.

138. VOCABULARY 22.

Whole (ὅλος). *Body, person* (σῶμα). *Month* (μήν, ὁ). *Name* (ὄνομα).
To strike (πλήσσω, *Att.* πλήττω : used by the Attics only in *perf. act.*
and in the *pass.* For other tenses πατάσσω, ξω, used). *Unjust* (ἄδικος).
Do injustice to, injure (ἀδικέω, acc. of *person*, and *also* of thing). *Injustice*
(ἀδικία. ἀδικεῖν ἀδικίαν, *to commit an injury*). *Staff* (ῥάβδος, f.). *Insult*
(ὑβρίζω, acc. ; ὑβρίζειν εἴς τινα, *to act insolently towards*). *Insult, insolence* (ὕβρις, f.) *Reverence* (αἰδέομαι, ἔσομαι and aor. 1. *pass.*: acc.).
Run away from (ἀποδιδράσκω [g], acc.). *To have no fear of, to be without
fear of* (θαρρέω, acc.). *Mild, gentle* (πρᾶος [h]). *Disposition* (ἦθος, n.).
To be distant from (ἀπέχω ; mid. *abstain from*, gen.). *Use, do with*
(χράομαι, dat.). *Stadium* (στάδιος or στάδιον).

Exercise 24.

[Why is ὅστις used in 134, *b* ? 67, [l].]

139. The boy is of a mild disposition. He told me that his
daughter was of a mild disposition. If any one of your slaves
should run away from you, and you should take him, what
would you do with him [36]? A certain philosopher, Socrates by
name, was there, *to see* the man. Accustom yourself to have-

---

[f] = τὸ ἐναντίον.

[g] διδράσκω, δράσομαι, δέδρāκα. ἔδραν (δρᾶθι, δραίην, δρῶ (ᾷς, &c.), δρᾶναι,
δράς).

[h] πρᾶος B. (πρᾶος P. R. K.) takes *all fem.* and *neut. plur.* as if from πραύς,
πραεῖα, n. pl. πραέα.
Plur. mas. πρᾷοι, πραεῖς; G. πραέων; D. πρᾴοις, πραέσι(ν); A. πρᾴους,
πραεῖς.

no-fear-of death. I am not without fear of the king of the Persians. I have been struck on my head [41]. He struck the boy with a staff. Accustom yourself to reverence your parents. Insult nobody. The injury (*nom.*) which they committed against you. We ought to do [38] what is just [13], and *abstain* [i] from what is unjust. The city is three stadia off. Let us avoid insolence. We must pursue what is just. Let us insult nobody. Let us no longer act insolently towards those who [1] manage the affairs of the state.

§ 24. *The Genitive.*

[The fundamental notion of the genitive is *separation from, proceeding from ;* i. e. the notion of the prepositions *from, out of.* B.]

140. *a.* οἱ φρόνιμοι τῶν ἀνθρώπων, *sensible persons.* οὐδεὶς Ἑλλήνων, *none of the Greeks.* ἡ μεγίστη τῶν νόσων, *the greatest of diseases.* *b.* τρὶς τῆς ἡμέρας, *three times a day.* ποῖ γῆς; *to (at) what part of the world?* ποῦ γῆς; *in what part of the world?* πόρρω τῆς ἡλικίας, *far advanced in years.* *c.* ἔδωκά σοι τῶν χρημάτων, *I gave you* (some) *of my money.* πίνειν ὕδατος, *to drink some water.* ἐσθίειν κρεῶν, *to eat* some *meat* (of a particular time : with the *accusative* the meaning would be, to do it habitually). *d.* στέφανος ὑακίνθων, *a crown of hyacinths.* δένδρον πολλῶν ἐτῶν, *a tree many years old.* ἦν γὰρ ἀξιώματος μεγάλου, *for he was of great consideration.* *e.* διαρπάζουσι τὰ ἐμὰ τοῦ κακοδαίμονος, *they are plundering my property,* wretched man that I am ! τῆς ἀναιδείας, *what impudence !*

141. (*a*) Partitives, numerals, superlatives, &c. govern the genitive.

---

i The *verbal adj.* from ἀπέχεσθαι is ἀφεκτέος, a word not found in Passow's Lexicon, but used by Xenophon. It, of course, governs the *gen.*

142. (*b*) The genitive is used with adverbs of *time* and *place*.

143. (*d*) The genitive also expresses the *material* out of which any thing is made; and generally such *properties*, *circumstances*, &c. as *we* should express by '*of*.'

Obs. 1. (*b*) Our *indef. art.* must be translated by the Greek (*def.*) *art.* in expressions like ' once *a* day,' &c., where ' a ' is equivalent to ' each.'

Obs. 2. (*e*) The *gen.* stands after *possessive pronouns* in a kind of apposition to the personal pronoun implied. It may often be translated as an exclamation. The gen. is also used alone, or after interjections, as an *exclamation*.

144. VOCABULARY 23.

Sensible, prudent (φρόνιμος). Greek ("Ελλην). Greece ('Ελλάς, άδος, f.). To what place? whither? (ποῖ;)—where? (ποῦ;) Far, far on (πόρρω). A person's age (ἡλικία). To drink (πίνω [k]). To eat (ἐσθίω [l]). Flesh, meat (κρέας [m], n.). Crown (στέφανος). Tree (δένδρον [n]). Year (ἔτος, n.). Consideration, reputation (ἀξίωμα). Violet (ἴον, Fίον). Lily (κρίνον [o], n.). Golden (χρύσεος, χρυσοῦς [p]). Place on (ἐπι-τίθημι), dat.). Worthless, despicable (φαῦλος). Arrive (ἀφ-ικνέομαι [q]). To be given (δοτέος, from ἐδόθην). Plunder (διαρπάζω, fut. mid.). Wretched, unfortunate (κακοδαίμων). Alas (φεῦ,—οἴμοι).

PHRASES.

Till late in the day (μέχρι πόρρω τῆς ἡμέρας). Willingly at least (ἑκὼν εἶναι [r]). So to say, to speak generally (ὡς ἔπος εἰπεῖν [r], showing that a general assertion is not *absolutely* true).

---

[k] πίνω, (irreg. *fut.*) πίομαι, πέπωκα, πέπομαι. ἔπιον, ἐπόθην.

[l] ἐσθίω (from ἔδω), (irreg. *fut.*) ἔδομαι, ἐδήδοκα, ἐδήδεσμαι. ἔφαγον (from root φαγ), ἠδέσθην.

[m] G. αος, ως, &c.

[n] δένδρον, D. plur. δένδρεσι (also plur. δένδρεα, δενδρέοις from another *Ionic* form).

[o] κρίνον has in *plur.* a collateral form κρινέα, D. κρίνεσι, as if from κρίνος, n.

[p] B. p. 24. W. p. 21, Obs. 2.

[q] ἰκνέομαι, ἵξομαι, ἶγμαι, ἱκόμην.

[r] Such short phrases with the *infin.* are inserted in the sentence: ὅθεν δὴ ἐκοῦσα εἶναι οὐκ ἀπολείπεται ἡ ψυχή. See 151, a.

Exercise 25.

145. I will place a crown of violets on the boy's head. The mother placed a crown of lilies on her daughter's head. Let us imitate sensible persons. Let us not imitate *worthless persons* [47]. I will be with you three times every year. If he were not (*a person*) of great consideration [36], the citizens would have put him to death. At what part of the earth am I arrived? I will give each of them a golden crown. He told me that we ought to give to each of them a golden crown (72). If he had not been advanced in years, he would not have died. They slept (*used to sleep*) till late in the day. Let us bear whatever the gods please [33] (91*). All men, *so to say,* admire rich men. No Grecian will do this, *at least willingly.* I will not drink *any* of the wine, at least willingly. I will give *some* of the flesh to this eagle. My property was plundered, *wretched man that I am!* Alas, what injustice! Alas, for my possessions! Let us fly from the greatest of diseases, shamelessness.

---

§ 25. *The Genitive continued.*

146. *a.* πρακτικὸς τῶν καλῶν, *apt to perform* (or, *in the habit of performing*) *honorable actions.*

    b. μεστόν ἐστι τὸ ζῆν φροντίδων, *life is full of cares.* ἄξιος τιμῆς, *worthy of honour.* δεῖσθαι χρημάτων, *to want money;* also δεῖσθαί τινος (*gen.* of person), *to beseech a person.*

    c. ὄζειν μύρων, *to smell of perfumes.* ἅπτεσθαι νεκροῦ, *to touch a corpse.* ἀκούειν παιδίου κλαίοντος, *to hear a child crying.*

τοὺς δούλους ἔγευσε τῆς ἐλευθερίας, *he allowed his slaves to taste of liberty.*

ἄγευστος τῆς ἐλευθερίας, *one who has never tasted of liberty.*

d. ἔχεσθαί τινος, *to cling to,* or *be next to.* σωτηρίας
ἔχεσθαι, *to provide* (carefully and anxiously) *for
one's safety.*

e. ἄπαις ἀρρένων παίδων, *without male offspring.* ἐγγύ-
τατα αὐτῷ εἰμι γένους, *I am very nearly related
to him* (literally, *very near to him with respect to
birth*). δασὺς δένδρων, *thick with trees; thickly
planted with trees.*

f. εὐδαιμονίζω σε τοῦ τρόπου, *I think you happy in
your disposition.* οἰκτείρω σε τοῦ πάθους, *I
pity you on account of your affliction.*

147. (*a*) *Verbal adjectives* with a transitive meaning govern
the genitive.

> That is, the object of the verb stands in the *gen.* after the verbal
> adjective.

147*. (*b*) Words relating to *plenty, want, value,* &c., govern
the genitive.

148. (*c*) Verbs relating to the *senses,* except *sight,* govern
the genitive.

> ἀκούειν, *hear,* generally takes a *gen.* of the sound, and an *acc.* of the
> *person* producing it : but in neither case without exception.

149. (*e. f.*) The genitive is often used where we may supply
' *in respect to* ' in English.

> In this way, the *gen.* restricts a general expression to a particular
> meaning ; to some particular *circumstance, object,* &c.
> The genitive so used may often be *supposed* governed by ἕνεκα, *on
> account of.* It is very frequently used in this way after words compounded
> with a *privative.*

150. VOCABULARY 24.

> *Apt to do* or *perform ; in the habit of doing* or *performing* (πρακτικός [s]).
> *Apt,* or *fit, to govern* (ἀρχικός). *To govern* (ἄρχω, gen.). *To smell of,*
> i. e. *emit a smell* (ὄζω [t]) *Ointment, perfume* (μύρον). *Touch* (ἅπτομαι).

---

[s] ικός, appended to *verbal* roots, denotes *fitness to do* what the verb expresses.
Appended to the root of substantives, it has the same latitude of meaning as ιος
(20, n.).

[t] ὄζω, ὀζήσω, ὄδωδα (with meaning of *pres.*).

Corpse (νεκρός, m.—adj. *dead*). *Free* (ἐλεύθερος). *Freedom, liberty*
(ἐλευθερία). *Hear* (ἀκούω u). *Child* (παιδίον v). *Cry* (κλαίω w). *Give to
taste, allow to taste* (γεύω). *One who has not tasted* (ἄγευστος). *Childless* (ἄπαις, δος). *Male* (ἄρρην x). *Near* (ἐγγύς, gen.). *Race, family,
birth* (γένος, n.). *Thick, crowded* (δασύς). *Think or pronounce happy*
(εὐδαιμονίζω). *Disposition* (τρόπος y). *Pity* (οἰκτείρω). *Suffering,
affliction* (πάθος, plur. *the passions*). *Worthy* (ἄξιος.) *Honour* (τῑμή).
Want, beseech (δέομαι, —ήσομαι, ήθην). *Full of* (μεστός). *Life* (τὸ
ζῆν). *Cares* (φροντίδες). *Not at all* (οὐδέν, μηδέν, often followed by τί:
οὐδέν τι, &c.).

　　　What is the *verbal adj.* in τέος from εὐδαιμονίζω? (εὐδαιμονιστέος.)
　　　Who in the world? (τίς ποτε z ;)
　　　What is the meaning of ἔχεσθαι with *gen.? * [146, *d.*]

Exercise 26.

151. I asked whether (67, *c*) the children of the judge were
in the habit of performing just actions. If you are in the habit
of performing just actions, you will be happy. I will make the
boy fit to govern men. I am not at all in want of money. I
would not touch a corpse, at least willingly. If the physician
had been present, my child would not have died. Let us ask
the next (subjects) to these. I think you happy on account of
your virtue. They pitied the mother on account of her affliction. The boy is nearly related to Socrates (*e*). He told me
that the boy was very nearly related to Socrates. We ought
to think the temperate happy. I would not *willingly* touch a
corpse a. I asked the boy whether he thought life full of cares.
What in the world am I to do with him (134, *b*)?

---

u ἀκούω, ἀκούσομαι, ἀκήκοα, ἤκουσμαι, ἤκουσα.

v —ιον the principal termination of *diminutives :* παῖς, παιδίον. Those that
form a dactyl are *paroxytone ;* the rest *proparoxytone.*

w κλαίω (κλαύσομαι, κλαυσοῦμαι); but aor. ἔκλαυσα. *Att.* κλάω (ᾱ).

x In *old Att.* ἄρσην.

y τρόπος from τρέπω, *to turn ;* as *we* say, *a man's* turn of mind.

N. B. Nouns in ος, from verbal roots, generally change ε of the root into ο.

z ποτέ (enclitic), *at any time ;* used with interrogatives, it expresses *surprise.*

a ἑκὼν εἶναι is confined to negative sentences.

Exercise 27.

152. Who *in the world* admires these things? Who in the world is this? If these things *are so*, let us carefully provide for our safety. Let us speak what[1] comes next (146, *d*) to this. What in the world are you admiring? I asked the judge, what in the world the citizens were admiring. The boy is nearly related to Sophroniscus. Xenoclides will be general, with three others[21]. Let us rule over our passions. We must set about[38] the task of ruling over our passions. He told me that he was one-who-had-never-tasted-of liberty. Let us cling to our liberty. He told me 'that the whole[20] country was thickly planted with trees. The judge is most worthy of honour. What *in the world* shall we do with the boy?

---

§ 26. *The Genitive continued.*

153. *a.* Most verbs that express such notions as *freeing from, keeping off from, ceasing from, deviating* or *departing from*, &c. govern the *gen.*

    b. Most verbs that express *remembering* or *forgetting; caring for* or *despising; sparing; aiming at* or *desiring; ruling over* or *excelling; accusing of* or *condemning*, &c. govern the *genitive;* but not without many exceptions.

154. VOCABULARY 25.

    (*a*) [Verbs governing the *genitive :* the transitive ones with *acc.* also of course.]

      To free from (ἀπαλλάττω, γ ; also, *to come out of an affair, come off, get off,* ἐκ, ἀπό. Mid. *take oneself off;* aor. 2. pass. with *mid.* meaning). *Exclude from* (εἴργω[b]). *Make to cease* (παύω, mid. *cease*). *Leave off,*

---

    [b] In *Attic* Greek, εἴργω is *excludo*, εἵργω *includo*. B.

desist from (λήγω). *Miss, err* (ἁμαρτάνω [c]; also *to sin,* εἰς or περί, with acc. *against*). *Differ* (διαφέρω, 60, *b*). *Way* (ὁδός, f.). *Chase, hunting* (θήρα). *Sea* (θάλασσα). *Disease* (νόσος, f.). *Physician* (ἰατρός). *With impunity* (χαίρων, *part.* literally *rejoicing*). *Toil, labour* (πόνος, also *trouble*). *Market-place* (ἀγορά). *Heavy-armed soldier, Hoplite* (ὁπλίτης, ῐ).

Exercise 28.

155. Death will free us from all our toils. They will exclude the Persians from the sea. He told me, that the Athenians were excluding the Persians from the sea. They are here *to exclude* (67, *b*) the Grecian [d] Hoplites from the market-place. Speaking [14] fast is a different thing (*differs*) from speaking well. A good king does not *at all* * differ from a good father. The physician was there, that he might free the boy from his disease. He told me, that the physician had missed his way. If the judge had been there, you would not have escaped with impunity. If the king is there, they will not escape with impunity. They who have sinned [1] against the state, will not escape with impunity. The boy is desisting from the chase. If I had known this, I would not have tried *at all* [54] to persuade him.

§ 27. *The Genitive continued.*

156. Vocabulary 26.

(*b*) [Verbs governing the *genitive*.]

Remember (μέμνημαι [e]). *Forget* (ἐπιλανθάνομαι [f]). *Care for, have*

---

[c] ἁμαρτάνω, ἁμαρτήσομαι, ἡμάρτηκα. ἥμαρτον.

[d] *Of the Greeks.*

* οὐδέν τι, not ἀρχήν : for ' *at all*' does not here refer to an *action*.

[e] The *third* (*paulo post*) *fut.* is the *fut.* used for verbs that have a *perf.* of the *pass.* form with the meaning of a *present*: as μέμνημαι, μεμνήσομαι.

[f] λανθάνω, λήσω, λέληθα. ἔλαθον.
  Mid. λανθάνομαι, λήσομαι, λέλησμαι. ἐλαθόμην.

E

any regard for (κήδομαι). *Hold cheap* (ὀλιγωρέω). *Despise* (καταφρονέω). *Spare* (φείδομαι). *Desire* (ἐπιθυμέω : *desire,* ἐπιθυμία). *Aim at* (στοχάζομαι). *Master* (κρατέω). *Overcome* (περιγίγνομαι). *Get the better of, surpass* (περίειμι). *Accuse, charge* (κατηγορέω; pass. *to be laid to the charge of*). *Condemn* (καταγιγνώσκω ᵍ).

[*Obs.* κατηγορέω may have acc. of the *charge* or *crime,* gen. of the person : or, if no crime is mentioned, *gen.* of *person.*

καταγιγνώσκω has *accus.* of the *charge,* or *punishment ; gen.* of *person.* In the *pass.* the *acc.* will of course become the *nom.,* and the *gen.* of the *person* remain.]

Impiety (ἀσέβεια ; *impious,* ἀσεβής, 87, z). *Piety* (εὐσέβεια; *pious,* εὐσεβής). *Banishment* (φυγή). *Former* (ὁ πρίν, 27). *Folly* (μωρία). *Laughter* (γέλως, ωτος). *I at least, I for my part* (ἔγωγε). *Far =* much, greatly (πολύ). *Forefather, ancestor* (πρόγονος).

Exercise 29.

What is the usual opt. of contracted verbs? [οίην, ψην.]

157. I remember my *former* ¹¹ troubles. They asked him whether he despised the Persians. Do not despise your neighbour. Let us spare our money. They accuse the judge himself of injustice. They condemned them all to death (*Obs.*). Do not aim at producing ¹⁴ laughter. The men of the present day ¹¹ have forgotten the virtue of their ancestors. Much injustice is laid to the charge of Xenoclides. The father of Xenoclides was found guilty ²⁷ of impiety. Most persons desire money. Let us master our desires. Do not desire the property ¹⁰ of your neighbour. Let us fly from the company of the impious. Let us not only speak well of the pious, but let us also confer benefits ¹⁶ upon them.

Exercise 30.

158. They have condemned Sophroniscus to banishment (*Obs.*). He accuses the others of folly. If you had done this³⁶, I for my part should have accused you of folly. If you do this,

---

ᵍ γιγνώσκω, γνώσομαι, ἔγνωκα, ἔγνωσμαι. *Aor.* ἔγνων.
(ἔγνων, γνῶθι, γνοίην, γνῶ, γνῶναι, γνούς.)

I for my part shall accuse you of folly. If any one should do this, the prudent would accuse him of folly. He said that, if any man did this, the prudent would accuse him of folly. I think you happy on account of your piety (146, *f*). This boy far surpasses his brother in virtue (*dat.*). Alas what folly [50] ! These things happened in the time of [26] our forefathers. He said, that to be prosperous was not in our (own) power [26].

---

§ 28.　*The Genitive continued.*

158*. *a.* δραχμῆς ἀγοράζειν τι, *to buy something* for a drachma.

b. πλείστου[h] τοῦτο τιμῶμαι, *I value this* at a very high price (very highly).

c. τρεῖς μνᾶς κατέθηκε τοῦ ἵππου, *he laid down three minæ* for the horse.

χρήματα τούτων πράττεται, *he exacts the money* (or *payment*) for this.

d. νυκτός, *by night;* ἡμέρας, *by day;* χρόνου συχνοῦ, *for a considerable time.*

e. πολλῶν ἡμερῶν οὐ μεμελέτηκα, *I have not practised* for many days.

f. λαβεῖν (generally λαβέσθαι) ποδός, *to take (a person)* by the foot. ἄγειν χειρός, *to lead* by the hand.

g. τὸν λύκον τῶν ὤτων κρατῶ, *I get hold of the wolf* by the ears.

h. τοῦτο οὐκ ἔστιν ἀνδρὸς σοφοῦ, *this is not* the part of a wise man.

i. οὐ παντὸς εἶναι, *not to be a thing* that every body can do. ἑαυτοῦ εἶναι, *to be* one's own master.

---

[h] πολύς, πλείων or πλέων, πλεῖστος.

159. (*a. b.*) After verbs of *price* and *value*, the *price* or *value* is put in the *genitive*.

160. After verbs that express or imply *exchange*, the thing *for which* we exchange another is put in the *genitive*.

161. (*d. e.*) A noun of *time* is put in the *gen.* in answer to the questions *when?* and *since*, or *within what time?*

[If the point of time is defined by a *numeral* adjective, *the time when* is put in the *dative :* it stands however in the *gen.* with *the former, the same, each*, &c.]

162. (*f. g.*) The *gen.* expresses the part *by which* a person *leads, takes*, or *gets hold of* any thing.

163. VOCABULARY 27.

Purchase, buy (ἀγοράζω [i]—properly, *am in the market-place*, ἀγορά).
Drachma (δραχμή). To value (τιμάομαι). Mina (μνᾶ). Lay down
(κατα-τίθημι). To exact, to exact payment (πράττεσθαι). Considerable, long—of time (συχνός, properly *continuous*). To practise (μελετάω).
To take hold of (λαβέσθαι, 92, o). To get hold of (κρατέω, properly *to
master*). Equestrian exercises (τὰ ἱππικά).

Exercise 31.

164. The king will not fight (these) ten days.   No one has arrived for a long time.   I should like to purchase [29] this for three minæ.   It is the part of a good man to confer benefits upon his friends.   He told me that he valued this very highly. He said that, if he had a talent, he would lay it down for this horse (102).   It is not every man that can master [56] his desires. He took hold of the boy by his foot.   The mother leads her daughter by the hands.   I have not practised equestrian exer-

---

[i] (*a*) The *being* or *having* what the root denotes, is expressed by verbs in

άω, έω, εύω, ώσσω (ώττω), άζω, ίζω.

(*b*) The *making* a thing *into*, or *furnishing it with* what the root denotes, is expressed by verbs in

όω, ίζω, ύνω (ῠ), αίνω.

Obs. These meanings are not invariably observed : *e. g.* those in ίζω are set down as belonging to both classes.   The least subject to change are those in έω, εύω, όω.   R.

cises for a long time. Two dogs had got hold of the same
wolf by the ears. Three dogs had got hold of the wolf by the
same ear. The boys are practising equestrian exercises.
They exact payment for the horse. If you care for yourself,
provide for your safety. If they cared for the boy, they would
not do this. I had got hold of the wolf itself by the ears. It
is not every man who can get hold of a wolf by the ears [k]. It
is not every man that is-without-fear-of death. A slave is not
his own master. I will go away by night. The Scythians
went away by night.

---

§ 29. *Comparison.*

165. *a.* μείζων ἐμοῦ, *taller* (greater) *than I.*

　　b. κάλλῑον ἐμοῦ ᾄδεις, *you sing better* (more beauti-
　　　fully) *than I* (do).

　　c. δυνατώτεροι αὐτοὶ αὑτῶν[1] ἐγίγνοντο, *they became
　　　more powerful* than ever (literally, *more powerful
　　　themselves than themselves,* i. e. than themselves
　　　were at any other time).

　　d. μείζω ἢ κατὰ δάκρυα πεπονθέναι, *to have suffered
　　　afflictions too great for tears.*

　　　νεκρὸς μείζων ἢ κατ' ἄνθρωπον[m], *a corpse* of
　　　　superhuman size.

　　　ὅπλα πλέω ἢ κατὰ τοὺς νεκρούς, *more arms than
　　　　could have been expected from the number of
　　　　the dead* (*quam pro* numero).

　　e. νεώτεροί εἰσιν ἢ ὥστε εἰδέναι οἵων πατέρων ἐστέ-
　　　ρηνται, *they are* too young to know *what fathers
　　　they have lost.*

---

[k] *To get hold of,* &c. . . . . . *is not the part of,* &c.

[1] So in *superl.* δεινότατος σαυτοῦ ἦσθα.

[m] Literally, *greater than in proportion to* (or *according to*) *man.*

166. (*a*) The thing with which another is compared, is put in the genitive.

The fuller construction is with ἤ, *than;* which however is used only where the genitive cannot be employed.

(*b*) The *gen.* is sometimes used, where it is not the *immediate* object of comparison : e. g. in *b*, the things compared are not '*I*' and '*your singing ;*' but '*my singing*' and '*yours.*'

167. (*c*) *Greater,* &c. *than ever, than at any other time,* is expressed by using αὐτός, before the *gen.* of the reciprocal pronoun.

168. (*d. e.*) *Too great,* &c. is expressed by the *comparative* with ἤ κατά [n] before a *substantive; ἤ ὥστε* before a *verb* in the *infinitive.*

168*. VOCABULARY 28.

Sing (ᾄδω [o]). *Sing better* (κάλλιον ᾄδειν). *Powerful* (δυνατός). *Tear* (δάκρυον). *Suffer* (πάσχω [p]). *Arms* (ὅπλα [q]). *Young* (νέος). *Deprive* (στερέω [r]—ἀποστερέω). *Dance* (χορεύω). *Master, teacher* (διδάσκαλος). *Pupil* (μαθητής).

[Words that go with comparatives to mark the *degree* of excess or defect.]

Still (ἔτι). *Much* (πολλῷ [s]). *Little, a little* (ὀλίγῳ). *The—the* (ὅσῳ —τοσούτῳ, quanto—tanto).

Exercise 32.

169. The boy is taller than his father. The boy is wiser than his master. The daughter sings better than her mother. You have become more powerful *than ever* (*c*). The Athenians have become more powerful than ever. The good judge is

---

[n] Or ἤ πρός.

[o] ᾄδω (ἀείδω), *fut.* ᾄσομαι, but *aor.* ᾖσα.

[p] πάσχω, πείσομαι, πέπονθα. ἔπαθον.

[q] Properly, *instruments* or *tools* of any kind.

[r] This verb is most common in the *pass.* form, with fut. mid., in the sense, *am deprived of :*

στεροῦμαι, στερήσομαι, ἐστέρημαι. ἐστερήθην, &c.

Ἀποστερέω (123, c.) is more common than στερέω. [στερίσκω is the common form of the pres. act. : στέρομαι of the pres. pass.]

[s] Sometimes the *acc.* is used ; μέγα, πολύ, &c.

suffering afflictions too great for tears (*d*). More arms were taken than could have been expected from the number of the dead (*d*). He told me, that the corpse was of a superhuman size. If I had practised, I should have sung[t] better than my mother. If you do this, you will become more powerful than ever. If they *were* to do[36] this, they would become more powerful than ever. If they had done this, they would have become more powerful than ever. He said that, if they did this, they would become more powerful than ever (102). He said that, if they had done this, they would have become more powerful than ever. He is too wise (*e*) to be deceived by his slave. The masters are too wise to be deceived by their pupils. The pupils practise by night, that they may become wiser than their masters. He said that he should have died *but for*[39] the dog. The boys dance better than their masters. Practise virtue, that you may become really wise. They are too young to know that virtue ought[38] to be desired. The boy is still taller than his father. The girl is a little taller than her mother. The daughter sings much better than her mother. *The* more they have, *the* more they desire.

---

§ 30. *Comparison continued.*

170. *a.* ταχύτερα ἢ σοφώτερα (*Herod.*), *with more haste than wisdom.*

     b. ὡς τάχιστα, *as quickly as possible.* σιγῇ ὡς ἀνυστὸν προσῄεσαν, *they came up* as silently as possible. ὅτι μέγιστος, *as great as possible.*

     c ὅσους ἠδύνατο πλείστους[u] ἀθροίσας, *having collected* as many men as he possibly could.

     d. καίπερ, εἴ τις καὶ ἄλλος, ἔχεις πρὸς τὰ ἔτη μέλαιναν τὴν τρίχα, *though* if any body *has black*

---

[t] *Imperf.*, because the meaning is, '*I should now be* a better singer.'

[u] Or, ὅτι πλείστους ἀθροίσας.

hair for his years, it is you (*i. e.* you have remarkably black hair for your years).

e. τοὺς ἀγωνιζομένους πλεῖστα εἰς ἀνὴρ δυνάμενος ὠφελεῖν, *being able to be of* more service *to the contending parties*, than any other individual.

f. περιττὰ τῶν ἀρκούντων, *more than enough* (of money, &c.). πολλαπλάσιοι ἡμῶν αὐτῶν, *many times as numerous as ourselves*.

171. (*a*) Two comparatives are to be translated by *more— than*, or *rather—than*, with the *positive*.

For adverbs it is often convenient, as in the example, to use a substantive.

172. (*b*) Ὡς and ὅτι (like the Latin *quam*) are used to strengthen superlatives. (So also ὅπως, ᾗ, &c.)

173. (*d. e.*) εἴ τις καὶ ἄλλος (*si quis alius*), and εἷς ἀνήρ (*unus omnium maxime*), have the force of superlatives.

(εἷς γε ἀνὴρ ὤν is also used.)

174. (*f*) περιττός (*exceeding, over and above*), and adjectives in -πλάσιος (*-fold*), govern the genitive from their *comparative* meaning.

175. VOCABULARY 29.

Silently (σιγῇ). *To come on, come up* (πρός-ειμι). *As many as* (ὅσοι). *Most* (πλεῖστοι). *Feasible* (ἀνυστός, from ἀνύτειν, *to perform*). *Although* (καίπερ). *For your years* (πρὸς τὰ ἔτη). *Hair* (θρίξ, τριχός, f.). *Collect* (ἀθροίζω). *To be enough* or *sufficient* (ἀρκέω, *f.* ἔσω). *Many times as many* or *much* (πολλαπλάσιοι). *Twice as many* (διπλάσιοι). *Brave* (ἀνδρεῖος). *Slow* (βραδύς). *Slowly* (βραδέως). *Gift* (δῶρον). *To give a share of, give some* (μετα-δίδωμι, gen. of thing ; dat. of person).

Exercise 33 ᵛ.

176. One could not find (84) a blacker dog than this. They

ᵛ In doing the exercises of the form : " *if any one—it is* " (*d*), replace mentally '*it is*' by the verb ; " if any man practises temperance, it is he" = *if any man practises temperance, he* practises temperance, i. e. *he, if any other man* (does), *practises temperance*.

In those of the form "*more than any other single person*," replace this form by πλεῖστα εἰς ἀνήρ, or εἷς γε ἀνὴρ ὤν.

are more wise than brave. If any man practises temperance, it is he. He received more gifts than any other one man. If you had done this, you would have done more bravely ᵂ than wisely. I shall collect as many men as possible (*c*). The Persians came on *as slowly as possible.* He has injured the state more than any other single person. He has collected as many ships as possible. When you have collected ³² as many men as possible, march against Cyrus. The just judge has been of more service to the state than any other single person. The army of the Persians comes on as silently as possible (*b*). If you have more than enough, give some to your friends. If they were bold, they would conquer twice as many as themselves. More hares were taken *than could have been expected from the* (small) *number of the dogs* ⁵⁹. One could not find a more beautiful woman than the mother of this Scythian. If any man has been of great service to the state, it is he.

---

§ 31. *The Dative.*

177. *a.* τὰ αὐτὰ πάσχω σοί, *I suffer* the same as you.

Θησεὺς κατὰ τὸν αὐτὸν χρόνον Ἡρακλεῖ γενόμενος, *Theseus who lived about* the same time as Hercules.

b. πατάσσειν ῥάβδῳ, *to beat with a stick.*

c. δρόμῳ παρῆλθεν, *he came running* (literally, *at a running pace*).

μεγάλῃ σπουδῇ, *in great haste.*

d. φόβῳ, *through fear.* κάμνειν νόσῳ, *to be suffering from* (or *ill of*) *a disease.*

ἀλγεῖν τινι, *to be pained at a thing.*

e. τῇ τρίτῃ ἡμέρᾳ, *on the third day.*

ᵂ *Comparative sing.* by rule 57 ; not *plur.* as in example.

f. ταῦτα λέλεκται ἡμῖν, *these things have been said by us.*

178.   The notion of the dative is *opposed* to that of the genitive, as its fundamental notion is that of *approach to.*

179.   The *dat.* expresses the person *to* or *for* whom a thing is done: it also follows words that express *union* or *coming together*, and those that express *likeness* or (*a*) *identity*.

180.   (*b*) The *instrument*, (*c*) the *manner*, and (*d*) the *cause*, are put in the dative.

181.   (*e*) The *definite* time at which a thing is done, is put in the dative.

182.   (*f*) The dative sometimes expresses the *agent*; especially after the *perfect pass.* and *verbals* in τέος, τός.

183.   VOCABULARY 30.

   To live about the same time, to be contemporary with (κατὰ τὸν αὐτὸν χρόνον γενέσθαι). Fear (φόβος). Running, a running pace (δρόμος). To be suffering, or ill of, a disease (κάμνω,—καμοῦμαι, κέκμηκα. ἔκαμον). On the next day (τῇ ὑστεραίᾳ). Heavy, severe (βαρύς). Thales (Θαλῆς[x]). Solon (Σόλων, ωνος). Why? (τί; or διὰ τί;) Haste (σπουδή). Hercules ('Ηρακλῆς[y]). Staff, stick (ῥάβδος, f.).
   [Verbs that govern the *dative.*]
   Associate with, keep company with (ὁμῑλέω). Follow (ἕπομαι[z]). Envy, grudge (φθονέω[a]—φθόνος, envy). To meet, fall in with (ἐντυγχάνω[b]). Blame (μέμφομαι). Find fault with, rebuke (ἐπιτιμάω). Scold, rail at, speak calumniously of (λοιδορέομαι—λοιδορέω, takes the acc.). Accuse of, charge with, blame (ἐγκαλέω). Plot against (ἐπιβουλεύω). Fight with (μάχομαι). Contend or dispute with (ἐρίζω—ἔρις, ιδος [acc. a and ν], contention, strife). Am angry with (ὀργίζομαι). Am in a passion or rage (χαλεπαίνω). Like (ὅμοιος).
   [*Obs.* Verbs of *reproaching*, &c. take *acc.* of the *thing* (as well as dat. of person), especially when it is a *neut. pronoun.* (ἐγκαλεῖν, &c. τί τινι.)]

---

[x] Θαλῆς, G. Θαλέω, D. Θαλῇ, A. Θαλῆν. (ητος, ητι, ητα, later.)

[y] B. p. 17. (where *voc.* should be 'Ηράκλεις, not -κλεῖς): W. 17, Obs. 1.   The *voc.* ὦ "Ηρακλες occurs only in this exclamation.

[z] ἕπομαι, ἕψομαι. Imperf. εἱπόμην, aor. ἑσπόμην.

[a] φθονέω takes gen. of the object that excites the envy, or of the thing grudged (See 146,*f*).

[b] τυγχάνω, τεύξομαι, τετύχηκα. ἔτυχον.   With a gen. to *obtain, receive* (παρά from, with gen.); also, to *hit* (a mark—σκοπός).

Exercise 34.

184. Do not associate with the bad (67, *a*). If you associate (68, 2) with the bad[36], you will become bad yourself.
The boys are following the dog. Most men follow their
neighbours. I envy you your wisdom (*note* a). Do not envy
your neighbour. Do not envy me. If you had struck[36] the
judge with a stick, you would not have got off *with impunity*[53].
They set out the next day. What do you charge me with
(*Obs.*)? I asked whether (67, *c*) they were suffering the same
as the geometer. If you had plotted against the general, you
would not have come off *with impunity.* He will not fight
with the king (these) ten days (161). I knew that he had
suffered the same as I (had). I plotted against the king from
envy. Do not contend with your parents. I suffer similar
treatment[c] to you. I should blame the citizens, if they had
done this. He scolds, *not only*[28] the others, *but also* the
judge himself. I should have scolded the boy, if he had
done this. Why are you in a passion with your slave? I
have not met you, (these) two days. I am angry with those
who transact the affairs of the state. O Hercules! what *in
the world*[51] am I to do (98, *c*)? Through fear he did not hit
the mark.

Exercise 35.

185. Do you wish, then (98, *a*), that I should strike him
with this stick? He told me that his father was suffering from
a severe disease. Thales *was contemporary with* Solon. I
admire the wisdom of Thales. Hercules lived about the same
time as Theseus. If any one was brave, it was Hercules[63].
O father, do not scold your son. If you had kept company
with the bad, you would have become bad yourself. I asked

---

[c] *Like things.*

the boy, whether we ought to envy [38] our neighbours. The
damsel has very beautiful eyes [12]. Let us aim at speaking [14]
well of all the good. Let us abstain from acting insolently.
All, *and you among the first* [34], admire these things. Let us be
contented with our present condition. He said that, if Xenoclides had been wise, he would not have plotted against the
general. He told me that he wished to *give* his slaves a *taste*
of liberty (146, *c*). Let us keep company with sensible persons. Let us obey the laws of the state. *I should like to hear* [29]
the boy sing (*part.*). Do not associate with those who [1] pursue
what is disgraceful [13]. Why do you charge me with injustice [65]?
Through fear he missed the mark. I admire both [d] your horses
and those [6] of your friend. *The rest of the country* [19] has been
laid waste by the Greeks. He told me that we ought to persuade the judge (114, *c*).

§ 32. *Middle voice.*

186. The middle voice denotes:

1) That the agent does the action *upon himself;* or
2) That the agent does the action *for his own advantage ;* or
3) That the agent *gets* the action *done* for his own
advantage.

The strict reflexive meaning is found but in very few verbs; principally
those that describe some simple action *done to our own persons ;* as *to clothe,
crown,* &c.

The reflexive sense is often equivalent to a new simple meaning ; which
may be either *transitive* or *intransitive.*

187. The tenses that have the middle meaning, when the
verb has it at all, are

---

[d] τὶ following the *article.*

1) *Pres.* and *imperf.*   } of the *passive form.*
2) *Perf.* and *pluperf.*   }

3) *Futures* and *aorists* mid.

And in some verbs

4) The *aor.* 1. *pass. i. e.* of the *passive form.*

188. VOCABULARY 31.

1) λούειν, wash : M. *wash myself, bathe* [e].

ἀπάγχειν, ἀπάγξαι, strangle : M. *strangle* (or *hang*) *myself.*

[With new *intrans.* meaning.]

στέλλειν, to send : M. (to send oneself) *to journey* [f].

παύειν, to make to cease : M. (to make myself cease) *to stop, cease, leave off.*

[With new *trans.* meaning.]

περαιοῦν (τινα), to put a man over (a river) : M. *to cross* (a river, *acc.*).

τίλλειν, to pluck : M. *to mourn for* (acc.), *i. e.* by tearing one's hair.

2) σύμμαχον ποιεῖσθαί τινα, to make a man one's ally (*to form an alliance with a person*), *i. e.* for one's own advantage.

καταστήσασθαι [g] φύλακας, to place guards (over one's own property ; for one's own protection).

αἴρειν τι, to lift or take a thing up : M. *to take up for one's advantage*, *i. e.* to keep for one's self.

εὑρίσκειν, find : M. *find for myself, procure, get.*

παρασκευάζειν, provide : M. *provide (for one's own use).*

3) παρατίθεμαι τράπεζαν, I cause a table to be set before me.

μισθόω, let out for hire : M. *cause to be let to myself, i. e. hire.*

So διδάσκειν, teach : M. *get* or *have taught.*

[In general any remote reference of the action to *self* is expressed by the *Mid.*]

κατακλαίειν, weep for : M. *weep for* (one's own misfortunes, *acc.*).

ἐπιδεδειγμένος τὴν πονηρίαν, having shown his own wickedness.

θεῖναι νόμους, to enact laws,—of an absolute prince who does not make them *for himself.* θέσθαι νόμους, of the legislator of a

---

[e] It may have an *accus.* of a part of one's own person.

[f] στέλλεσθαι, *to clothe oneself*, and *to send for*, has aor. στείλασθαι : στέλλεσθαι, *to travel*, σταλῆναι.

[g] καθ-ίστημι, W. 84. B. p. 102.

free state, who makes them for himself as well as for his fellow-citizens [h].

Wicked (πονηρός). *To weigh anchor* (αἴρειν, *anchor* understood). *To commence* or *engage in a war against* (ἄρασθαι πόλεμον πρός, &c. acc.). *Sail away* (ἀπο-πλέω [i]).

Exercise 36.

189. Solon enacted laws for the Athenians. Wash yourselves, O boys. The son of Xenoclides hung himself. All (of them) washed their hands and their feet. Hire your neighbour's eyes. I will let you my house. I will take into my pay (*hire*) as many Hoplites *as possible* [62]. The mother wept for her sufferings. I provided [k] myself long ago with this stick. O daughters, mourn for your mother. The citizens, fearing, placed guards. O ye rich, cease to act-insolently (*partic.* 238). The soldiers crossed over the river. Let us form an alliance with the Athenians. If we had been wise, we should have formed an alliance with the Athenians. What-kind-of laws has the king of the Persians enacted? The boy has shown his wicked disposition. If you do this, you will get something good. The Athenians engaged in a war with the Persians. The Athenians, having weighed anchor, sailed away. He told me that we ought to obey the laws of the state (114, *c*).

---

§ 33. *Middle Voice continued.*

190. VOCABULARY 32.

   a. αἱρεῖν [l], *take ;* αἱρεῖσθαι, *choose* (followed by ἀντί with *gen.*). λαβεῖν, *take, receive ;* λαβέσθαι, *take hold of.*

---

[h] This difference is not, however, strictly observed. B.
[i] πλέω, πλεύσομαι and πλευσοῦμαι,—ἔπλευσα.
   Pass. πέπλευσμαι, ἐπλεύσθην.
[k] *Perfect,* as I still *keep* it.
[l] αἱρέω, &c. εἷλον, εἱλόμην, ᾑρέθην.

b. [Verbs whose middle voice seems to have a *reciprocal meaning.*]

βουλεύειν, *consult* ; βουλεύεσθαι, *consult together, deliberate :* but also (with regular *mid.* signification) *to counsel myself, adopt a resolution.* In the sense of *deliberate* it is followed by περί with *gen.*

διαλύειν [m], *to reconcile* others ; διαλύεσθαι, *to be reconciled to each other* (πρός with *acc.*).

c. [Middle forms, of which there is *no active,* and which must therefore be considered simply as deponents.]

δέχομαι, *receive* ; αἰσθάνομαι [n], *perceive, am informed of.*

d. [Aorists *pass.* with *mid.* meaning.]

κατεκλίθην (ῐ) [o] *laid myself down ; laid down.* ἀπηλλάγην, *took myself off :* so ἐπεραιώθην, ἐφοβήθην, ἐκοιμήθην, ἠσκήθην (from περαιοῦσθαι, φοβεῖσθαι, κοιμᾶσθαι, ἀσκεῖσθαι).

e. [Some futures 1. of *mid. form* have a *pass.* meaning.]

ὠφελήσομαι, ὁμολογήσομαι, φυλάξομαι, θρέψομαι : from ὠφελέω ; ὁμολογέω, *confess ;* φυλάττω, *guard ;* τρέφω, *nourish ; maintain —bring up.*

f. φυλάττεσθαι, mid., *to be on one's guard ; to guard against,* with *acc.* ot *thing* or *person.*

g. ' *By* ' (agent after pass. verb—ὑπό with *gen.;* also παρά and πρός).

Exercise 37.

191. They will choose to obey rather than [p] to fight. I would choose liberty before wealth. Xenoclides was chosen general with three others. The multitude often choose ill. He took hold of his hair (*plur.*). Let us consult about the state. To deliberate quickly is a different thing (*differs*) from deliberating [14] wisely. Let us consult together what we ought to do [38]. They consulted together what they should do with (134, *b*) the unjust judge. I exercised-myself-in (*d*) that art. Go to sleep. Having said this, he took himself off. The boy, having shown (p. 61, 3) much virtue and temperance, died.

---

[m] λύω, λύσω, &c.—λέλυμαι, ἐλύθην.

[n] αἰσθάνομαι, αἰσθήσομαι, ᾔσθημαι. ᾐσθόμην.

[o] κατα-κλίνω.　　　　　　　　　　[p] μᾶλλον ἤ.

O boys, receive this. I have received this. The city will receive
many times as much (170, *f*) as this (*plur.*). O slaves, receive
some[48] of the wine. The physician being informed of what
had happened, came in great haste. I crossed over the river
in great haste. If you do this, you will be greatly benefited.
I will guard against this danger. Having a pain in both my
ears, I lay down. This will be confessed by all. This will be
confessed, *willingly at least*[45], by none. The army shall be
maintained from the king's country. I am glad that[5] the
children are well brought up. The city shall be well guarded
by the citizens. I feared the very men (*those themselves*) who[1]
guarded the city.

§ 34. On the Perfect 2.

192. The *Perf.* 2. (improperly called the *Perf. mid.*) prefers
the *intransitive* signification, but *never has the pure reflexive
meaning* of the *middle*.

> (1) If the verb has both the *trans.* and *intrans.* meaning, the *perf.* 1. has
> the former; the *perf.* 2. the latter. (2) If the *intrans.* meaning has gone
> over to the *mid.*, or to the *pass.* (as often happens), the *perf.* 2. belongs in
> meaning to that voice. (3) If the verb is *intrans.*, the *perf.* 2. has the
> same relation to it that any other *perf.* has to its verb.

193. VOCABULARY 33.

	Perf. 1.	Perf. 2.
ἀνοίγω q, *open*,	ἀνέῳχα,	ἀνέῳγα, *stand open*.
ἐγείρω, *arouse*,	ἐγήγερκα,	ἐγρήγορα, *am awake*.
πείθω, *persuade*,	πέπεικα,	πέποιθα, *am confident, trust, have confidence*.
ἄγνυμι r, *break*,		ἔαγα, *am broken*.

---

q This verb prefixes the temporal to the syllabic augment—
ἀνέῳγον, ἀνέῳξα, inf. ἀνοῖξαι.

ἀνέῳγα belongs to later Greek writers: ἀνέῳγμαι was used by the older
authors.

r ἄγνυμι, ἄξω, aor. ἔαξα, ἐάγην (ă).

	Perf. 1.	Perf. 2.

ὄλλυμι[s], *destroy*,　ὀλώλεκα,　ὄλωλα, (perii,) *am undone*.

πήγνυμι [t], *fix*,　　　πέπηγα, *am fixed, am congealed,*
　　　　　　　　　　　　　　　　　　　&c.

(N.B. ἀπόλλυμι, κατάγνυμι, more common than the simple verbs.)

Pot, pitcher (χύτρα). One more (ἔτι εἶς). Gate (πύλη). Spear (δόρυ [u], n.). Breast (στέρνον). To watch over (ἐγρηγορέναι περί with gen.). To raise a war (ἐγείρειν πόλεμον—pass., arise). Safety (ἀσφάλεια). Roman (Ῥωμαῖος). Jupiter (Ζεύς, Διός, &c. V. Ζεῦ). Early in the morning (πρωΐ).

Exercise 38.

194. The pitcher is broken. If we conquer the Romans *in* one more battle [42], we are undone. The spear was fixed in his breast. All the water [20] is congealed. I broke the boy's head. The boy's head is broken. I have watched over your safety for many years. Having lost [v] all his property, he took himself off. The gates are open. The servants opened the gates early, as their custom was. Brave men have confidence in themselves. Then only (89, *c*), when they obey the laws, will the citizens be prosperous. If we do not bear *what comes from the gods* [25], we are undone. Who *in the world* [51] has broken this pitcher? It is *the part* [55] of a general to watch over the safety of his army. O Jupiter, the folly of the man [50]! If a war should arise (*be raised*), we are undone. If you break one pitcher more, O worst of slaves, you shall not come off *with impunity* [53]. My property was plundered, *wretched man that I am* [49]! If any man is in the habit of performing just (actions), it was he [63]. I have not met either my friend or my brother's [6].

---

[s] ὄλλῡμι, ὀλῶ, ὀλώλεκα. ὤλεσα.

ὄλλῡμαι, ὀλοῦμαι, ὄλωλα. ὠλόμην.

[t] πήγνυμι, πήξω, &c.—πέπηγα, ἐπάγην (ᾰ).

[u] δόρυ, δόρατος, &c.—Poet. δορός, δορί : of which δορί is found in Attic prose, in the phrase δορὶ ἐλεῖν.

[v] ἀπόλλυμι.

F

66 MOODS AND TENSES. [§ 35.

§ 35. *Additional Remarks on some of the Moods and Tenses.*

195. *a.* ἡ πολιτεία τελέως κεκοσμήσεται, ἐὰν ὁ τοιοῦτος αὐτὴν ἐπισκοπῇ φύλαξ, *the constitution* will have been *perfectly* arranged, *if such a guardian superintends it.*

b. φράζε καὶ πεπράξεται, *speak and it* shall (*immediately*) *be done.*

c. τὰ δέοντα ἐσόμεθα ἐγνωκότες ʷ, καὶ λόγων ματαίων ἀπηλλαγμένοι, *we* shall have voted *on the subject as we ought, and be freed from empty speeches.*

d. εἴθε ὁ υἱὸς νενικήκοι, *would that my son had conquered !*

e. εἶπεν ὅτι ἥξοι ἡμέρᾳ τρίτῃ, *he said that he* should come *on the third day.*

f. πεπειράσθω, *let it be attempted.*

196. (*a*) The *fut.* 3. expresses a *future* action *continuing* in its *effects.*

197.   The *fut.* 3. differs, therefore, from the Latin *futurum exactum*, in not being used to express merely the future *completion* of a *momentary* action.

198. (*b*) The *fut.* 3. is, however, sometimes used to express (1) the *speedy completion* of an action, or (2) the *certainty of its completion* in the most positive manner.

199.   The *fut.* 3. is obviously the natural future of those perfects, that, from their marking a *continued* state, are equivalent to a *present* with a new meaning : *e. g.* μέμνημαι, κέκτημαι.

200.   Some verbs have the *fut.* 3. as a simple future : *e. g.* δεδήσομαι ˣ, πεπαύσομαι, κεκόψομαι.

201. (*c*) In the active voice a *continued future state*, or a *future action continuing in its effects*, is expressed by ἔσομαι

ʷ γινώσκειν interdum de plebiscitis vel populi jussis. Bremi ad Demosth. Phil. I. 54.

ˣ From δέω *to bind.*

with *perf. participle :* a circumlocution which is also used in
the *passive* (as in the example).

202. (*d. e.*) The *perf.* has also a subjunctive and optative,
and the future an *optative*, which are used whenever that kind
of uncertainty or contingency peculiar to those moods agrees
with the time of these tenses.

Only, however, when particular distinctness is required; and even
then, the *perf. part.* with εἴην or ὦ is generally preferred to the regular
opt. and *subj.* of that tense.

203. The *imperat. perfect* is principally used in those verbs
whose perfects have the meaning of a present : μέμνησο, &c.

204. (*f*) The third person of the *imperat. perf. pass.* marks
a *decided resolution :* it is a strong expression for *let it be done,*
&c.

205. (*d*) εἴθε with the optative—and also the optative alone ʸ—expresses a *wish.*
[If the wish expressed *has not been* (and now *cannot be*) *realized,* εἴθε *is*
used with *indic.* of aorist or *imperf.,* according as the time to which the
wish refers is *past,* or *present.*]

So ὤφελον (ες, ε) *alone,* or with εἴθε, εἰ γάρ or ὡς, and followed by
the infinitive.

206. VOCABULARY 34.

Constitution (πολιτεία). *Arrange, adorn* (κοσμέω). *Superintend, overlook* (ἐπισκοπέω). *What we ought* (τὰ δέοντα). *Empty, vain, useless*
(μάταιος). *I am come* (ἥκω ᶻ with perf.* meaning). *I am gone, am off*
(οἴχομαι ᵃ, perf.* meaning). *Endeavour* (πειράομαι). *Would that . . . . . !*
(εἴθε, εἴθ' ὤφελον ᵇ, ες, ε, &c. εἰ γὰρ ὤφελον, ὡς ὤφελον, or ὤφελον
alone). *To make to disappear* (ἀφανίζω). *If it is agreeable to you, if you
are willing* (εἴ σοι βουλομένῳ ἐστί). *And that too* (καὶ ταῦτα). *For the
present at least* (τό γε νῦν εἶναι). *As far as they are concerned* (τὸ ἐπὶ
τούτοις εἶναι).

ʸ As in ὦ παῖ, γένοιο πατρὸς εὐτυχέστερος.   See also 295, *e.*

ᶻ ἥκω, ἧκον, ἥξω ; no other tenses in use. βίου εὖ ἥκειν, *to have arrived at an*
advanced age (*Herod.*): a construction seldom found in Attic Greek.

ᵃ οἴχομαι, οἰχήσομαι, ᾤχημαι (οἴχωκα).

ᵇ ὀφείλω (debeo), *owe, ought.* ὀφειλήσω. *Aor.* ὤφελον (*un-Attic* ὄφελον) used
only in wishes.

ὡς ὤφελε ζῆν Σωκράτης (*how Socrates ought to be alive*), *would that Socrates*
were alive ! εἴθε κλέος ἔλαβες.

Exercise 39.

207. For thus we shall have done (*c*) what we ought. For thus what we ought (to do) will have been done (*b*). I will remember my *former* [11] folly. He told me that they had forgotten their former virtue (*c*). Let us place the wise and good as guardians of this most beautiful constitution. *If it is agreeable to you*, these things shall (*instantly*) be done. Let these things be done (*f*). Do not attempt to deceive the gods. If you do this, I am off. The physician told me, that he would come on the fourth day. If you obey God, your soul will be adorned with all virtues. *Would that* the wise superintended the state! *Would that* the prudent managed the affairs of the state! *Would that* the wise judge had superintended the whole constitution! *Would that* Thales were alive! *Would that* the man had escaped death! If you obey the physician, you will be freed from your disease. Would that the Greeks had conquered! They condemned him to death (156, *obs.*), and that too *though he was* (say: '*being*') your citizen. *For the present at least*, we will use him. I don't know what in the world [51] we are [38], *for the present at least*, to do [c] with him. *As far as that* (person) *is concerned*, I am undone. For the present at least, let us desist from the chase. O boy, may you become wiser!

---

§ 36. *On the Infinitive.*

208. *a.* ὁ ἄνθρωπος πέφυκε φιλεῖν, *it is the nature of man to love.*

b. παρέχω ἐμαυτὸν ἐρωτᾷν, *I offer myself to be questioned.*

c. ἦλθον ἰδεῖν σε, *I came* (or *am come*) *to see you.*

---

[c] χρηστέος is the verbal adj. from χράομαι.

d. ἡδὺς ἀκούειν, *sweet to hear.* δεινὸς λέγειν, *clever at speaking.* χαλεπὸς λαβεῖν, *hard to take (or catch).*

e. οὕτως ἀνόητός ἐστιν, ὥστε πόλεμον ἀντ᾽ εἰρήνης αἱρεῖσθαι, *he is so senseless* as to *choose war in preference to peace.*

οὕτως ἀνόητός ἐστιν, ὥστε πόλεμον ἀντ᾽ εἰρήνης αἱρεῖται, *he is so senseless,* that he *(actually)* chooses *war in preference to peace.*

f. φιλοτιμότατος ἦν, ὥστε πάντα ὑπομεῖναι τοῦ ἐπαινεῖσθαι ἕνεκα, *he was very ambitious,* so as to bear *any thing for the sake of being praised.*

209.　The use of the Greek infinitive is much nearer to that of the English than that of the Latin is ; thus :—

210.　(*b. c.*) It expresses the *purpose,* and (*b. d.*) is often used in the active, after both verbs and adjectives, where the passive would be *admissible,* but *less common.*

Hence it must often be translated into Latin by the *participle in* dus, or by the *supine in* u.

211.　The particle ὥστε [d] expresses a *consequence,* and is used with *the infinitive ;* or, if the consequence be a definite consequence that has actually occurred, the indicative.

212.　{ *So—as to* = ὥστε with *infinitive* always.
 { *So—that* = ὥστε with *infinitive* or *indicative.*

With the infinitive the consequence is more closely connected with the principal clause, as *contemplated* or *resulting immediately* and *naturally* from what is there stated.　The consequence may be equally *real.*

213.　' *So that* ' should not be translated by the indicative, except where the sense would allow us to substitute *therefore* or *consequently (itaque)* for *so that.*

Thus: "the road was so bad that I did not reach my inn till midnight" = " the road was very bad; *consequently* I did not reach my inn till midnight :" here the *indicative* would be properly used.

ὥστε properly answers to οὕτως, or some other demonstrative, in the preceding clause.

---

[d] More rarely ὡς.

214. VOCABULARY 35.

To put forth naturally (φύω. πέφῦκα and ἔφυν are *intrans.* ; *I am produced* = *I am by nature*, or *it is my nature to*, &c.). *Supply, afford, offer* (παρέχω [e]). *Sweet, pleasant, agreeable* (ἡδύς). *Terrible* [f], *clever* (δεινός). *Hard, difficult* (χαλεπός). *Senseless* (ἀνόητος). *In preference to, instead of* (ἀντί). *Peace* (εἰρήνη). *Ambitious, fond of honour* (φιλότῑμος). *Undergo, bear* (ὑπομένω). *On account of, for the sake of* (ἕνεκα, *gen.*). *Leaf* (φύλλον). *Bring up, educate* (παιδεύω). *Very* (πάνυ [g]). *Wing* (πτερόν. πτέρυξ, ὕγος, f.). *Young bird* (νεοσσός). *Art, also contrivance, trick* (τέχνη). *Long* (μακρός). *Not yet* (οὔπω [h]). *Endure, bear* (ἀνέχομαι [i]).

φύω = *to get* teeth, feathers, &c.

πόνον or πράγματα παρέχειν = to give one trouble, *to molest, harass*, &c.

Exercise 40.

215. It is the nature of man (*a*) to love those who confer benefits upon him. The city is a difficult one to take. The woman is a terrible one to find out contrivances. The man is unable to hold his tongue. He told me that his daughter had been well brought up. If you give me any trouble, I will not endure it, *at least* (not) *willingly*[45]. The eagle has long wings[12]. He had been so brought up as very easily to have enough. He is so beautiful as to be admired by all. You are so senseless, that you are always hoping for what is impossible[13]. They are too wise[60] to choose war in preference to peace. The young birds have already got[k] feathers. The trees are already putting

---

[e] παρέχεσθαι, *mid.* is also used for *to afford*, without any *perceptible* difference of meaning. See example in 295, *b*.

[f] —νος, an old *pass.* termin. (like τέος, τός), whence δεινός, *terrible*, στυγνός, *hateful*, &c. B.

[g] This word is often strengthened by the addition of τί (πάνυ τι).

[h] πώ, πώποτε, *ever yet, ever up to this time.* The former is joined to οὐ, μή ; the latter to οὐδέ, μηδέ ; and both relate to the *past*. Οὐδέποτε, μηδέποτε, are commonly employed only *generally*, or with reference to the *future*. See 236*, u.

[i] This verb has a double augment: *imperf.* ἠνειχόμην, aor. ἠνεσχόμην.

[k] *Aor.* 1., as *perf.*, has a different meaning.

forth their leaves.   The child has not yet got (any) teeth.   If you molest me, you shall not come off with impunity[53].   They harassed them so, that the army was not able (*indic.*) to advance[1].   This wine is pleasant to drink.   It is the nature of boys to pursue what is pleasant.

§ 37.   *The Infinitive continued.*

216. *a.* ἐτειχίσθη δὲ καὶ 'Αταλάντη, τοῦ μὴ λῃστὰς κακουρ-γεῖν τὴν Εὔβοιαν, and *Atalanta also was fortified*, that *robbers* (or *pirates*) might not commit depredations *in Euboea*.

b. οὐδὲν ἐπράχθη διὰ τὸ ἐκεῖνον μὴ παρεῖναι, *nothing was done, because he was not present.*

c. οὐκ ὀρθῶς ἔχει τὸ κακῶς πάσχοντα ἀμύνεσθαι ἀντιδρῶντα κακῶς, *it is not right* for one who suffers wrong to avenge himself *by doing wrong in return.*

d. δέομαί σου παραμένειν, *I beseech* (or *entreat*) *you to stay with us.*   ἔφη σπουδάζειν, *he said that he was in a hurry.*   συνειπεῖν ὁμολογῶ, *I confess that I assented.*

e. ὁ 'Αλέξανδρος ἔφασκεν εἶναι Διὸς υἱός, *Alexander used to say* that he was the son *of Jupiter.*

ἔπεισα αὐτοὺς εἶναι θεός, *I persuaded them that I was a god.*

ἐδέοντο αὐτοῦ εἶναι προθύμου, *they entreated* him *to be* zealous.

ἔξεστί μοι γενέσθαι εὐδαίμονι, *I may* (if I please) *become* happy.

---

[1] πορεύομαι.

217. (*a*) The infinitive with the article in the *gen.* sometimes denotes a *motive* or *purpose.*

It may be considered as governed by ἕνεκα understood.

218. (*b*) When the infinitive has a subject of its own, the general rule is, that it stands in the accusative.

This rule holds good, when the *infin.* is used with τό, as in (*c*).

219. (*b*) A *preposition* with the *infin.* may be equivalent to a sentence introduced by a conjunction.

220. (*d*) But when the subject of the infinitive belongs to and is expressed with the former verb, it is generally not expressed with the infinitive.

The examples show that this rule holds good, whether the subject of the *infin.* be the subject of the preceding verb or an oblique case governed by it.—In the second example the accusative would be expressed even in Latin : *dixit* se *festinare.*

221. (*e*) When the subject of the infinitive is omitted because expressed with the other verb, an adjective or substantive that forms the predicate with the *infin.* is mostly put in the same case that the subject of the infinitive stands in *in the other clause.*

Thus in (*e*) υἱός conforms to Ἀλέξανδρος· θεός to ἐγώ· προθύμου to αὐτοῦ, &c.

(This construction is called *Attraction.*)

222. VOCABULARY 36.

To *wall, to fortify* (τειχίζω). *A wall* (τεῖχος, n.). *Evil-doer, rascal, villain* (κακοῦργος. κακός, ἔργον). *Villainy* (κακουργία). *Misdeed* (κακούργημα). To *do evil towards, do harm to, to inflict damage on,* &c. (κακουργέω.) *Ward off* (ἀμύνειν τί τινι : also with dat. only, ἀμύνειν τινί, to *defend.* In Mid. *ward off from myself ; repel, requite, revenge myself on,* with acc. of person : also without case, to *protect oneself*). To *return a man like for like* (τοῖς ὁμοίοις ἀμύνεσθαι). To *remain with* (παραμένω). *Say* (φάσκω = *give out,* ' with a slight intimation that the thing is not exactly so.' *Vömel.*). To *feel* or *be thankful for, return thanks for* (χάριν εἰδέναι : gen. of thing). *One may* (ἔξεστι, licet, one might, ἐξῆν). *It is right* (ὀρθῶς ἔχει). *Master* (δεσπότης). *Laugh* (γελάω, with fut. mid. -άσομαι).

Exercise 41.

223. The city was fortified, that no one^m might do injury to the citizens. Nothing was done, because (*b*) that villain gave us trouble. Let us beseech our friends to be zealous. He said that he would be with us, *if it was agreeable to us*⁶⁶. I persuaded them that I was a philosopher (*e*). I persuaded the judges that Abrocomas was a rascal. It is a hard thing (65) to conquer one's temper. He is too young⁶⁰ to have mastered his temper. If you ward off from me this danger, I shall feel thankful to you for your zeal. I will revenge myself on him who has injured you. If you return like for like to him who has treated you ill, you commit a sin. You used to say (*e*) that you were master. We ought to defend the laws of the state. It is in our power²⁶ to become happy. You may (if you please) become a philosopher. He says that he will deliberate. Nothing was done, because (*prep.*) all the citizens envy the judge. He says that he will brave this danger. It is not right, that a citizen should plot against the constitution. If all the citizens defend the laws, it will be well.

---

224. VOCABULARY 37.

[Preposition ἐκ, before vowel ἐξ, (*gen.*) *out of, forth from.* Hence of cause (*in consequence of ; from, for*) ; and of succession in time.]

Out of the city (ἐκ τῆς πόλεως). *For this cause* or *reason* (ἐκ ταύτης τῆς αἰτίας). *This being the case, for this reason, therefore* (ἐκ τούτου). *After our former tears* (ἐκ τῶν πρόσθεν δακρύων). *Unexpectedly* (ἐξ ἀπροσδοκήτου—ἀπροσδόκητος, *unexpected*).

Exercise 42.

225. We are now laughing after our former tears. The men from (*out of*) the city are plotting against the king. He

---

^m μηδείς, as a *purpose* is expressed.

says that he is watching over the safety of all. The Grecian
cavalry, unexpectedly charging the ranks of the Persians,
conquer (them). It is sweet to laugh after troubles. The
physician says that diseases are from Jupiter. This being the
case, it seemed good to the generals to depart. The slave
says that the pitcher is broken. He says that he is glad⁵ the
citizens are rich. He says that he takes pleasure in sleeping.
He said that the judge had an upper-chamber, whenever he
stayed in town. This being so, let every man provide for his
own safety. I asked him how much he thought the geometer's
possessions would fetch³⁷, if sold. I wonder at what has been
done¹ by the general. It is not every man⁵⁶, that can bear
unexpected (evils). This man has inflicted more damage upon
the city than any other single person⁶⁴. Would that the physician had remained with (us)! Would that the physician
were here! Would that the physician had been here!

§ 38. *The Infinitive continued.*

226. *a.* πρὸς τὸ συμφέρον ζῶσι, διὰ τὸ φίλαυτοι εἶναι, *they
make self-interest the object of their lives, because
they are lovers of themselves.*

b. ἐκπέμπονται ἐπὶ τῷⁿ ὅμοιοι τοῖς λειπομένοις εἶναι,
*they are sent out, on the understanding that they
are to be equal (on an equal footing) with those
that are left behind.*

c. οὐδεὶς τηλικοῦτος ἔστω παρ' ὑμῖν ὥστε, τοὺς νόμους
παραβὰς, μὴ δοῦναι δίκην, *let no one be so powerful amongst you, as not to be punished if he transgresses the laws.*

227. *Attraction* may take place, (that is, the *predicate sub-*

ⁿ ἐπί with *dat.* often marks a *condition.* 288.

stantive or *adjective* be in the *nominative*), when the infinitive is introduced by the article or ὥστε.

228. VOCABULARY 38.

It is expedient or *profitable* (συμφέρει, *dat.*). *Expediency, utility* (τὸ συμφέρον— τὰ συμφέροντα, *what is expedient*). *To make self-interest the object of one's life* (πρὸς τὸ συμφέρον ζῆν). *Self-loving, a lover of self, selfish* (φίλαυτος). *Self-love, selfishness* (φιλαυτία). *Transgress* (παραβαίνω º, *of a law*, &c. *to break*). *So great, so powerful* (τηλικοῦτος). *To be punished, suffer punishment* (δίκην διδόναι, *gen. of thing ; dat.* of *person by whom*). *Infinitely many, very many, a vast number of* (μυρίοι). *Ten thousand* (μύριοι). *Soldier* (στρατιώτης). *Country* (πατρίς P, ίδος, f.). *Treaty* (σπονδαί, *pl.* properly *libations*). *Excessively* (ἄγᾱν). *Excessive* (ὁ ἄγαν).

'Αντί (*gen.*), *instead of ; in preference to* (208, *e.*) ; *equivalent to.*

Exercise 43.

229. Let us fly from excessive self-love. Let us pursue the honorable rather than the expedient. They choose war in preference to peace, because they have not tasted the evils of war. They undergo every toil, because they are ambitious. He says that a king is equivalent to very many soldiers. All men, *so to say* [46], are lovers of self. If he were not ambitious, he would not endure this. I am come *on an understanding*, that I am to be on-an-equal-footing with the other citizens. Do not transgress the laws of your country. They bear every thing for the sake of being praised, because (*prep.*) they are excessively ambitious. Let us choose what is honorable in preference to what is expedient. *It is not right*, to make self-interest the object of one's life. It does not *belong to* a pious man, to fear death excessively. It is not every man that can [56] master self-love. I have not fallen in with Abrocomas for a

---

º βαίνω, βήσομαι, βέβηκα, ἔβην. βήσω and ἔβησα, *trans.* (ἔβην, βῆθι, βαίην, βῶ, βῆναι, βάς.)

παραβαίνω has also *perf. pass.* παραβέβᾰμαι, *aor.* παρεβάθην.

P Properly a poetical *fem. adj.* agreeing with γῆ.

long time. I love both the children of Abrocomas ^q and those of Philip. Every body aims at becoming happy. It is profitable to men to be pious. If you do this, you shall be punished for your villainy. All the laws of the state, *so to say* ⁴⁶, were transgressed by this villain. He thinks that the treaty has been broken.

§ 39. *The Participle.*

230. *a.* γυνή τις χήρα ὄρνιν εἶχε καθ' ἑκάστην ἡμέραν ὠὸν αὐτῇ τίκτουσαν, *a certain widow woman had a hen* which laid *her an egg every day.*

b. τὰ χρήματα ἀναλώσας ἀπήγξατο, *when, or after, he had spent all his money, he hanged himself.*

c. χαλεπόν ἐστι λέγειν πρὸς τὴν γαστέρα, ὦτα οὐκ ἔχουσαν, *it is difficult to speak to the stomach, because it has no ears.*

d. γιγνώσκοντες ὅτι κακά ἐστιν, ὅμως ἐπιθυμοῦσιν αὐτῶν, *though they know that they are hurtful, they nevertheless desire them.*

e. ληϊζόμενοι ζῶσιν, *they live* by plundering.

f. κρατῶν δὲ ἡδονῶν καὶ ἐπιθυμιῶν, διαφερόντως ἂν σωφρονοῖ, *but if he gained the victory over pleasure and his desires, he would be temperate in an uncommon degree.*

g. λαβὼν, ἔφη, τοῦτον, μαστίγωσον, take *this fellow,* said he, and *flog him.* ῥίψας δ' ὁ ποιμὴν πέτραν, τὸ κέρας αὐτῆς κατέαξεν, *but the shepherd* threw *a stone* and *broke her horn.*

231. A participle *assumes* an assertion ; or rather states it *attributively*, not *predicatively*. Whenever it is convenient to express this assertion by a

---

q Nouns in *ας* have the Doric gen. in *ā* (for *ου*), when they are the names of *foreigners*, or of Doric Greeks of no celebrity; as Ἀβροκόμας, G. Ἀβροκόμα. R.

complete sentence, we may do so ; connecting it with the principal sentence by a *relative* pronoun, or a conjunction (or conjunctional adverb) of
time, cause, condition, or *limitation.* Hence *vice versâ*—

232. (*a. b. c. d.*) Relative sentences, and sentences introduced by *when, after, if, since, because, although,* &c. may be
translated into Greek by omitting the relative or conjunction,
and *turning the verb* into a *participle.*

In translating from Greek into English, the proper *particle* to be used
must be found by considering the *relation* in which the participle stands
to the principal verb.

Thus, "I visited my friend νοσοῦντα," may mean, '*who was ill,*' or
'*because* he was ill,' or '*when* he was ill.'

233. (*e*) The English *verbal* or *participial substantive* under
the government of a preposition, may often be translated by a
participle agreeing with the nominative case of the sentence.

234. (*g*) A past participle may often be translated into
English by a verb, connected with the principal verb by '*and.*'

Of course, *vice versâ,* the first of two verbs connected by '*and*' may be
translated into Greek by a past participle.

235. VOCABULARY 39.

A widow (χήρα). *To know* (γιγνώσκω [r]). *To consume, spend* (ἀνᾱ-
λίσκω, *fut.* ἀνᾱλώσω, *aor.* ἀνάλωσα). *Stomach, belly* (γαστήρ, ἑρος [s], f.).
The future (τὸ μέλλον). *To plunder* (ληΐζομαι). *Remarkably, in an
uncommon degree* (διαφερόντως). *To scourge, flog* (μαστῑγόω). *To throw*
(ῥίπτω). *Stone* (πέτρος. πέτρα in good authors is *rock*). *Bare,
uncovered* (ψῑλός).

[Participles with peculiar meanings.]

At first, at the beginning (ἀρχόμενος). *At last* (τελευτῶν). *After
some time* (διαλῐπὼν χρόνον [t]). *With* (often translated by ἔχων, ἄγων,
φέρων, χρώμενος: of course in choosing *which* may be used, we must
consider whether the persons merely *had,* or *led,* or *brought,* or *used* the
thing or person *with which* he performed the action).

---

[r] γιγνώσκω, γνώσομαι, ἔγνωκα, ἔγνωσμαι, ἔγνων. (ἔγνων, γνῶθι, γνοίην,
γνῶ, γνῶναι, γνούς.)

[s] As πατήρ, B. p. 15. W. 15. *Obs.* 3.

[t] So διαλ. πολύν or ὀλίγον χρ.

Exercise 44.

[*Obs.* Sentences in *Italics* are to be translated by participles.]

236. I shall be happy, *if I know myself.* The judge himself shall be punished, *if he transgresses the laws of the state.* The master himself *took the slave* and flogged him. He fled for refuge into the temple, that [70] he might not be punished. *Since you see this,* are you not without fear of death? *If you do what you ought,* you will be happy. That shameless (fellow) lives by flattering the rich. What impiety [50]! He set off *with* ten thousand Hoplites. Cyrus was riding *with* his head uncovered. *Take the boy* and punish him. He has spent both his own money and his [6] father's. It is not every man who can [56] be without fear of the future. *He threw a stone* and broke the eagle's head. He crossed the river, *though it was flowing with a full stream.* The wolf *was persuaded,* and went away. The physician, *with* much skill (*art.*), freed the boy from his disease. At last he went away. At first you spoke ill of every body. After some time I will be with you.

---

§ 40.   *The Participle continued.*

236*. *a.* ἐγὼ ἔρχομαι ὑμῖν ἐπικουρήσων, *I am coming* to aid *you.*

τὸν ἀδικοῦντα παρὰ τοὺς δικαστὰς ἄγειν δεῖ δίκην δώσοντα, *he who wrongs another should be taken before the judges* to be punished (literally, *one should take,* &c.).

τοὺς τοῦτο ποιήσοντας ἐκπέμπει, *he sends out men* to do *this.*

b. ᾔδειν τοὺς παῖδας θνητοὺς γεννήσας, *I knew that I had begotten mortal children* (or, *I knew that the children I had begotten were mortal*).

ἠσθόμην αὐτῶν οἰομένων εἶναι σοφωτάτων, *I per-ceived* that they thought *themselves extremely wise.*

σύνοιδα ἐμαυτῷ σοφὸς ὤν (or σοφῷ ὄντι), *I am conscious* of being wise (*or*, that I am wise).

οὐδέποτε[u] μετεμέλησέ μοι σιγήσαντι, *I have never repented* of having held my tongue.

237. (*a*) The participle of the *future* is used to express a *purpose*[v].

238. (*b*) Many verbs that signify *emotions, perception by the senses, knowledge, recollection, cessation* or *continuance,* &c., take the participle, where *we* should use the *infinitive* mood, the *participial substantive,* or '*that,*' &c.

239. VOCABULARY 40.

> *To bring assistance, to aid, succour* (ἐπικουρέω, *dat.* : it may have besides an *acc.* of the thing[w]. ἐπικουρεῖν νόσῳ, to bear help against a disorder; *to combat* it). *Judge* (δικαστής[x]). *Beget* (γεννάω). *Dare, attempt* (τολμάω[y]).
>
> [Verbs that take the participle.]
>
> *See* (ὁράω). *Learn, am aware* (μανθάνω[z]). *I repent* (μεταμέλει[a] μοι). *Make to cease, stop* (παύω). *Cease* (λήγω, παύομαι), *Am ashamed* (αἰσχύνομαι[b]). *Remember* (μέμνημαι). *Appear* (φαίνομαι[c]). *Am*

---

[u] See 214, h.: "but οὐδέποτε, like *nunquam,* is occasionally found with *past tenses* even in the best writers." P.

[v] The intention is spoken of in a less *certain* way by the addition of ὡς. He had Cyrus arrested, ὡς ἀποκτενῶν.

[w] εἰ τῷ χειμῶνα ἐπεκούρησα, Xen.

[x] The δικαστής decides in a court of justice according to *right* and *law* : the κριτής in the other relations of life according to *equity* and his knowledge of human nature. Pass.

[y] Of things requiring *courage.* It has also the meaning of *sustinere, to bear* to do so and so.

[z] μανθάνω, μαθήσομαι, μεμάθηκα. ἔμαθον.

[a] μετα-μέλει, μετα-μελήσει, &c.

[b] αἰσχύνομαι ποιεῖν = *I am ashamed* to do it: αἰσχύνομαι ποιῶν or ποιήσας, I am ashamed of *doing,* or *having done it.*

[c] ἐὰν φαίνωμαι ἀδικῶν, *if* it should appear *that I have acted unjustly.*

evident (δῆλός εἰμι [d] = *am evidently*). *Know* (οἶδα). *Am conscious*
(σύνοιδα ἐμαυτῷ). *Rejoice* (χαίρω). *Perceive* (αἰσθάνομαι).

Exercise 45.

239*. I am ashamed of having flattered Xenoclides. Remember that you are a man. He was conscious of acting
unjustly. He rejoices in being praised, because he is ambitious. I have ceased to be a flatterer. I am conscious of fearing
death. I am not ashamed of having conferred many benefits
upon him. I know that I am mortal. I do not repent of
having ravaged the whole country. I am conscious of wishing
to destroy whatever I may take (*shall have taken* [e]). He is
evidently doing disgraceful things. He evidently cannot either
speak well of his friends or treat them well. Cyrus knew that
the son he had begotten, was mortal (*b*). I will put a stop
to his inflicting damage on the city. I knew that the children
he begot were mortal. Do not cease to love your mother.
Know that you shall be punished for your injustice. The
physician is here to (*p*) combat the boy's disease. Take the
villain before the judges to be punished. They will evidently
attempt this. I knew that he had done more service to the
state than any other single person [64]. I will send out men
to (*p*) [f] inflict damage on the city.

---

§ 41. *The Participle continued :* τυγχάνω, λανθάνω, φθάνω.

240. *a.* ὁ Κῦρος, ἅτε [g] παῖς ὤν, ἥδετο τοῖς τοιούτοις, *Cyrus,*
as being a boy, was pleased with such things.

---

[d] δῆλός ἐστιν ἀνιώμενος, *he is evidently vexed.*

[e] 89, *e.*

[f] A (*p*) after the first word of a clause shows that it is to be turned into a *parti-*
cipial clause, as explained in the two preceding sections.

[g] *Often* ἅτε δή. See 371.

b. ἔτυχον παρόντες, *they happened to be present.*

τυγχάνει ὤν, *he happens to be* (or simply, *is*).

c. λανθάνω τι ποιῶν, (1) am concealed from *myself* doing it = do it *without knowing it; unconsciously, unknown to myself.* (2) am concealed from *others* doing it = do it *without being observed ; secretly ; without being seen* or *discovered.*

d. ἔφθην αὐτοὺς ἀφικόμενος, *I arrived before them.*
ἔφθην ἀφικόμενος[h], *I arrived first.*

e. οὐκ ἂν φθάνοις ποιῶν τοῦτο, *you cannot do this too soon.*

f. οὐκ ἂν φθάνοις ποιῶν τοῦτο; *won't you do this directly?* = do it directly.

g. λέγε φθάσας, *speak* quickly; at once. ἀνύσας[i] τρέχε, *run* immediately.

241. Φθάνω[k] (*come* or *get before*) and λανθάνω[l] (*am concealed*) are generally construed by *adverbs;* the participle that accompanies them must then be turned into a *verb.*

242. The participle λανθάνων or λαθών may be construed by *secretly, without being observed, seen,* &c. Hence ἔλαθεν εἰσελθών is nearly equivalent to εἰσῆλθεν λαθών, but gives more prominence to the notion of *secrecy.*

243. VOCABULARY 41.

[Preposition Ἀπό, *from :* gen.]

To fight on horseback (ἀφ' ἵππων). To have done supper (ἀπὸ δείπνου γενέσθαι). To do a thing of themselves (ἀφ' ἑαυτῶν). At the suggestion of others (ἀπ' ἀνδρῶν ἑτέρων). Openly (ἀπὸ τοῦ προφανοῦς, from *adj.* προφανής).

---

[h] ἱκνέομαι (commonly ἀφικνέομαι), ἵξομαι, ἷγμαι. ἱκόμην.
[i] From ἀνύειν or ἀνύτειν, *to accomplish.*
[k] φθάνω, φθήσομαι, ἔφθακα. ἔφθασα, ἔφθην. Fut. φθάσω in later writers. (ἔφθην—φθαίην, φθῶ, φθῆναι, φθάς).
ἔφθην is the *older* aorist: but ἔφθασα is used once even by *Thuc.*, and from *Xenophon* downwards is the more common form. B.
[l] λανθάνω, λήσω, λέληθα. ἔλαθον. See 156.

πρό (*before*, of time, place, and preference—*in behalf of, for*).

For (= in behalf of) *the king* (πρὸ τοῦ βασιλέως). *To value very highly, to attach great importance to* (πρὸ πολλοῦ ποιεῖσθαι, *to value before*, i. e. *more than, much.* See 282). To choose war *before*, in preference to, *peace* (πρὸ εἰρήνης, for which ἀντί is used in 208, *e*).

Exercise 46.

244. The physician happened to be present. You cannot punish the boy too soon (*e*). The enemy arrived at^m the city before us. Go away immediately (*g*). Won't you go away directly (*f*)? If you do this before our enemies (do it), we have conquered. If you do this before me, I am undone. If we arrive at the city before them, all will be well. The slave broke the pitcher *without being discovered*. The Scythians fought on horseback. The father went in to the general *without being observed*. These Hoplites were drawn up before the king himself. He is too sensible [60] to choose war before peace. He has done supper. Speak at once (*g*), if it is agreeable [66] to those who are present. To incur danger in behalf of the state is honorable. It is the part of a good man, to incur dangers himself for his friends. He did this at the suggestion of other persons. I should never have done this of myself. If Xenoclides had not been their general, they would never have dared to commence a war openly. Men enact laws, *that* [70] they may not be injured. *Having done supper*, they practised equestrian exercises.

---

§ 42. *The Genitive Absolute*, &c.

245. *a.* ἐμοῦ καθεύδοντος, whilst *I was asleep.* τούτων οὕτως ἐχόντων, *this being the case ;* or, *as this is the case.*

---

m εἰς, if they went *into* it.

b. διὰ τί μένεις, ἐξὸν ἀπιέναι; *why do you remain,*
when you are at liberty to go away?

c. So δέον ἀπιέναι, when, whereas, &c. *you ought to*
go away. δόξαν ἡμῖν ἀπιέναι, when we have
determined *to go away.* Also δόξαν ταῦτα °,
this being determined.

d. ἐπὶ Κύρου βασιλεύοντος, *in the reign of Cyrus.*

e. ἐσιώπα ὡς πάντας εἰδότας (or πάντων εἰδό-
των), *he held his tongue, as supposing that all*
knew.

246. (*a*) The case *absolute* is in Greek the genitive : it marks
the *time,* or generally any such relation to the principal sentence, as *we* should express by *when, after, since, as, because,*
though, if, &c.

247. (*b. c.*) The participles of impersonal verbs are put
absolutely in the *nominative ;* of course without a noun, and in
the neuter gender.

248. (*d*) When the time relates to a *person,* ἐπί is generally
expressed.

249. (*e*) When a *motive* is attributed to *another person,* the
particle ὡς is generally used with the *gen.* or *acc.* absolute.

250. VOCABULARY 42.

[Words used in *nom.* absol.]

When, or *whereas, it was said* or *told* (εἰρημένον). *It being disgraceful*
—possible—impossible—plain or *evident* (αἰσχρὸν—δυνατὸν—ἀδύνατον
—δῆλον ὄν). *There being an opportunity, when I may* or *might* (παρόν ᴾ).
It being fit or *incumbent* (προσῆκον. προσῆκει, dat., it belongs to. οἱ
προσήκοντες, those that *belong* to us = *relations*). *When, whereas, one*
ought (δέον).

ⁿ So δοκοῦν, δεδογμένον.

º Also δόξαντος τούτου, δοξάντων τούτων, and δόξαντα ταῦτα.

ᴾ ἔστιν, ἔνεστι, πάρεστιν, ἔξεστι, &c. πράττειν, all signify, *one can* or *may :*
but ἔνεστι relates to *physical possibility* (it is *possible*) ; ἔξεστι to *moral possibility*
(it is *allowed*) ; ἔστι and πάρεστι stand between these two meanings, without
being confined to either of them ; the latter implying also the notion of *facility.* B.

G 2

As far at least as this is concerned, as far as depends on this (τούτου γε
ἕνεκα). For the sake of (χάριν with gen. = propter ; but χάριν ἐμὴν,
for my sake). After the manner of a dog, like a dog (κυνὸς δίκην).
Without (ἄνευ, gen.).

PHRASE.

ἕνεκα τῶν ἑτέρων ἄστρων, for any thing the other heavenly bodies could
do to prevent it.

Exercise 47.

251. Without you I should have perished *for any thing my
other friends could have done to prevent it.* Why do you remain, *when we have determined* to succour our friends? Why
do you hold your tongue, *whereas you ought to speak?* Why
do you remain, *now that you have an opportunity* to depart?
He asked the boy, why he remained, when it was his duty to
depart. Though they were told * to be present, they are not
come. If it is agreeable to you[60], we will go away. I hope
that we shall thus arrive before[77] the Persians. He had the
same upper-chamber, whenever he wished. The slave told
me, that the physicians were come (*p*) *to combat* the boy's disorder. If you act unjustly towards your slaves, know[74] that
you will be punished by the gods. I knew that all the rest of
the country had been ravaged by the Persians. Why did you
choose war, *when you might* have chosen peace? He told me
that all were permitted to go in to the general, whenever he
was at leisure.

Exercise 48.

252. Cyrus *evidently*[73] desired to be praised. I perceived
that he wished to disobey the laws of his country. O boy,
cease to do this, since (*p*) it is disgraceful to despise your
father. The boy went *secretly* (242) into his father's house.

---

* *It being told.*

But this being determined, we cannot set out too soon [77]. The master, *as* being a fool, was deceived by his slave. Do not practise many arts, *since it is impossible* to do every thing well. Let us not despise our relations. As far as money is concerned, you will rule over all the Greeks. Know that you will get off well, as far at least as this is concerned. He told me that, if any man was well suited to govern men, it was Cyrus [63]. The physician told me, that he had come for my sake. This animal runs like a dog. This being the case, I will go away at once. All men, *so to say*, desire what is absent. It is the part of a senseless man, to hold cheap what is present, from the desire of what is absent. He said nothing himself, as supposing [78] that all felt grateful to Xenoclides.

§ 43.　*The Relative.*

253. *a.* θαυμαστὸν ποιεῖς ὃς ἡμῖν οὐδὲν δίδως, *you act strangely* in giving *us nothing.*

b. ἐμακάριζον τὴν μητέρα, οἵων τέκνων ἐκύρησε, *they pronounced the mother happy in having* such *children.* (Here οἵων = ὅτι τοιούτων.)

c. ἡ ναῦς πρεσβεῖς ἄγει, οἵπερ τὰ σφέτερα φράσωσιν [q], *the ship is bringing ambassadors* to make (or, that they may make) *their own statement.*

ὅπλα κτῶνται, οἷς ἀμυνοῦνται τοὺς ἀδικοῦντας, *they are procuring arms to defend themselves with against those who injure them* (or, *with which to repel,* or *punish, those who injure them*).

d. {οὗτός ἐστιν, ὃν εἶδες ἄνδρα,} This is the man you
{ὃν εἶδες ἄνδρα, οὗτός ἐστιν,} saw.

---

q More probably, φράσουσιν. Krüger.

ATTRACTION OF RELATIVE.

e. μεταδίδως αὐτῷ τοῦ σίτου, οὗπερ αὐτὸς ἔχεις, *you
give him a portion of the food which you have
yourself.*

f. τῷ ἡγεμόνι πιστεύσομεν ᾧ ἂν Κῦρος δῷ, *we will confide in any general whom Cyrus may give us*[h] (for
ὃν ἄν[i]).

g. ἀπολαύω[k] ὧν ἔχω ἀγαθῶν, I enjoy *the good things
I possess.* μεμνημένος ὧν ἔπραξε, *remembering
what he had done.*

h. μετεπέμπετο ἄλλο στράτευμα, πρὸς ᾧ πρόσθεν εἶχε,
*he sent for another army, in addition to the one
he had before.*

254. (*a. b. c.*) The relative is often used to introduce a *cause,
ground, motive,* or *design* of what is stated.

Obs. 1. When it expresses a *cause* or *ground* it takes the *indic.*; when
it expresses a *purpose* (as in *c*), the *fut. indic.* [or the *subjunctive*[1]].

Obs. 2. The relative is not used merely to *connect* a sentence with the
one before it so frequently as in Latin. When so used, it is probably
always expressive of some emotion. B.

Obs. 3. ὅδε is not used as a *mere* antecedent to the relative, but οὗτος,
which is not so strongly demonstrative.

255. (*d*) The antecedent is often expressed in the relative
clause, and omitted in the principal clause.

When this is the case, the relative clause often stands first; the subst.,
which mostly loses its article, is then not to be placed immediately after
the relative.

256. (*e*) The relative is often made to agree in *case* with
the antecedent in the principal clause.

---

[h] *Dederit.*   [i] See 95.

[k] This verb (which is probably from the same root as λαβεῖν. P.) is properly *to
receive from;* to receive whether *advantage* or *disadvantage* from any thing. So
that (like our, *to reap the fruits of*) it is used in both a good and a bad sense.

[1] '*Conjunctivus* cum pronominibus adverbiisve relativis consociatus nonnisi in
veterum epicorum sermone *fini indicando* inservit.' Herm. ad Œd. Col. 190. So
Krüger, Lachmann, &c. Some MSS. read ὅπως in the passage of Thucydides,
253, *c.*

This is called *Attraction of the Relative* : it seldom takes place except where the relative should *regularly* stand in the *accusative,* the antecedent being in the *gen.* or *dat.* and *without* a demonstrative pronoun (as οὗτος, ἐκεῖνος).

257. (*g*) When the relative is *attracted,* the antecedent is often placed in the relative clause, but in the case in which it would stand in the principal clause.

258. (*g*) The antecedent is sometimes wholly omitted.

As, for instance, when it is some general or indefinite notion (*man*, *thing*, &c. as in *g*, ex. 2), or has been before mentioned, as in *h*.

In (*h*) the *rel.* seems under the government of a preposition belonging to the other clause. As in English sometimes,—" she would have the head *of whosoever* advised it."

259. VOCABULARY 43.

Surprising, strange (θαυμαστός). *To act strangely* (θαυμαστὸν ποιεῖν). *Corn* [m], *food* for man in general (σῖτος). *Ambassador* (πρέσβυς). *To send for* (μεταπέμπομαι). *To enjoy* (ἀπολαύω [n]).

ἐν (*in,* in answer to *where?—dat.*). *the first of all* (ἐν τοῖς πρῶτος [o]). *It depends upon you* (ἐν σοὶ ἔστι).

ἀνά (properly *up ; acc.—in, on, through,* of a large space or time).

Through the whole country (ἀνὰ πᾶσαν τὴν γῆν). *Through the whole day, all day* (ἀνὰ πᾶσαν τὴν ἡμέραν). *Every day* (ἀνὰ πᾶσαν ἡμέραν). *Every year* (ἀνὰ πᾶν ἔτος). *By fives,* or *five-and-five* (ἀνὰ πέντε).

εἰς (into, *acc.—towards, against, in reference to*).

εἰς διδασκάλου φοιτᾶν [p] (understand οἰκίαν), *to attend a master.*

εἰς διδασκάλου πέμπειν, *to send* (a boy) *to a master.*

Exercise 49.

260. I pity the mother for having been deprived of such a daughter (*b*). I will give him some of the wine *which* I have.

---

[m] *Plur.* often σῖτα in Att. Greek, which is also found in Herodotus.

[n] ἀπολαύω, ἀπολαύσομαι. *Imp.* ἀπέλαυον, *aor.* ἀπέλαυσα, though no simple verb is found. ἀπήλαυον, ἀπήλαυσα are later forms.

[o] This phrase is elliptical: ἐν τοῖς πρῶτοι παρῆσαν = ἐν τοῖς παροῦσιν πρῶτοι παρῆσαν. Thuc. uses ἐν τοῖς even with a *fem.* superlative. See iii. 81.

[p] Properly, *to go frequently into his house.*

He sent for more wine in addition to what he had drunk already (*h*). This is the hare you saw (*d*). You act strangely in speaking ill even of your friends. He knew that I should enjoy the good things I possess (*g*). Receive the good things you desire (*g*). I have a stick *to beat* you *with* (*c*). The Hoplites arrived *first of all.* All these things depend on you. They harassed us all the day, so that (212) the Hoplites could not march. They went into the city by fives. Those who had plotted against the king entered (*went into*) the city by threes *without being observed*[76]. Say *quickly*, what your opinion is (*what seems good to you*). I, for my part, would choose peace in preference to all that I possess. I knew that (*p*) the citizens *would* choose[31] peace in preference to war. Why do you wait, *when it is your duty* to succour your friend? The Athenians used to do this every year. They are not aware that (*p*) they are despised[74] by every body. They do this, *not only* every year, *but also* every day. I admire your lilies, but not[q] your brother's. The boy attends no master. We send our boys to masters.

Exercise 50.

261. I repented of having flogged[74] the slave. I indeed eat that I may live, but others live that they may eat. Socrates said, that he indeed ate that he might live, but that others lived that they might eat. The beauty of the city was admired by all who were-there[1]. He said that if the citizens obeyed the laws of the state, they would prosper (102). I wonder at the water being turned into wine. The widow *would have died*[37] *but for*[39] her hen, which (*p*) laid her an egg every day. The beauty of the boy was admired by Socrates himself. The Persian cavalry unexpectedly charged the ranks of the Greeks. He says that he (220) has a pain in his head. I perceived that

---

[q] *οὐ* should stand last : it then takes an accent (οὔ).

he rejoiced [74] in the wealth of the citizens [5]. I am ashamed of
being glad [74] that my daughter is beautiful [6]. He *is evidently* [73]
vexed at the misdeeds of his brothers. Henceforth let us
despise nobody. The judge told me that we must persuade
(114, *c*) the citizens. Would that you had done what you
ought! Would that you would do what you ought! I am at
a loss what to do (99).

<hr/>

§ 44. *The Relative continued.*

262. *a.* φόβος, ἣν αἰδῶ καλοῦμεν, *the fear* which *we call*
bashfulness.

b. ἀπὸ τῶν ἐν Σικελίᾳ πόλεων ἔστιν ὧν, *from* some
of the cities in Sicily.

c. οὕσπερ εἶδον ἔστιν ὅπου, *whom I saw* somewhere.

d. ἔστιν οὕστινας ἀνθρώπους τεθαύμακας ἐπὶ σοφίᾳ;
are there any persons whom *you have admired
for their wisdom ?*

e. λέξω σοι, ἐφ' ᾧ σιγήσει, *I will tell you,* on condition
that *you will hold your tongue.*

f. ᾑρέθησαν ἐφ' ᾧτε συγγράψαι νόμους, *they were
chosen on* the condition that *they should draw up
laws* (i. e. *to draw up laws*).

g. χάριν σοι οἶδα ἀνθ' ὧν ἦλθες, *I feel thankful to
you* for *coming.*

h. ἔφθειρον εἴ τι χρήσιμον ἦν, *they destroyed* every
thing of value.

263. (*a*) When the relative, with such a verb as *to be, call,
believe,* &c. stands in *apposition* to a noun, it generally agrees
in gender with *it*, rather than with its proper antecedent.

264. (*b*) ἔστιν-οἵ [g] = ἔνιοι, *some,* and may be declined
throughout:—

<hr/>

ᵍ For '*sunt qui dicant*' the Greeks said, ἔστιν οἳ λέγουσιν, or εἰσὶν οἱ λέγοντες,
or εἰσὶν οἳ λέγουσιν. Examples of the last construction are *not* uncommon. Kr.

N. ἔστιν οἵ, ἔστιν αἵ, ἔστιν ἅ.

G. ἔστιν ὧν.

D. ἔστιν οἷς, ἔστιν αἷς, ἔστιν οἷς, &c.

265. (c) In the same way ἔστιν ὅτε = *sometimes;* ἔστιν ὅπου, *somewhere,* &c.

266. (d) So also ἔστιν with ὅστις is used as an interrogative.

267. (e) Ἐφ' ᾧ or ᾧτε is, '*on condition that,*' with the *future* indic. or the *infin.*

The relative in this construction answers to the demonstrative ἐπὶ τούτῳ : which, or ἐπὶ τοῖσδε, is not unfrequently expressed.

268. (g) ἀνθ' ὧν, *because, for* (= ἀντὶ τούτου ὅτι).

It may, however, be used in its proper meaning : '*in return for* those things which,' &c.

269. (h) εἴ τις [h] does not express any *doubt* as to whether there *was any,* but is used as equivalent to ὅστις, *whosoever, whatsoever* (= *all that*).

269*. VOCABULARY 44.

To be banished (φεύγειν [i]). *To return from banishment* (κατέρχομαι, κάτειμι). *To wound* (τιτρώσκω [k]). *Some* (ἔστιν οἵ). *Somewhere* (ἔστιν ὅπου). *Sometimes* (ἔστιν ὅτε). *Hold my tongue* (σιγάω [l] : it cannot, like σιωπάω, take acc. of thing).

[Διά.]

Διὰ τοῦ is, '*through'* of space of time ; and of *means.*

Διὰ τόν is, '*on account of ;'* also, '*through'* of a *cause.*

On your account (διὰ σέ). *After a long time* (διὰ πολλοῦ χρόνου—also, διὰ χρόνου, *after some time*). *Every five years* (διὰ πέντε ἐτῶν [m]). *To pity* (δι' οἴκτου ἔχειν). *To be angry with* (δι' ὀργῆς ἔχειν). *To be at enmity with* (δι' ἔχθρας γίγνεσθαί τινι [n]). *At a little, at a great distance* (δι' ὀλίγου, διὰ πολλοῦ). *To have in one's hand* (διὰ χειρὸς ἔχειν).

---

[h] τὶς *indef.* has *gen.* του, *dat.* τῳ (both *enclitic*), for τινός, τινί. So ὅστις has ὅτου, ὅτῳ.

[i] φεύγειν is used for φυγεῖν, *to be in banishment.* Heindorf.

[k] τιτρώσκω, τρώσω, &c.

[l] *Fut.*, generally, σιγήσομαι.

[m] Also διὰ πέμπτου ἔτους and διὰ πέμπτων ἐτῶν.

[n] So διὰ φιλίας ἰέναι τινί. Xen. Anab. iii. 8.

Exercise 51.

270. I deem you happy in having received [80] such good things. Most men *evidently desire* [73] the good things which their neighbours possess. I will go away *on condition that* the physician shall stay. *Some* of them were wounded by the enemy. I will tell you, on condition that the others shall hold their tongue. Is there *any* person *whom* (d) you have praised for [o] his forwardness? I will endeavour to do this so that (212) even you shall praise [p] me. I *would choose* liberty before all the good things I possess (253, g). He chose war, *when he might* have peace. Xenoclides was chosen general, *with three others* [21]. I rejoice to have been elected [74] general by the Athenians. Why am I wretched, *when I may* become happy? I am at enmity with Abrocomas. He was banished through the Athenians. I rejoice in seeing you [74] after some time. Know that it is through the gods [q] that you are doing well. Know that it is through me that you have returned from banishment. The physician is come on your account. They do this every five years. The boy pursues the dog with (*having*) a stick in his hand.

---

§ 45. ὁ οἷος σὺ ἀνήρ.

271. *a.* G. ἔραμαι οἷου σοῦ ἀνδρός, *I love* such a man as you.

D. χαρίζομαι οἵῳ σοὶ ἀνδρί, *I gratify* such a man as you.

---

o *Gen.—*αἰνέω takes *acc.* of person, *gen.* of thing.

p *Infin. pres.*

q i. e. *know, doing well* (nom. partic.) *through the gods.* The other sentences of this kind (having '*it is*' followed by '*that*') are to be turned in the same way.

A. ἐπαινῶ οἷον σὲ ἄνδρα, *I praise* such a man
as you.

b. N. ὁ οἷος σὺʳ (ἀνήρ), such a man as you.

G. τοῦ οἵου σοῦ (ἀνδρός), of such a man as you,
&c. &c.

c. θαυμαστὸν ὅσον προὐχώρησε, *he made* astonishing
progress.

d. θαυμασίως ὡς ἄθλιος γέγονε, *he has become* surprisingly *miserable.*

272. These constructions may be resolved thus:
ἔραμαι ἀνδρὸς τοιούτου, οἷος σὺ εἶ.
θαυμαστόν ἐστιν, ὅσον προὐχώρησε.

273. (*d*) In this construction ὅσος follows such words as θαυμαστός, πλεῖστος,
ἄφθονος : and ὡς the adverbs θαυμασίως, θαυμαστῶς, &c.

274. VOCABULARY 45.

To love (ἐράω ˢ). *To gratify* (χαρίζομαι). *Advance, make progress*
(προχωρέω). *To leap* (ἅλλομαι ᵗ). *To throw* (ῥίπτω). *The truth* (τὸ
ἀληθὲς—ἀληθής, *true ;* ἀλήθεια, *truth*). *True happiness* (ἡ ὡς ἀληθῶς
εὐδαιμονία). *To dwell* (οἰκέω). *Miserable, wretched* (ἄθλιος).

κατά properly expresses a motion from a higher place *downwards.*

κατὰ τοῦ, *down from, down, under ;* but more commonly *against,* with
verbs of *speaking, thinking,* &c.

κατὰ τὸν, *at, by, near, during,* in.an indefinite way : also, *according to,*
and with the distributive sense of our ' *by* ' (*by twos,* &c.).

According to reason (κατὰ λόγον ; also with gen., *in proportion to*).
During, in, or *at* the time of the disease (κατὰ τὴν νόσον). *In villages,*
vicatim (κατὰ κώμας). *Two by two* (κατὰ δύο). *In all respects* (κατὰ
πάντα). *Sensual pleasures* (αἱ κατὰ τὸ σῶμα ἡδοναί). *According to*
Plato (κατὰ Πλάτωνα).

ʳ πέρ is often added : οἱ οἷοί περ ὑμεῖς ἄνδρες.

ˢ ἐράω, poet. ἔραμαι, ἐρασθήσομαι, ἠράσθην (gen.) *love.* See Index.
Pres. pass. ἐρῶμαι, (ἐρᾶσθαι, ἐρώμενος,) *to be loved.*

ᵗ ἅλλομαι, ἁλοῦμαι. aor. 1. ἡλάμην with ᾱ in the moods, aor. 2. ἡλόμην with
ᾰ. *Aor.* 1. should probably be preferred for *indic.* and *part. ;* aor. 2. for *optat.* and
infin. B. Hermann rejects the *indic.* and *imper.* of aor. 2.

Exercise 52.

275. They cling to sensual pleasures, because [71] they have never tasted true happiness. They are too wise [60] to cling to sensual pleasures. (Men) gladly gratify *such a man as you are.* I would gladly gratify *such men as you.* They leapt down from the wall. Do you wish (99) that I should speak the truth against my friend? The boy is like his father in every respect. This is (65) hard, and for men like us impossible. The king loved such men as you are. The boy has made astonishing progress. He said that he would [37] very gladly gratify a man like you. Men like you always speak well of the good. A man like you is praised by every body. I would rather see men like you, than the king of the Persians himself. He has become very wretched, *unknown to himself* [76]. I cannot gratify a man like you *too soon* [77]. Will you not gratify a man like me *directly* [77]? Sophroniscus, *as* being selfish, obliged nobody, *willingly at least* [45]. All men, *so to say* [46], like to oblige such men as you. All men, so to say, rejoice in praising [77] such a man as you are. These things happened *in the time* of the disease. I know that they dwell [74] in villages. The eagle has wings *in proportion to* its body. To live according to reason is a different thing (from living [u]) according to passion. I will tell you *on condition* that you (will) send your boy to some master (259).

---

§ 46. *οὐδεὶς ὅστις οὐ.*

276. N. οὐδεὶς ὅστις οὐκ ἂν ταῦτα ποιήσειεν.
G. οὐδενὸς ὅτου οὐ κατεγέλασεν.

---

u The *art.* must be expressed, though the *infin.* is to be omitted.

D. οὐδενὶ ὅτῳ οὐκ ἀπεκρίνατο.

A. οὐδένα ὅντινα οὐ κατέκλαυσε.
There is no one who *would not do this.*
There was no one whom *he did not laugh at.*
There was no one whom *he did not answer.*
There was no one whom *he did not weep for.*

277. In οὐδεὶς ὅστις οὐ (*nemo non*) the declinable words are put under the immediate government of the verb.

Kühner calls this *inverted attraction*, because the noun (or word representing it) conforms to the relative, not the relative to the noun.

Sometimes adverbs are affected by this kind of attraction : βῆναι κεῖθεν, ὅθεν περ ἥκει (for κεῖσε).

278. VOCABULARY 46.

To laugh at (καταγελάω ᵛ). *To answer* (ἀποκρίνομαι ʷ). *To weep for* (κατακλαίω). *Especially* (ἄλλως τε καί, both otherwise and also). *There is nothing like hearing* (οὐδὲν οἷον ἀκοῦσαι). *As fast as they could* (ὡς τάχους εἶχον ˣ). *The agricultural population* (οἱ ἀμφὶ γῆν ἔχοντες).

Exercise 53.

279. There is no one who would not weep for *such men as you* [85]. There is nobody whom he does not despise. There is no one whom he does not hold cheap. There is no one whom they do not gladly oblige. There was none of those present ʸ whom he had not plotted against. I act strangely *in not gratifying* [79] a man like you [85]. I know *that I shall love* [74] a man like you. I am ashamed *of having plotted* [74] against a man like you. He *evidently wished* [73] to oblige such men as you. That *is* a hard thing, and for a man like me at least ᶻ, impossible. To

---

ᵛ γελάω, ἄσομαι, but ἐγέλασα. Short α.

ʷ *Aor.* 1. ἀποκριθῆναι is *passive*, from ἀποκρίνω (*secerno*), except in *late* writers, who use it for ἀποκρίνασθαι. B.

ˣ Gen. of τάχος.

ʸ Put the *partic.* after the negatives. Οὐ$\hat{\varsigma}$ενὸς ὅτου οὐ πάντων ἂν ὑμῶν καθ' ἡλικίαν πατὴρ εἴην. Plato, Protag. 317, c.

ᶻ οἵῳ γε ἐμοί.

live according to reason is unpleasant (*not pleasant*) to most persons, *especially* (when they are) young. *There is nothing like hearing* the ambassadors themselves. The agricultural population are doing well. They pursued the dog *as fast as they could.*

---

§ 47. οἷος. δέω. μέλλω.

280. *a.* οἷός τέ εἰμι, *I am* able (i. e. *am such as* to do a thing). οἷον τέ ἐστι, *it is* possible.

b. οἱ πρόσθεν ὀδόντες οἷοι τέμνειν εἰσίν, *our front teeth* are adapted for cutting.

οὐ γὰρ ἦν οἷος ἀπὸ παντὸς κερδαίνειν, *he was not* of a character [a] *to do any thing whatever for the sake of gain.*

c. ὀλίγου δέω δακρῦσαι, *I could almost cry;* or *am near crying.*

ὀλίγου δεῖν ἐδάκρυσα, *I was near crying.*

ὀλίγου πάντες, nearly *all* (δεῖν omitted). τοῦτο γὰρ πολλοῦ δεῖν εἴποι τις ἄν, *for a man would not assert that,* far from it.

d. δυοῖν δέοντα [b] εἴκοσι, *eighteen.*

e. μέλλω γράψειν, γράφειν, γράψαι, *I am going to write.*

f. εἰ μέλλει φιλόσοφος γενέσθαι, *if he is to become a philosopher.*

281. (*e*) Μέλλω is followed by an *infin.* of the *future*, present, or *aorist.*

The *future infin.* is the *most,* the *aorist* the *least* common [c]. P.

---

[a] Or, *was not a man to*, &c.

[b] The construction δυοῖν δεόντοιν has disappeared, under the influence of modern criticism, from the works of the great writers, with the single exception of *Xen. Hell.* i. 1, 5 : ἐπεισπλεῖ δυοῖν δεούσαιν εἴκοσι ναυσίν, where δεούσαις is undoubtedly the proper reading. Krüger.

[c] There is a large class of verbs, the object of which, expressed by an *infin.*, relates to *future* time, and *may*, therefore, be in the *future*, though it often *is* in the

282. VOCABULARY 47.

Cry, shed tears (δακρύω). *I am far from* (πολλοῦ δέω). *Nearly, almost* (ὀλίγου δεῖν, used as an adverbial phrase; or ὀλίγου only). *Far from it* (πολλοῦ δεῖν). *Am going to* (μέλλω—also *am likely to*, and *am to*, &c.). *To gain* (κερδαίνω). *Gain* (κέρδος, n.). *Stove* (κάμῑνος, f.). *Mostly* (τὰ πολλά). *Front*, adj. (ὁ πρόσθεν).

ἀμφί, περί (gen., dat., acc.).

ἀμφὶ, or περὶ τὸν, '*about*,' in answer to both *where?* and *whither?*—ἀμφὶ or περί τι or τινὰ ἔχειν or εἶναι is: *to belong to* [d], *to be* or *be employed about.*

περὶ τῷ denotes *care about:* it follows verbs of *fearing* (δεδιέναι), *being at ease about* (θαῤῥεῖν), &c.

ἀμφὶ and (more commonly) περὶ τοῦ are *of, about (de)*, as in '*to talk about.*' Also φοβεῖσθαι, φιλονεικεῖν (*to contend*) περί τινος.

περὶ πολλοῦ ποιεῖσθαι or ἡγεῖσθαι [e], *to value very highly, to make a great point of,* or *attach great importance to.*

Exercise 54.

283. He asked whether this was possible.   We cut with our front teeth.   He told me that his father had the tooth-ache in one of his front teeth.   He has large [12] front teeth.   He was not of a character to fear death.   He says that he does not choose to go in to the general, since (*p*) he is not at leisure.   The Athenians sailed *with* (*part.*) nineteen ships.   It is not

---

pres. or *aor.*   " The *pres.* is preferred when either the *certain definite occurrence* of the action is to be marked, or its *immediate commencement* from the time the words are uttered." (K.)   Buttmann properly observes, that a distinction should be made between verbs whose object is *necessarily future* (e. g. *hope, promise, expect*) and those where the object is not necessarily future (e.g. *say, think*, &c.) : with the latter the *pres.* or *aor.* might be misunderstood ; with the former, not.   But the MSS. often agree in giving the *pres.* or *aor.* (with reference to *future* time) after such verbs.   B. ad *Plat. Crit.* 14. 3.

d οἱ ἀμφὶ (or περὶ) Ἄνυτον, *Anytus and his followers* or *party :* a phrase employed by Attic writers, when they chiefly allude to *only one individual ;* leaving it at the same time, for some reason, undecided and in the dark, whether they mean that individual alone, or others besides.   B.

e So περὶ πλείονος, πλείστου, &c. περὶ μικροῦ.   See 243.

possible that one man *should* ever *do*[37] all this.   You will not
escape from (84, *b*) death.   He is[f] mostly about the stove.
Do not think that I do this from insolence.   Young men are
of a character to desire many things.   *Nearly* all (of them)
wish to entrust the arbitration to Socrates.   They will be
entrusted with this[41] by nearly all (of them).   I am far from
desiring all that you have.   He fears the same things *that we
do* (177).   He says that he (220) is without fear of death.   He
says that the mother is afraid about her daughter.   The agricultural population are doing well.   I asked the general,
whether he was going to march against the king.   He says
that *he* has been entrusted with this[41].

---

§ 48. ὅπως. οὐ μή.

284. *a.* φρόντιζε ὅπως μηδὲν αἰσχρὸν ποιήσεις, *take care
to do nothing disgraceful.*

b. ξυνεβούλευεν οὕτω ποιεῖν, ὅπως ὁ σῖτος ἀντίσχῃ,
*he advised them to do this, that the provisions
might hold out.*

c. ὅπως ἀνὴρ ἔσει, *see that you behave* (or *quit yourself*)
like a man.

d. ὅπως μὴ ποιήσητε, ὃ πολλάκις ὑμᾶς ἔβλαψεν, *be sure
not to do what has often been detrimental to you.*

e. οὐ μὴ λαλήσεις; *do not chatter, pray.*
οὐ μὴ γένηται τοῦτο, *this will assuredly not happen.*

285. (*a. b.*) Ὅπως[c], when it refers to the *future*, has either
the *subj.* or the *future indic.*[*], and retains them even in con-

---

[f] ἔχω.

[c] ὅπως is properly ' *how*,' and it cannot be used for ' *that*,' except where for ' *that* '
we might substitute ' *that by this means*,' or ' *that so.*'   With the *future indic.* it is
always strictly ' *how*,' ὅτῳ τρόπῳ.

[*] The *fut.* with ὅπως expresses a definite intention, for the accomplishment of
which vigorous measures are to be pursued. R.

nexion with *past* time, when the *optative* might have been expected (70).

286. (*c. d.*) The verb on which the sentence with ὅπως depends, is often omitted.

This construction is equivalent to an *energetic imperative:*—ὅρα or ὁρᾶτε may be supplied.

287. Οὐ μή [d], with the *fut. indic.* or *aor. subj.*, is used as an emphatic *prohibition* or *denial.*

This construction is probably *elliptical*: οὐ (δέος ἐστὶ) μὴ . . . &c.

With the *sec. pers. sing.* of the *future indic.* it is a *prohibition*; with the *subj.*, and other persons of the future, a *denial.*

Elmsley says: "οὐ μή cum futuro *vetantis* est, cum subjunctivo vero *negantis*;" but Hermann shows, that the *prohibitive* meaning depends on the *person*, not on the *tense*.

Elmsley explained this phrase in what seems the simpler way, by joining the μή to the verb. Thus οὐ μὴ λαλήσεις; = *will you not not-talk?* = *will you not hold your tongue?* = *hold your tongue.*

But Hermann (who at first agreed with Elmsley), Rost, Kühner, &c. adopt the other explanation, supposing δέος ἐστί, or some such phrase, understood.

288. VOCABULARY 48.

To bethink myself, consider, take care (φροντίζω). *Talk, chatter* (λαλέω). *Whilst he was walking* (μεταξὺ περιπατῶν). *Nevertheless* (ὅμως). *To be at dinner* (δειπνέω: δεῖπνον, cœna, the principal meal of the day, taken towards the evening).

ἐπί, ' on,' in answer to *where?* generally with *gen.*, sometimes with *dat.* (ἐφ' ἵππου ὀχεῖσθαι—ἐφ' ἵππῳ πορεύεσθαι). With *acc.* in answer to *whither?* (ἐπὶ λόφον τινά, *to a certain hill*;) and, more generally, *on, in, towards, to,* &c.

They marched *to Sardis* (ἐπὶ Σάρδεων). They sailed *to Chios* (ἐπὶ τῆς Χίου). *Towards home* (ἐπ' οἴκου).

ἐπὶ τῷ denotes ' *in addition to*,' ' *besides*;' ' *close by* ' (ἐπὶ τῷ ποταμῷ); an *aim* or *condition* (267), and the *being in one's power* (65).

ἐπὶ τοῦ often marks the *time* by means of something *contemporary*, generally a *contemporary person* (65).

---

d Dawes laid it down as a rule, that the subjunctive of the *aor.* 1. *act.* and *mid.* was never used with ὅπως, οὐ μή, but that the *fut. indic.* was used instead. This rule is now given up by the best scholars; but Buttmann thinks that the *subj.* of the *aor.* 2. was employed with a *kind of predilection,* and that, when the verb had no such tense, the *fut. indic.* was used in preference to the *subj.* of the *aor.* 1.

ἐλθεῖν ἐπὶ τούτῳ, to come for this (to *effect* it).
——— τοῦτο, ——————— (to *fetch* it).
To be drawn up four deep (ἐπὶ τεττάρων τετάχθαι). To be named after a person (ὄνομα ἔχειν ἐπί τινος). To endure a thing for the sake of praise (ἐπ᾽ ἐπαίνῳ).

Exercise 55.

289. Be sure to be here yourself (*d*). Take care that your children may be as good [e] *as possible* [62] (*a*). Be sure to behave like men worthy of the liberty you possess. Take care not to say what has often hurt you. Take care to injure nobody. The Grecian Hoplites were drawn up three deep. Cyrus marched for Sardis with (*part.*) his Grecian Hoplites. He said that these things *were not in his power* [26]. They made (*mid.*) a treaty on these conditions. He is named after the great king. He said that his boy was named after Thales, the philosopher. They killed him whilst he was at dinner. The Athenians, though (*p*) they were able to take the city, nevertheless sailed back home. In addition to all this, the Athenian generals have already sailed home. He told me that the general was not of a character [88] to act unjustly by the citizens. They are not sent out (*on an understanding that they are*) to be slaves (226, *b*). He says that *he* dwells close by the river. He is very ambitious, so as (212) to do every thing for praise. He said that the corpse was *of a superhuman size* [59]. He said that he had suffered things *too great* for tears [59]. Do not do this, *pray*. They will assuredly not obey the laws of the city. Leave off chattering.

---

[e] βέλτιστος.

§ 49. μή. μὴ οὐ.

290. *a.* { δέδοικα μὴ θάνω, *I fear that I* shall die.
{ δέδοικα μὴ οὐ θάνω, *I fear that I* shall not die.

b. φοβοῦμαι μὴ εὑρήσομεν, *I fear* we shall find.

φοβοῦμαι μὴ ἀμφοτέρων ἡμαρτήκαμεν, *I fear* that we have missed (lost) *both.*

c. ἀλλὰ μὴ οὐκ ᾖ διδακτόν, *but perhaps it is a thing that cannot be taught.*

d. εἰ δὲ γενησόμεθα ἐπὶ βασιλεῖ, τί ἐμποδὼν μὴ οὐχὶ πάντα τὰ δεινότατα παθόντας ἀποθανεῖν; *but if we shall fall into the power of the king, what will prevent us from being put to death, after suffering all that is most terrible?*

e. ἀποκωλῦσαι τοὺς Ἕλληνας μὴ ἐλθεῖν, *to prevent the Greeks from coming.* ἠρνοῦντο μὴ πεπτωκέναι, *they* (denied that they had fallen) *said that they did not fall.* ἀπιστοῦντες αὐτὸν μὴ ἥξειν, *not believing that he would come.*

f. σὺ γὰρ ὑπέσχου ζητήσειν [f], ὡς οὐχ ὅσιόν σοι ὂν μὴ οὐ βοηθεῖν δικαιοσύνῃ, *for you promised to investigate it* (with us), *as holding it impious in you not to come to the assistance of justice.*

g. οὔτε μὴ μεμνῆσθαι δύναμαι αὐτοῦ, οὔτε μεμνημένος μὴ οὐκ ἐπαινεῖν, *I can neither not remember him, nor remembering not praise him.*

291. (*a. b.*) After expressions of *fear, solicitude, uncertainty,* &c. μή is used with the *subjunctive* or *indic.*

The indic. is used when the speaker wishes to intimate his conviction that the *thing feared,* &c. has or *will really* come to pass.

Of course the subj. becomes the *opt.* in connexion with *time past,* and in a *dependent proposition.* (71, 72.)

292. (*c*) The notion of *fear* is often omitted before μὴ οὐ, the verb being then generally in the *subj.*

---

[f] 281, *c.*

293. (*f. g.*) μὴ οὐ is also used with the *infin.* after many negative expressions.

(1) After *to hinder, deny, feel misgiving*, &c. when they have a negative with them; if not (*e*), they are used with μή, where *we* use *no* negative *.

(2) After such expressions as δεινὸν εἶναι, αἰσχρόν or αἰσχύνην εἶναι, αἰσχύνεσθαι.

(3) After such negative expressions as, to be *unable, impossible, not right*, &c.

(4) μὴ οὐ is also sometimes used with the participle ᵍ and with ὥστε and *infin.*, after negative expressions.

293*. VOCABULARY 49.

Capable of being taught, that can be taught (διδακτός). *Science* (ἐπιστήμη). *Know, know how* (ἐπίσταμαι ʰ). *To fall into a person's power or hands* (γίγνεσθαι ἐπί τινι). *To prevent a person* (ἐμπόδων εἶναι μή, or, after *negatives* or in questions implying a negative, μὴ οὐ. ἐκποδών is, *out of the way of*). *Right, lawful*, as determined by *divine* or *natural* laws (ὅσιος ⁱ—δίκαιος of what is permitted by *human* law). *Fall* (πίπτω ᵏ). *Hinder, prevent* (κωλύω, ἀποκωλύω). *To deny* (ἀρνέομαι). *Fear* (δείδω ˡ). *Suspect* (ὑποπτεύω, acc. of person).

[μετά.]

μετὰ τὸν, *after*; μετὰ τοῦ, *with*; μετὰ τῷ (only in the poets), *among, inter*.

Exercise 56.

294. I fear his coming to some harm (*lest he should suffer something*). I feared the boy would come to some harm. I fear we shall find, that (*p*) these things are not so. I fear about my boy lest he should come to some harm. The father,

---

* But the μή is not always expressed after verbs of *hindering, preventing*, &c. σχήσω σε πηδᾶν, &c.

ᵍ Thus δυσάλγητος γὰρ ἂν | εἴην τοιάνδε μὴ οὐ κατοικτείρων ἕδραν. Soph. *Ant.* 96.

ʰ ἐπίσταμαι, ἐπιστήσομαι, ἠπιστήθην. Imp. ἠπιστάμην. 2 sing. pres. ἐπίστασαι.

ⁱ But as opposed to ἱερός, ὅσιος relates to *man*, i. e. to *natural* laws: hence ἱερὰ καὶ ὅσια, 'divine and human things.'

ᵏ πίπτω, πεσοῦμαι, πέπτωκα. ἔπεσον.

ˡ δείδω, δείσομαι, δέδοικα and δέδια (both with meaning of *pres.*). Aor. 1. ἔδεισα.

though he feared about his boy, nevertheless went away. I
cannot *either* go *or* stay (111). I knew that they would prevent[74] the king from coming (*e*) into the country. I fear that
we have treated them ill. I fear that the rascal will not die.
It is disgraceful not to defend the laws of our country. Nothing
prevents this from being (*e*) true. What prevents us from
dying at once? It is a disgrace not to be without fear of
death. It is a terrible thing, not to bear what comes from the
gods. It is not right, not to choose to fight for one's country.
It is not right not to die for one's country, if it be necessary.
I am ashamed not to appear to have conferred great benefits
upon my country. I fear this will happen. After this, what
prevents us from dying? They sent out *men to prevent them**
from coming into the country.

§ 50. *μή with Relatives, the Infinitive*, &c.

295. *a.* τίς δὲ δοῦναι δύναται ἑτέρῳ, ἃ μὴ αὐτὸς ἔχει; *but
who can give to another what he has not got himself?*

b. ἀσφάλειάν σοι παρέξονται, ὥστε σε μηδένα λυ-
πεῖν, *they will afford you security, so that no man
shall annoy you.*

πράγματα παρεῖχον, ὥστε οὐκέτι ἐδύνατο τὸ στράτευμα πορεύεσθαι, *they harassed them, so that the
army could not advance any further (any longer).*

c. οὐδεὶς ... ὅστις μὴ παρέσται, *no one who shall not be
present* (or, *who is not present*[m]). ὁ μὴ πιστεύων,

* See 236, the third example.

[m] In connexion with future time, the Greeks and Romans marked the *futurity*
of the condition or connected notion. *We* generally do not. Thus in the example
we should say, ' *a man who* is not present,' taking that as a *general notion*, without
referring it to the time of the other verb. The future must be used when it is

he who does not believe. τὰ μὴ καλά, *dishonorable things.*

d. τὸ μὴ τιμᾷν γέροντας ἀνόσιόν ἐστι, *it is wrong* (an unholy thing) *not to honour old men.*

e. μὴ γένοιτο [t], *may it not be so!* μὴ ἴδοις τοῦτο, *may you never see this!*

296. (*a. c.*) μή is used in *relative* sentences and with *participles, adjectives,* &c., whenever the negative does not *directly* and *simply* deny an assertion with respect to some *particular mentioned* person or thing.

Hence relative sentences, participles, and adjectives take μή, whenever they might be resolved into a sentence with '*if*,' or describe only a *supposed* case ; not particular *individuals*, but individuals of a *class* [u].

297. (*d*) The infinitive generally takes μή, except where the opinions or assertions of *another* person are stated (*in sermone obliquo*). See 110.

298. (*b*) With ὥστε [v] the *infinitive* takes μή, the *indicative* οὐ.

299. VOCABULARY 50.

One who has slain a man with his own hand, the actual murderer (αὐτόχειρ). Wrong, wicked, impious (ἀνόσιος, see 293). Security, safety from danger (ἀσφάλεια. ἀσφαλής, safe. ἐν τῷ ἀσφαλεῖ εἶναι, to be in safety, to be safe). Voluntarily (ἐθελοντής, οῦ, properly, as a volunteer). Lazy, idle (ἀργός [w], from ἀ, ἔργον).

[παρά.]

Besides his bread (παρὰ τὸν ἄρτον). Beyond, more than, the others

necessary to mark this out ; but to use it always, as some writers do who plume themselves upon their accuracy, is against the idiom of our language ; of which any one may convince himself by examining a few consecutive pages of the English Bible. See '*English Grammar for Classical Schools,*' p. 39, c.

[t] Translated by, '*God forbid !*' in the English Bible.

[u] The thing to be considered, with respect to a relative or participial clause, is, whether it introduces some *new particular* concerning the object spoken of, or *forms one complex notion* with it. In this way it merely *restricts* the general notion to a *particular* sense ; the thing spoken of being, *not* the *substantive itself,* but the *substantive so limited.*

[v] Or ὡς, which is used (though less frequently) in the same way.

[w] ἀργός, 2 *termin.*

(παρὰ τοὺς ἄλλους). *Against* the laws of the gods (παρὰ τοὺς τῶν θεῶν θεσμούς). *Contrary to* or *beyond* what was expected (παρὰ δόξαν).

παρὰ τοῦ, *from,* after such verbs as to *receive, learn, bring, come ;* and with the *agent* after the passive verb.

παρὰ τὸν, *to,* and (in answer to *where ?*) *at.*

παρὰ τὸν has also the meaning of the Latin *præter ;—besides, beyond, against.*

PHRASES.

I had a narrow escape from death (παρὰ μικρὸν ἦλθον ἀποθανεῖν). *I had a narrow escape* (παρ' ὀλίγον διέφευγον).

Exercise 57.

300. He who (*p*) does not love his father, is impious. I fear it may be impious not to honour old men. No one who is not present (*c*), shall receive money. I entreat you not to stay. The sons of the Persians *of the present day*[11] pursue what is dishonorable. He who (*p*) does not trust God, *has become miserable, unknown to himself*[76]. Not to love one's own children is wicked. It is not possible for me to give you what I do not possess myself. He is too wise[60] not to know that. Not to do good to your friends, when (*p*) you can, is wicked. Pursue those things which are not (*p*) against the laws of the gods. He said that, if there was any occasion, he *would* labour[37] more than the rest. Know that I will incur[74] this danger with you (*pl.*). Besides his bread he has wine. I am conscious[73] of having had a narrow escape from death. He was very lazy, so as to undergo no labour *voluntarily.* He was very lazy, so that he underwent no labour, *at least willingly*[45]. I had a narrow escape from those who were pursuing me. These things happened contrary to what was expected. If we conquer the barbarians *in*[42] one more battle, we shall be in safety. I have received this wine from the faithful slave. They denied that they were (290, *e*) the actual murderers. I suspect[x] that this is impious. He went away, because (*p*) he

---

[x] ὑποπτεύω is followed by *acc.* and *infin.,* or (when it implies, *fear*) by μή. ὑποπτεύσας μή τι πρὸς τῆς πόλεως ὑπαίτιον εἴη, &c. Xen. An. iii. 1, 5.

suspected that it was impious to remain. Shall we say this (98) or not?

§ 51. *Some Adverbs of Time, &c.*

301. *a.* ἀξίως ἡμῶν πολεμήσομεν, *we will conduct the war in a manner worthy of ourselves.*

b. εἰσῆλθεν ὡς ἐμέ, *he came in to me.*

c. παρέσομαι ὁπότε κελεύσεις, *I will be with you whenever you bid me.*

d. περιμενῶ ἕως ἂν (or μέχρις ἂν) ἐλθῇ, *I will wait till he comes* (venerit).

πoίησον τοῦτο ἕως ἔτι ἔξεστι, *do this* whilst *you still* may.

ἔστε (μὲν) αἱ σπονδαὶ ἦσαν, οὔποτε ἐπαυόμην ἡμᾶς οἰκτείρων, as long as *the treaty* lasted, *I never ceased to think upon ourselves with pity.*

οὔποτε λήγουσιν ἔστ᾽ ἂν ἄρχωσιν αὐτῶν, *they never leave off* till they rule over *them.*

e. πρὶν ἢ ἐλθεῖν ἐμέ (or πρὶν ἐλθεῖν ἐμέ[y]), *before I came.*

πρὶν ἂν ἔλθω, *till I come* (= till I *shall have* come ; *venero*).

302. (*a*) Some adverbs govern a noun in the same case as the adjectives from which they are derived.

Hence comparatives and superlatives take the *gen.*

303.   Some particles are sometimes simply *adverbs*, and sometimes *prepositions* governing a case : *e. g.* ἅμα, ὁμοῦ, *together :*—ἅμα (*or* ὁμοῦ) τοῖς ἄλλοις.

304. (*b*) ὡς, as a preposition (= πρός), is only joined to *persons.*

---

[y] Also πρὶν ἦλθον ἐγώ. The preceding clause has often πρόσθεν in it, which makes the πρίν appear superfluous.

305.   Some adverbs, especially relative ones, refer to *verbs* and *whole clauses*, and thus connect propositions.

This is the origin of conjunctions.

306.   (*d*) Ἄχρι or μέχρι, ἕως [z] and ἔστε, both in the sense of '*until*' and in that of ' *as long as*,' govern the *subj.* or *opt.* when there is any *uncertainty;* the *indic.* when not.

Of course the *opt.* will appear without ἄν *in oratione obliqua*, even where there is no uncertainty.

307.   Hence, when a thing is spoken of as an *object* or *purpose contemplated*, the *subj.* with ἄν [a] will be used in connexion with *pres.* or *future* time; the *optative* [b], in connexion with past time and the *oratio obliquâ*.

308.   (*e*) πρίν, as being a *comparative*, takes ἤ (which however is often *omitted*), and generally the *infinitive;* but the *subj.* with ἄν, if the event is *future*.

Hence the *subj.* with ἄν will be used after the *imperative* and *future* with *negatives :* i. e. when *before* = *till.*

309.   VOCABULARY 51.

Near (ἐγγύς: *near the city,* ἐγγὺς τῆς πόλεως). *Apart* (χωρίς: *apart from,* or *without, the rest,* χωρὶς τῶν ἄλλων. So δίχα τινός). *Immediately, directly* (εὐθύς). *Directly,* or *straight to, the city* (εὐθὺ [c] τῆς πόλεως). *Immediately on his arrival* (εὐθὺς ἥκων). *From our very birth, as soon as we are born* (εὐθὺς γενόμενοι). *Most of all* (μάλιστα πάντων). *Except a very few* (πλὴν πάνυ ὀλίγων). *Except if* (πλὴν εἰ). *Out of, without, the city* (ἔξω τῆς πόλεως).

---

[z]   μέχρις οὗ is often found : So ἕως οὗ, &c.

[a]   With πρίν and ἡνίκα, and (in *poetry*) with μέχρι, ἄχρι, ἕως, the *subj.* is sometimes found without ἄν.   K.

[b]   And according to Hermann (against Elmsley) *with* ἄν. "Ubi in rectâ oratione πρὶν ἄν et similes particulæ conjunctivum requirunt, in oratione obliquâ manet ἄν, sed conjunctivo substituitur optativus ut proprius orationis obliquæ modus." Præf. ad *Trach.* p. 8.—Hartung says : " When the optative thus takes (in oblique narration) the place of the subjunctive (in *direct*), the particle ἄν may, *whenever one pleases*, be left at his old post." *Partikellehre*, ii. 304.—Poppo, however, rejects ἄν from *Xen. An.* vii. 7, 35. ἐδέοντο μὴ ἀπελθεῖν πρὶν ἂν ἀπαγάγοι τὸ στράτευμα (which in direct narration would be, μὴ ἀπέλθῃς πρὶν ἂν ἀπαγάγῃς . . . .), a passage quoted by Hartung.

[c]   εὐθύς and εὐθύ are no more different words than μέχρις and μέχρι; but the Attics generally used εὐθύς of *time*, εὐθύ of *place*.   It is only accidentally, that εὐθύς is identical in form with the *masc.* adjective.

Exercise 58.

310. Do not go away till I come.   I will not cease fighting till I have conquered you.   It is not possible for you to conquer your enemies out of the city, till you have chastised those in the city itself.   He went away before I came.   I was banished myself before you returned-from-banishment.   Whilst you are still at leisure, speak.   We were afraid, till (μέχρις) the Greeks sailed away.   They did not cease till (*before*) they sent for the boy's father.   We used to wait about [d] till the gates were opened.   I will not go away till (*before*) I have conquered you.   He said, that he would come to us, whilst he still might.   Do not cease, till you have mastered your temper.   Whilst you remain, combat the boy's disorder.   He said that he feared the gods most, whenever he was most prosperous (*was doing best*).   The general went in to the king.   And they (*of persons before mentioned,* 39) obeyed, except if any man stole any thing.   He said that he was nearly related [52] to him.   They march straight to the city.   Immediately on his arrival, he told me that we ought to set about [38] the task.   From our very birth we want many things.   He died as soon as he was born.

---

§ 52.   On Interrogative Sentences.

311. *a.* ἆρ᾽ εὐτυχεῖς ; *are you prosperous ?*

b. $\begin{cases} \text{ἆρ᾽ οὐκ ἔστιν ἀσθενής ; } \textit{is not he ill ?} \\ \qquad\qquad\qquad\qquad \textit{he is ill, isn't he ?} \end{cases}$ } [Yes.]

$\begin{cases} \text{ἆρα μὴ ἔστιν ἀσθενής ; } \textit{is he ill ?} \\ \qquad\qquad\qquad\qquad \textit{he is not ill, is he ?} \end{cases}$ } [No.]

c. ἦ που τετόλμηκας ταῦτα ; *you have not surely dared to do this ?* [No.]

---

[d] περιμένω.

d. ἢ γὰρ, ἐάν τι ἐρωτᾷ σε Σωκράτης, ἀποκρινεῖ; *if Socrates puts any question to you, you will answer him, will you not?* [Yes.]

e. οὔτι που ἐγὼ ἀγροικίζομαι; *surely I am not behaving rudely, am I?* [No.]

f. μῶν τί σε ἀδικεῖ ᵉ; *he has not injured you in any respect, has he?* [No.]

g. μή τι νεώτερον ᶠ ἀγγέλλεις; *you bring no bad news, I hope, do you?* [No.]

h. εἶτ' ἐσίγας Πλοῦτος ὤν; *and did you* then *hold your tongue, you Plutus?*

i. ἔπειτ' οὐκ οἴει θεοὺς ἀνθρώπων τι φροντίζειν; *do you* then really *not think that the gods regard mankind?*

k. ἄλλο τι ἢ περὶ πλείστου ποιῇ, ὅπως ὡς βέλτιστοι οἱ νεώτεροι ἔσονται; *do not you look upon it as a thing of extreme importance, that the rising generation should turn out as well as possible?*

ἄλλοτι οὖν οἵγε φιλοκερδεῖς φιλοῦσι τὸ κέρδος; *what! do not the covetous love gain?*

312.   Besides the interrogative adverbs and pronouns, the following particles are used in questions.

313.   ἄρα is mostly used in questions that imply something of *uncertainty, doubt,* or *surprise.*

314.   The answer '*Yes*' is expected by,—

ἆρ' οὐ; ἦ γάρ; οὐ; οὔκουν; ἄλλο τι ἤ;

315.   The answer '*No*' is expected by,—

ἆρα μή; ἦ που (*num forte?*); μή or μῶν ᵍ;

ᵉ The *pres.* of this word is used for the *perfect,* for a man *continues* to wrong us till he has made us reparation. Heindorf, *Protag.* 463.

ᶠ νεώτερον for νέον (*a new thing; news*), and that *per euphemismum* for κακόν. Heind. *Prot.* 461.

ᵍ μῶν = μὴ οὖν : but the etymology being forgotten, οὖν is sometimes used with it. Also μῶν μή ; and μῶν οὐ ; the latter requiring an assenting answer (= *nonne?*).

Obs. οὐ expects *yes;* μή, *no.*—οὐ is often followed by μέντοι : also by δή, δή που, with which it has an *ironical* force, *I imagine, forsooth,* &c. Also οὔτι που.

316. (*h. i.*) εἶτα, ἔπειτα (*then—and yet—and nevertheless*) express *astonishment* and *displeasure,* implying that what they suppose has been done, is inconsistent with something before mentioned.

317. (*k*) From the frequent use of ἄλλο τι ἤ, it came to be used as a *simple interrogative particle,* and the ἤ was often dropt[h]. It is then better to write it as one word, ἄλλοτι (K.).

318. τί παθών ; (*having suffered what?=*) *what possesses you*
to . . . &c. ?

τί μαθών; (*having learnt what? =*) *what induces you*
to . . . &c. ?

These phrases are used in *indignant, reproachful* questions : the former obviously relates to the *feelings ;* the latter to the *understanding,* and consequently to more deliberate offences.

319. VOCABULARY 52.

Strike (τύπτω). *Free* (ἐλεύθερος). *Weak, ill* (ἀσθενής: ἀ, σθένος, *strength.* ἀσθένεια, *weakness, infirmity, a complaint*). *Fond of gain,* (φιλοκερδής).

[πρός.]

πρός, *to, close by,* generally takes the *acc.* in answer to *whither?* the *dat.* in answer to *where?*

πρὸς τὸν is also *towards, against, in reference to, with a view to, in comparison of.*

πρὸς τοῦ is *from, by,* after to *hear,* to be *praised* or *blamed by,* and frequently after the passive verb.

πρὸς τοῦ is also used of *situation* and in *adjurations.*

I am wholly wrapt up in this (πρὸς τούτῳ ὅλος εἰμί). *To pay close attention to one's affairs* (πρὸς τοῖς πράγμασι γίγνεσθαι). *In addition to this* (πρὸς τούτοις). *To fight against a person* (πρός τινα). *To calculate with oneself* (λογίζεσθαι πρὸς ἑαυτόν. So with σκέπτεσθαι, σκοπεῖν, *to consider*). *To be dishonoured by* (ἀτιμάζεσθαι πρός τινος). *On the father's side* (πρὸς πατρός).

εἶναι πρός τινος is (1) *to be consistent with, like,* or *characteristic of;*

---

[h] Stallbaum thinks it was dropt in *animated, impassioned* questions, and retained in those of a more *sedate* and *sober* character.

(2) *to be on his side;* (3) *to make for him, to be for his interest; to be a good thing* for him.

Exercise 59.

320. Are not these things for our interest rather than for that of our enemies (*b*)? Is not he wholly wrapt up in these things? You do not *surely* wish to have wine in addition to your bread (*c*)? I do not *surely* act insolently, do I (*e*)? You are not come to bring us (*p*) any bad news I hope (*are you*)? [No.] And are you, *then*, not without fear of death, though (*p*) a pious man (*h*)? And do you, *then*, not think that you shall be punished for what you have done (*p. pass.*) against the laws of the gods? *What possesses you* to strike [1] a free man? *What induces you* not to choose to stay with us any longer? *What possesses you*, that you will not cease to behave-insolently [74] towards your friends? These things are not more *for the interest of* our enemies than of us, are they? [No.] Have you been in any respect dishonoured by Xenoclides? Do you not think it a most important thing, that your children should be brought up as well as possible (*h*)? It is not like a pious man to fear death excessively. The other party are more on Cyrus's side. Know that these things are [74] for the interest of Cyrus. I know that he is on the side of the Athenians. Do we not both see and hear *from our very birth* [95]?

---

§ 53. *Indirect single Questions.*

321. *a.* οὐκ οἶδα (*or* οὐκ ἔχω) ὅποι τράπωμαι. (See 67, *b.*)

 οὐκ οἶδα ὅστις ἐστί, *I don't know who he is.*

 οὐκ οἶδα ὅπως τὸ πρᾶγμα ἔπραξεν, *I don't know*

Translate as if it were, '*having suffered* what *do you strike* ?' &c.

how he did the thing. ἀπόκριναι ἀνδρείως ὁπό-
τερά σοι φαίνεται, *answer boldly which of the
two is your opinion.*

b. ἴσμεν [k] πόσα τέ ἐστι καὶ ὁποῖα, *we know both how
many they are, and of what kind.*

c. ὁρᾷς οὖν ἡμᾶς, ἔφη, ὅσοι ἐσμέν; *do you see, said he,
how many we are?* (*or how many there are of
us?*)

d. οὗτος [l], τί ποιεῖς ;—ὅ,τι ποιῶ ; *you there, what are
you doing?—what am I doing?*

322. (*a*) The proper forms for *indirect* questions are those
pronouns and adverbs which are formed from the direct interrogatives by the prefixed *relative* syllable ὁ —, which gives
them a connecting power.

> Thus from πόσος; ποῖος; ποῦ; πόθεν; πῶς; &c. are formed ὁπόσος,
> ὁποῖος, ὅπου, ὁπόθεν, ὅπως, &c.
>
> So ὅστις, formed by prefixing the relative to τίς, is the proper *depend-
> ent* interrogative. See 67, 1.

323. But as the Greeks often pass from *oblique* to *direct*
narration, so they often use the *simple interrogatives* in dependent questions; and even, as in (*b*), *intermix* the two.

324. (*c*) Occasionally, though very seldom, the *relative
forms themselves* are used in dependent questions.

> (*c*) When, as in this example, a pronoun or noun is the *accus.* after the
> first verb, and the *nom.* before the second, it is generally expressed in the
> *accus.* [m], and not in the *nominative.*

325. (*d*) When the person *of whom the question is asked*
repeats it, he uses the forms beginning with ὁ —.

326. VOCABULARY 53.

[ὑπό.]

ὑπὸ τὸν, '*under,*' after verbs of *rest* as well as verbs of *motion.* Also
'*about*' of time.

---

[k] See 73, c.

[l] οὗτος, αὕτη, are used (instead of *voc.*) in exclamations ; *you there !*

[m] The accusative is generally retained in the English Bible ; "I know *thee*, who
thou art," &c.

ὑπὸ τῷ, ' under,' after verbs of *rest* only : sometimes, instead of the *gen.*, after passive verbs (δαμῆναι ὑπό τινι).

ὑπὸ τοῦ, ' by,' after *passive* verbs and active verbs with a passive notion.   Also, to express a *cause ; from, out of, through.*

To die *by the hands of* (ἀποθανεῖν ὑπὸ—gen.).   To learn *by compulsion* (ὑπ' ἀνάγκης).   He did it *through* or *from fear* (ὑπὸ δέους.   δέος, n.).   To *be mad from intoxication* (ὑ π ὸ μέθης μαίνεσθαι).   *Sub noctem, at* or *about nightfall* (ὑπὸ νύκτα).

Exercise 60.

327. The slave died by the hands of his master. Most boys learn by compulsion. I perceived (*p*) that the boy learnt by compulsion. I do not repent of having learnt [74] these things by compulsion. He said that the shameless flatterer was mad from intoxication. The few are wounded by the many. I will go away *on condition that* (262, *e*) you will yourselves set out at nightfall. Do you see, said he, how many men are wounded by a few? I don't know how the eagle had his eye knocked out [41]. I shall praise (all) whom I see (95, 1) marching in good order. How much would your possessions fetch, if they were sold? He says that he will hold his tongue, *though he should have* [31] much to say. If the slave should die by your hands, you will be punished. Do you see how many there are of the enemy? He says that he has been entrusted with these things [41]. These things happened about the same time.

§ 54.   *Double Questions.*

328. *a.* πότερον ἕψονται Κύρῳ, ἢ οὔ ; *will they follow Cyrus or not ?*

πρὶν δῆλον εἶναι . . . πότερον ἕψονται Κύρῳ, ἢ οὔ, *before it was known,* whether, &c.

b. τούτῳ τὸν νοῦν πρόσεχε, εἰ δίκαια λέγω, ἢ μή, *attend to this,* whether *what I speak is just* or *not.*

c. σκοπῶμεν εἴτε εἰκὸς οὕτως ἔχειν, εἴτε μή, *let us consider whether it is likely to be so, or not.*

329. *Direct double* questions are asked by πότερον (or πότερα)—*ἤ*, less commonly by ἄρα—*ἤ*.

μῶν—*ἤ* is still less common; *ἤ*—*ἤ* belongs to poetry, especially *epic* poetry.

330. *Indirect* double questions are asked by—

εἴτε—εἴτε,

εἰ—*ἤ*,

πότερον—*ἤ*.

ἤ—*ἤ* belongs to *epic* poetry, though occasionally found in Attic poets.
εἴτε—*ἤ*, and εἰ—εἴτε, are also used by poets.

331. VOCABULARY 54.

The road home (ἡ οἴκαδε ⁿ ὁδός). *To suffer a thing to be done, to allow it to be done with impunity* (περιοράω ᵒ). *Boldly* (θαρρῶν, part.). *Restore an exile* (κατάγω). *To pay attention to, to attend to* (τὸν νοῦν προσέχειν, or προσέχειν only, with *dat*.). *Likely, natural* (εἰκός ᴾ).

Exercise 61.

332. I don't know whether he is alive or dead. If you attend to your affairs yourselves, all will be well. If you attended to your affairs yourselves, all would be well. If you had attended to your affairs yourselves, all would be well. I will not allow our land to have been ravaged with impunity. Are the same dogs pursuing the sheep, or not? Go away boldly *on condition* of holding your tongue.

ⁿ οἴκαδε is from the *acc.* of a *shorter* form (such as οἴξ, οἰκός) of οἶκος. Though *this* form does not occur, several *similar* ones do; e. g. ἀλκί, κρόκα, for ἀλκῇ, κρόκην. B.

ᵒ It takes the *infin.* if the thing is to be *prevented;* the *part.* if it is to be *avenged.* Of course (by 73, r) περιϊδεῖν will be used for *aor.*, περιόψεσθαι for *fut.*—The phrase brings to one's mind our '*to stand by and see*' (a man injured); but it *gets* its meaning in a different way; *i. e.* not from the notion of *seeing* and yet not acting, but from that of *not seeing*, of looking *round about* an object instead of *at* it. Hence it agrees more nearly with our to *overlook* (an offence).

ᴾ Neut. of εἰκώς, *part.* of ἔοικα (*am like*), which has *three forms* of *part.* ἐοικώς, εἰκώς, οἰκώς. B.

I

I fear that we shall forget our road home. I knew that they would not suffer[74] their country to be ravaged. O citizens, let us not suffer our country to be ravaged. They will not *stand by and see* us injured. They made peace *on condition* that both (parties) should retain (*have*) their own. He said that Xenoclides was too wise[60] to be deceived by his slaves. He says that more arms were taken *than could have been expected from the number of the dead*[59]. He says that *he*[72] is not afraid of death. The king sent persons to restore (*the exile*) Xenoclides (236*, third example).

---

§ 55.   *Observations on* εἰ, ἐάν.

333. *a.* ἀ γ α ν α κ τ ῶ εἰ οὑτωσὶ[q] ἃ νοῶ μὴ οἷός τ᾽ εἰμὶ εἰπεῖν, *I am indignant at being so unable to express my meaning.*

 οὐκ ἀγαπᾷ εἰ μὴ δίκην ἔδωκεν, *he is not contented with not having been punished.*

θαυμάζω εἰ μηδεὶς ὑμῶν ὀργίζεται, *I am astonished, that not one amongst you is angry.*

b. σκέψαι[r] εἰ ὁ Ἑλλήνων νόμος κάλλιον ἔχει, *consider whether the Grecian law is better.*

σκέψαι ἐὰν τόδε σοὶ μᾶλλον ἀρέσκῃ, *see whether this pleases you better.*

c. μηδὲ τοῦτο ἄρρητον ἔστω μοι, ἐάν σέ πως πείσω, *nor let me leave this unsaid, if I may by any means persuade you;* i. e. (*that I may see whether*) I can, &c.

---

q Demonstrative pronouns and adverbs are strengthened by what is called the *i demonstrativum*, which is a long accented ι answering to -ce in Lat. *Short* vowels are thrown away before it. οὑτοσί (*this man here*), οὑτηΐ, τουτί, &c. So οὑτωσί.

r The Attics use σκοπῶ, σκοποῦμαι, for *pres.* (*not* σκέπτομαι), but σκέψομαι, ἐσκεψάμην, and ἔσκεμμαι, from σκέπτομαι, depon. middle.

334. (a) εἰ is used for ὅτι (*that*) after θαυμάζω, and some other verbs expressive of *feelings*.

This arises from the Attic habit of avoiding *positiveness* in speaking; which, in this case, speaks of what may be *quite certain* as only probable.

335. (b) εἰ is (as we have seen, 80) used for '*whether:*' it has this meaning after verbs of *seeing, knowing, considering, asking, saying, trying,* &c.

336. (b) ἐάν is also used in this way with the *subjunctive* when the question relates to an *expected case that remains to be proved.* K.

337. VOCABULARY 55.

Am indignant (ἀγανακτέω, *dat.*; but it takes the *acc.* of a neuter pronoun). O Athenians (ὦ ἄνδρες Ἀθηναῖοι). Please (ἀρέσκω [s], *dat.*).

Exercise 62.

338. It is this very thing, O Athenians, that I am indignant at [t], that you *allow* half your country (59) to have been ravaged *with impunity.* This it is that I am indignant at. Cyrus, being indignant, sets out with (*part.*) five horsemen for Sardis. He pleases more men than any other single person [64]. He says that he is of a mild disposition (134, *a*)? I asked him whether the king was of a mild disposition or not. Do you see how many are suffering *the same as you* (177, *a*). Do you know of what kind the laws of the Persians are (324)? *You there,* what do you say?—What do I say! Although, if any man is of a mild disposition, it is he [63]. I wonder that you are not able to go in *without being observed* [76]. He says that he is not of a character to do any thing whatever for the sake of gain (280).

---

[s] ἀρέσκω, ἀρέσω, &c. perf. pass. ἤρεσμαι : ἠρέσθην.
[t] I am indignant at this thing itself.

§ 56. *Condensed Questions.*

339. *a.* τί ἂν ποιοῦντες ἀναλάβοιεν τὴν ἀρχαίαν ἀρετήν;
what must they do to recover their ancient virtue ?
(or, *by what conduct* can they, &c.?)

b. καταμεμάθηκας οὖν τοὺς τί ποιοῦντας τὸ ὄνομα
τοῦτο ἀποκαλοῦσιν; (have you learnt =) *do you
know, then,* what those persons do, to whom *men
apply this name ?*

c. τίνας τούσδ' ὁρῶ ξένους ; who are these strangers
whom *I behold?*

340. (*a. b. c.*) By attaching the interrogative to a *participle,*
or using it in an *oblique* case, the Greeks employ a *single* sentence in questions where *we* must use two.

Thus in translating from English into Greek, a relative clause attached
to an interrogative one will be got rid of.

341. VOCABULARY 56.

With what object or *view ?* (τί βουλόμενος;) *By Jupiter* (νὴ Δία or
νὴ τὸν ᵘ Δία). *No, by Jupiter* (μὰ Δία). *Apollo* ('Απόλλων ᵛ). *Neptune* (Ποσειδῶν ᵛ). *Minerva* ('Αθηνᾶ). *Swallow* (χελιδών ʷ). *Nightingale* (ἀηδών ˣ). *Spring* (ἔαρ, n.ʸ). *Once* (ἅπαξ). *Bring, lead* (ἄγω).
To burn out (ἐκκαίω). *Peacock* (ταώς).

Exercise 63.

342. One swallow does not make a spring. He told me
that one swallow did not make a spring. I asked *by what
conduct* I should please the gods. The eagle is having its

ᵘ The *art.* is generally used except in μὴ or μὰ Δία.

ᵛ 'Απόλλων and Ποσειδῶν (*G.* ωνος) have *acc.* 'Απόλλω, Ποσειδῶ, *voc.* "Απολ-
λον, Πόσειδον.

ʷ χελιδών, όνος. V. χελιδοῖ.

ˣ ἀηδών, όνος—also G. ἀηδοῦς, V. ἀηδοῖ.

ʸ In prose ἔαρ is *nom.* in use; but the *gen.* and *dat.* are of the contracted form,
ἦρος, ἦρι.

eyes burnt out[41]. He says that the eagle has had its eyes
burnt out. *With what view* did the other party march into the
country of the Scythians the same spring? The peacock lays
only once a year. He (*p*) who commits no injury[z], requires
no law. By Apollo, I will be with you, if I am wanted. By
Minerva, I will free the boy from his disorder. Who is this
physician that you are bringing (*c*)? Will you not go away
at once?—No, by Jupiter, not I (ἔγωγε). Even if you
should be unseen by others, you will at least be conscious[73]
yourself of having acted unjustly. What do those persons do
with whom all men, *so to speak*[46], are angry (*b*)? He envies
every body[86]. By Neptune, there is nobody he does not plot
against (276). Envy nobody. The nightingale sings most
beautifully.

---

§ 57. *Various Constructions.*

343. *a.* ἦ μὴν ἔπαθον τοῦτο, I protest *that I suffered this.*
　　ὄμνυμι[a] ἦ μὴν δώσειν, I swear that I will as-
　　suredly *give* (or, solemnly *swear that I will give*).

　b. ἀπώλοντο αἱ νῆες αὐτοῖς ἀνδράσιν, *the ships were
　　lost together with their crews.*

　c. διαφέροντες ἢ σοφίᾳ ἢ κάλλει ἢ ἀμφότερα, *distin-
　　guished either for wisdom, or beauty, or both.*

　d. τά τε ἄλλα εὐδαιμονεῖ καὶ παῖδας ἔχει κατηκόους
　　αὐτῷ, he is *happy* both in other respects and
　　especially *in having obedient children.*

　e. ὅπερ ἦα[b] ἐρῶν, *what I was going to say.*

---

[z] Who injures not at all.

[a] ὄμνυμι, ὀμοῦμαι, ὀμώμοκα. ὤμοσα. Perf. pass. ὀμώμοσμαι, but the other
persons and aor. 1. *pass.* more commonly without the ς.

[b] Imperf. of εἶμι, *ibo.*

f. πάλαι θαυμάσας ἔχω, *I have long been wondering.*

g. παίζεις ᶜ ἔχων, *you are joking.*

h. ὑπέβαλεν ἑαυτὸν φέρων Θηβαίοις, he went and flung himself into the hands of the Thebans.

344. (*a*) ἦ μήν is a solemn form of asseveration.

345. (*b*) The *prepos.* σύν is omitted before αὐτῷ, αὐτῇ, &c. which then = *together with, with.*

346. (*c*) ἀμφότερον is used *adverbially* (or *elliptically*) by the poets; *both; as well—as,* &c. So ἀμφότερα is used in reference to *two words*, without being made to conform to them in case.

347. (*d*) When καί refers to ἄλλος, it has the force of *especially, in particular.*

348. (*e*) ἔρχεσθαι, ἰέναι, with *part. fut.*, is *to be going to,* or *on the point of.*

349. (*f. g.*) Sometimes ἔχω makes an emphatic circumlocution with the *past partic.* : and with some verbs (e. g. the 2nd *pers.* of ληρεῖν, παίζειν, φλυαρεῖν) it is used to make a good-humoured observation.

350. (*h*) φέρων appears redundant in some expressions, but denotes a *vehemence of purpose, not altogether free from blame.*

Hence it answers to our *to go and do a* (foolish, impetuous) *thing : to take a thing and fling it away,* &c.

351. VOCABULARY 57.

To swear (ὄμνυμι, acc. of the God or thing sworn by). Just as he was (ᾗπερ or ὥσπερ εἶχεν).

Exercise 64.

352. The damsel is beautiful in person (134) in other respects, and especially has very beautiful eyes [12]. He swore that he would *assuredly* give them three talents, if he had them. I swear that I will *assuredly* do this. I swear *by* all the gods

ᶜ παίζω, παίξομαι, οὖμαι, πέπαισμαι. ἔπαισα. Later writers have ἔπαιξα, πέπαιγμαι. B.

that I will assuredly *confer a great benefit* upon the state.
Those with the king, with (*p*) their heads uncovered, charged
the ranks of the Greeks. He told me that the ships were lost,
together with their crews. He told me that, *but for* [39] the
general, the ships would have been lost, together with their
crews. Are you not trying (me)[d], whether I am mad? (321, *c.*)
You are not trying (me) whether I am mad, are you? Is he
distinguished from [e] other people by (his) wisdom, or (his)
temperance, or both (*c*)? Are you joking, or are you mad?
Cyrus set out just as he was, with five horsemen. *He went
and gave* (*h*) all his possessions to his neighbour. I have long
been wondering at the shamelessness of this flatterer (*f*).

---

§ 58. *Various Constructions continued.*

353. *a.* δίκαιός εἰμι τοῦτο πράττειν (= δίκαιόν ἐστιν ἐμὲ
τοῦτο πράττειν), *it is just* (or *right*) *that I should
do this.*

b. ἔφθασε τοσοῦτον ὅσον Πάχητα ἀνεγνωκέναι τὸ
ψήφισμα, *it arrived first* (*indeed*), *but only suffi-
ciently so, for Paches to have had time to read out
the decree.*

c. φθάνεις ἕλκων ἢ τὰ πτηνὰ φεύγειν, *you draw* (your
nets) *before the birds fly away.*

d. οὐκ ἂν φθάνοι ἀποθνήσκων [x], *he will* certainly *die*
(or, *be killed*).

e. τί ἄλλο οὗτοι ἢ ἐπεβούλευσαν; *what did these people
do but plot?*

---

[d] πειρᾶσθαι takes *gen.*, seldom *acc.* Thuc. i. 71.

[e] Does he differ from . . . ?

[x] That is, *he cannot die too soon* (for die he must). Buttmann gives a different
explanation.

f. ἀπεκρίνατο ὅτι βασιλείαν οὐκ ἂν δεξαίμην, *he answered,* " I would not receive a kingdom."

g. τί οὐκ ἐποιήσαμεν; (why have not we done it? =) *why don't we do it?   Let us do it directly?*

354. (*a*) With δίκαιος, ἄξιος, &c., the *personal* construction is preferred to the impersonal.

355. (*b*) ὅσον is used elliptically with the *infin.*

356. (*c*) Some words that *imply* a comparison (e. g. φθάνειν, διαφέρειν, ἐναντίος, διπλάσιος, ἴδιος, ὕπερθεν, πρίν) often take the construction with ἤ.

357. (*e*) The verb ποιεῖν is often omitted after οὐδὲν ἄλλο^y ἤ—, ἄλλο τι ἤ—; τί ἄλλο ἤ—; &c.

358. (*f*) A person's *quoted* words, when quoted exactly as he uttered them, are introduced by ὅτι.

> Here the Greek idiom differs from our own : *we* omit ' *that*' when a person's words are quoted exactly, and insert it when not.

358*. (*g*) After τί οὐ ^z—; (in questions) the *aor.* appears to be used for the *present.*

359. VOCABULARY 58.

> *Give orders, order* (ἐπιτάττω).   *Would* probably *have been destroyed* (ἐκινδύνευσεν ἂν διαφθαρῆναι).   *To be the slave of* (δουλεύω, dat.).

Exercise 65.

360. *But for* Xenoclides, the whole country would *probably* have been ravaged. But *it is just* that every man should defend the laws of his country. You do nothing but give orders. He answered, I should be a fool if (*p*) I were to do this. He answered, I will give you a portion of the food

---

^y When the ἄλλο is spelt with an *apostrophus* in this phrase, it mostly *drops its accent,* and thus looks like the abbreviated ἀλλά, *but.*   The accent was dropt, because in some *very similar* phrases the ἀλλ' *is* ἀλλά; and in some others it is difficult to say whether it stands for ἄλλο or ἀλλά.   Wherever it *certainly* stands for ἄλλο, it should retain its accent.   See 364, a.

^z τί οὖν, ἔφη, οὐ διηγήσω μοι; *quin tu mihi narres?* " Hæc interrogatio *alacritatem quandam animi* et *aviditatem sciendi* exprimit."   Weiske.

which I have myself. He went away before his friend arrived. It is right that every body should oblige *such a man as you are.* He answered, I have done more service to the state than any other single person. He answered, I will come to you if I am wanted. You do nothing but laugh at all the citizens. What do you do but hold all men cheap? He answered, I will collect *as many men as I possibly can.* He answered, I will come to you *as quickly as possible,* to (*p*) combat the faithful slave's disorder. He answered, if any body has done much service to the state, it is you. They arrived first, indeed, by just time enough to have destroyed those with the king (*b*). Why don't you make me also happy? Why don't you answer? He answered, if Xenoclides had not been present, the ships would have perished, *together with* their crews. If (*p*) you do this, you will certainly be the slave of your temper. If he were not ambitious, he would not undergo every labour.

---

§ 59. *List of Particles and short connecting and other Phrases.*

[Those with an asterisk cannot stand first in a sentence.]

A.

361.   ἄγε δή, ' but come ;' ' come now.'

362.   ἀεί (*Ion.* and *poet.* αἰεί, αἰέν), *always.*
       ὁ ἀεὶ ἄρχων, *the archon for the time being :* the person who *at any time* is archon.

363.   ἄληθες (accented in this way), ironically, *indeed ? itane ?*

364.   ἀλλά, *but.* It is often used to introduce *quick, abrupt retorts, objections, exhortations,* &c. ἀλλ' ἀδύνατον, ' nay but, *it's impossible* ' (or, why, *it's impossible*): ἀλλὰ βούλομαι, ' well, *I will !'*
       ἀλλά is also our ' *but* ' = ' *except* ' after general negatives : some case of ἄλλος generally stands in the preceding clause.

ἀλλ' ἤ [a], *unless, except ; nisi.*

ἄλλο τι ἤ (or ἄλλοτι) ; *used as an interrogative particle* (317).

ἄλλως τε καί, *especially, in particular.*

365.   ἄμα, *at the same time* (as prep. ' together with,' *dat.*).   ἄμα *followed by* καί *in the following clause ; as soon as* (omitting the καί [b]).   The two assertions are marked out as occurring at *the same time ;* and the particles may be variously translated, according to the view with which the *coincidence* is pointed out : *no sooner—than ; already—when ; when—at once,* &c.

366.   ἀμέλει (properly the *imperat.* of ἀμελέω, *don't mind,* or *be anxious about*), as *adv. doubtless, certainly.*

367.   *ἄν, see 75 : for ἐάν, see 77.

368.   ἄνα [c], *up! (for* ἀνάστηθι, *rise up!)*

369.   ἀνθ' ὧν, *because, for* (268).

370.   *ἄρα [d] (ἄρ, ῥά [e] in *Epic* poets), *therefore, consequently, then.*

   1) It is also used where it seems to be without power, but indicates *conformity with the nature of things* or *with custom ; as might have been expected ; ex ordine, rite.*   Hence it serves to mark a transition to an *expected* proposition.

   2) After εἰ, ἐάν, &c. it has the force of *indeed* or *perchance.—εἰ μὴ ἄρα (nisi forte)* has often an ironical meaning ; *unless forsooth* [f].

371.   ἅτε (with *part.*), *as being* (240, *a*).

372.   *αὖ (*backwards*), *again ;* 2) *on the other hand ;* 3) *further ; and then also.*

373.   *αὖτε, αὐτάρ (both Epic), and ἀτάρ *have the same meaning as* αὖ.

---

[a] ἀλλ' ἤ has this meaning after negatives and questions that imply a negative. The ἀλλ' *might sometimes* be supposed ἄλλο, used elliptically ; but frequently this is impossible ; and it is better, therefore, to understand it always to he ἀλλά. (Krüger.)—A case of ἄλλος often stands already in the sentence.   The construction probably arose from two nearly equivalent forms : οὐδὲν ἄλλο—ἀλλά, and οὐδὲν ἄλλο—ἤ. (K.)

[b] e. g. ἄμα ἀκηκόαμέν τι καὶ τριηράρχους καθίσταμεν. Ἅμα is also used with the *part.* like μεταξύ : ἄμα ταῦτ' εἰπὼν ἀνέστη.

[c] When propositions are used alone as *adverbs,* and thus become equivalent to verbs, they throw back the accent.

[d] The old derivation from ΄ΑΡΩ (to *fit,* trans. and intrans.) seems far preferable to Hartung's derivation from a common root with ἁρπάζω, *rapio, repente.* So Kühner.

[e] Enclitic.

[f] ΄Αρα, the *interrog.* particle, stands first in its sentence.   "Attic poets, however, allow themselves to interchange the quantity, and use ἄρα for *consequently,* ἄρα as the interrog. particle ; but without altering the proper *place* of each."   B.

So also the poetical *αῦθις, *Ion. αῦτις. *(αὐτάρ* and *ἀτάρ begin* a sentence or clause.)

374.   αῦτως, *thus* (emphatical): 2) *ut erat;* of things in their *original unchanged* state, or that are of *common every-day occurrence :* 3) it is attached to words expressing *reproach, contempt,* or *neglect,* e. g. *childish, useless, vain,* &c. Hence 4) it is used *alone* as equivalent to μάτην, *idly, vainly, uselessly.* It is a sister form of οῦτως g. B.

Γ.

375.   *γάρ (γε ἄρα) *for.*

It often refers to a short sentence *to* be mentally supplied (such as, *I believe it ; no wonder,* &c.). In questions h it answers pretty nearly to our ' *then,*' and implies *surprise* (= *why, what ?*).

τί γάρ ; *quid enim ?* or *quidni enim ?* = *certainly, to be sure.*

πῶς γάρ ; (*Att.*) is an emphatic *denial* = *by no means.*

376.   *γέ (a strengthening particle), *at least* i, *at all events, certainly.*

It adds strength and emphasis to the word to which it is added, answering the same purpose that an *elevation of the voice* does in speaking, or *italics* in a printed passage. It is used in *rejoinders* and *answers,* either to confirm or to restrict : also in *exhortations* to make them more impressive.

ἔγωγε, *I for my part*—εἰκότως γε, *quite naturally*—πάνυ γε, *quite so, certainly.*

γὲ δή k, *certainly.*

γέ τοι, *yet at least ; at least however ; however.*

γὲ μήν (certe vero ; vero), *certainly however ; but yet :* hence it is also a strengthened δέ.

---

g Hermann, on the other hand, says, that it should always be written αῦτως in Homer ; and Hartung thinks Buttmann's a strange mistake, the derivation being from αὐτός, *he and no other, self* (so that αῦτως = *thus and in no other way*). He considers that the rough breathing is only a dialectic peculiarity. αῦτως *Æol.,* αῦτως *Att.* Eustath.

h Especially after τίς ; πότε ; πῶς, &c.

i For which γοῦν is more commonly used.

k Interest hoc inter γὲ δή et γέ τοι, quod δή sententiam per γέ restrictam simpliciter confirmat, τοί autem eam sententiam indicat oppositam esse præcedentibus quodammodo. Hinc γὲ δή est *sane quidem, enimvero ;* γέ τοι autem *certe quidem.* Herm.

Δ.

377. διότι (= διὰ τοῦτο ὅτι), *because* : but later writers often use it for ὅτι, *that*.

378. *δέ (see μέν) has the three meanings of *and*, *but*, *for* [the last in the old writers only].

379. *δή[1], a strengthening particle, properly *now* (for which ἤδη is used) ; it is employed in various ways to enliven a speech :—

ἄγε δή, φέρε δή, *come now !*

τί δή ; *what then ?*

It also means *truly, forsooth.* After relatives it has the force of our '*ever.*' ὅστις δή, *whoever it may be,* &c.   It often follows superlatives.

380. *δήπου (confirms a conjecture proposed.   M.): it is a more emphatical πού (see πού), *I imagine* or *suppose ; doubtless.*

*δήπουθεν is used to hint, with a little irony, that the contrary is impossible.

*δῆθεν has also the ironical force of δή, *forsooth.*   M.

*δῆτα, like δή, is used in assuring and confirming (*surely, certainly*).

E.

381. εἰ, *if*; 2) *whether ;* and 3) after some verbs of feeling, *that.*   (See 334.)

εἰ καί, *if even, although.*
καὶ εἰ, *even if, even though.*

εἰ γάρ, *O that !*—a wish; like εἴθε.

εἰ μή, *unless.*

εἰ μὴ διά, *but for.*

εἴτις, εἴτι, properly, *if any one ; if any thing :* but it is used as equivalent to ὅστις with more emphasis ; *whoever, whatever.*

382. εἶτα,
      ἔπειτα, } 1) *afterwards, thereupon ;* 2) *then.*

They are used in *scolding, reproachful* questions (see 316), and often with verbs, to refer emphatically to a preceding *participle*[m].

383. ἔνθα, demonstr., *here, there ;* but also, and in prose generally, relat. *where*[n].   ἐνθάδε, demonstr., *here ; hither.*

---

[1] It is only in Homer and Pindar that δή stands at the beginning of a proposition or clause.   M.

[m] οὐ δυνάμενοι εὑρεῖν τὰς ὁδούς, εἶτα πλανώμενοι ἀπώλοντο.

[n] But ἔνθα or ἔνθα δή may stand at the beginning of periods for *ibi, there* or *then.*

ἐνταῦθα (*Ion.* ἐνθαῦτα), *here.*

ἔνθεν, *hence, thence, whence :* ἐνθένδε, *hence.*

ἔνθεν μέν—ἔνθεν δέ (*hinc—illinc*), *on the one side—on the other.*

ἔνθεν καὶ ἔνθεν (*hinc illinc ; ab utraque parte*), *on this side and that ; on both sides.*

ἐντεῦθεν, *hence, thence.*

(All these words relate also to *time.*)

384.　ἐπεί, *after ;* 2) *since,* quoniam.

Before *interrogatives* and the *imperat.*, it has the meaning of *for ; for else.*

ἐπειδή has the same meanings, but ἐπεί is far oftener used in the sense of *since.*

385.　ἔστε (= ἐς ὅτε *), *until, as long as.*

386.　ἔτι, *yet, still, further.*

οὐκέτι, μηκέτι, *no more, no longer.*

387.　ἐφ' ᾧ º, *on condition that :* ἐφ' ᾧτε, the same, but generally with the infinitive.

H.

388.　ἤ, *or* P *; in comparisons, than.*

389.　ἤ, *truly, certainly :* but generally a mere interrogative particle [—*ne*, but only in direct questions].

ἦ μήν, *assuredly,* in asseverations, promises, &c.

390.　ἤδη, *now, already.* Also, ' *without going any further* ᕪ.'

391.　ἤν = ἐάν (see 77). This is the form used by the Attic poets for ἐάν : never ἄν.

Θ.

392.　*θήν (*enclit.*), *I should imagine ; surely ;* in ironical, sarcastic speeches.

οὐ θήν, ἦ θήν. It is peculiar to Ionic and Doric poets.

---

* This derivation seems disproved by such passages as Xen. An. iv. 5, 6 : ἔστε ἐπὶ τὸ δάπεδον, *usque ad.* I believe it to be ἐς with the old connective τέ. See τέ.

º Here ἐφ' ᾧ (properly = ἐπὶ τούτῳ ὅ—) is equivalent to ἐπὶ τούτῳ ὡς—.

P It retains this meaning in questions : πόθεν ἥκει ; ἦ δῆλον ὅτι ἐξ ἀγορᾶς ; *where is he come from ?* or *is it plain that he is come from the market-place* (and so the question unnecessary) ?

ᕪ πάνυ γάρ μοι δοκεῖ ἤδη πολλοῦ ἂν ἄξιος εἶναι ἐπίτροπος, ὢν τοιοῦτος. Xen.

I.

393.   ἵνα, *where;* 2) *in order that* [r].

K.

394.   καί, 1) *and;* 2) *also, even.*

τέ—καί, *both—and* or *and also: as well—as.*

[But these particles are often used where *we* should only use '*and.*']

καὶ εἰ, κᾶν εἰ; see under εἰ.

καὶ μάλα, } before these words καὶ has a peculiar energy.
καὶ πάνυ, }

καὶ μήν, (immo,) *well! certainly!* 2) (atqui), *and yet.*

καίπερ, *although.*

καὶ ταῦτα (idque), *and that too.*

καίτοι, *and certainly;* 2) *and yet certainly; and yet;* 3) *although.*

καί (*also*) often seems to be superfluous in familiar conversation: ἵνα καὶ εἰδῶ, *that I may know,* &c.

καί is used in questions, to imply that *nothing* can be expected, &c. It may be often translated by *at all, possibly.* τί χρὴ προσδοκᾶν; asks for information, but τί χρὴ καὶ προσδοκᾶν; '*what can one* possibly *expect?*' implies that nothing can possibly be expected.

καί—δέ. When καί and δέ come together in a proposition, καί is *also:* but the two are often used where we should use '*and also.*'

395.   *κέ, κέν, an *enclitic* particle, used by the Epic poets for ἄν.

M.

396.   μά, *not by —;* a particle of *swearing.* It has a negative force when *alone,* but may have either ναί or οὐ (*yes* or *no*) with it.

397.   μάλιστα μέν—εἰ δὲ μή, &c. = *if possible—but if not,* &c.—mentioning what is *best* to be done, and also what is the *second best,* if that is not feasible [s].

398.   μᾶλλον δέ, *or rather.*

399.   *μέν [t], *indeed*—answered by δέ (*but*), or sometimes by ἀλλά, μέντοι, &c.

---

[r] ἵνα (= *in which case*) goes with indic. of a past tense to express what *would have happened, if,* &c. ἵν' ἦν τυφλός. ἵν' εἶχον, &c.

[s] With *numerals,* words of *time,* &c. μάλιστα (*about*) signifies that the statement made is *nearly exact* (according to the *belief* of the speaker), without pretending to be *quite so.*

[t] μέν and δέ are much more frequently used than *indeed—but,* which always

The answering δέ is sometimes omitted :—

1) When the *opposition* is clearly marked without it : e. g. by naturally *opposite* words, such as adverbs of *place* and *time*, with an opposite meaning : *here—there ; in the first place—secondly.*

2) When the opposition is suppressed : chiefly when *personal* and *demonstrative* pronouns are used with μέν at the beginning of a proposition. Thus, ἐγὼ μέν, *equidem.*

400. *μέντοι, *to be sure ;* 1) *I allow ;* 2) *but indeed, however.*

401. μή, *not ;* 2) *lest,* or *that not ;* 3) *that* (after verbs of *fearing,* &c.). In questions it expects the answer ' *no,*' being somewhat stronger than μῶν ; (*num ?*) After some verbs (e. g. *restrain, prevent, forbid,* deny, &c.) it is used where it seems to be superfluous, from *our* using no negative particle.

μὴ οὐ : see § 49.

402. μηδέ, } See οὐδέ.
μήτε,

403. *μήν, 1) *truly, indeed ;* 2) *but indeed, yet.*
τί μήν ; *why not ?*

404. μήτι γε, (nedum) *much less.*

N.

405. νή, ' *by,*' in oaths (with *acc.*).
406. *νύ, νύν, (enclit. ὔ) properly the same as νῦν, for which it sometimes stands ; 2) for οὖν, *then, now.*
407. νῦν δή, *now ;* 2) with a *past* tense, *just now.*

O.

408. ὁ μέν—ὁ δέ u, *the one—the other.*
οἱ μέν—οἱ δέ, *some—others.*
ὁ μέν, ὁ δ' οὔ often stand alone in reference to a preceding proposition. πάντας φιλητέον, ἀλλ' οὐ τὸν μὲν τὸν δ' οὔ, *we must love all, and not* (*love*) one man indeed, but not another. παρῆσαν οὐχ ὁ μὲν ὁ δ' οὔ, ἀλλὰ πάντες.

express a strong *opposition*, whereas the Greek particles connect any *different* propositions or notions. Thus a *section, chapter,* or even *part* of a whole work, often ends with (for instance) καὶ ταῦτα μὲν οὕτως ἐγένετο : when the next chapter will necessarily begin with something like τῇ δ' ὑστεραίᾳ (*on the following day*). It is only when the context clearly requires it, that μέν is to be rendered, *it is true, indeed.*

u For ὁ μέν—ὁ δέ we sometimes find ὃς μέν—ὃς δέ.

409. ὃ δέ (*quod vero est*), after which the τοῦτό ἐστι is omitted ᵛ.

410. ὀθούνεκα (= ὅτου ἕνεκα), *because, that*, in the Tragic poets.

411. οἷος (ποιεῖν), *of a kind or character* (to do, &c.).

        οἷός τε, *able, possible.*

        οἷον εἰκός, *as is natural ; as one may* (or *might*) *suppose.*

412. ὁπότε, *when, whenever ;* 2) *since :* as *quando, quandoquidem* are used
        for *quoniam.*

413. ὅπου, *where* (there were) ; 2) *since* (siquidem).

414. ὅπως, as adv., *how ;* 2) conjunct., *in order that, that.* ὅπως ἔσεσθε,
        see *that you be* = a strong imperative.

415. ὅσαι ἡμέραι or ὁσημέραι, *daily ; properly, as many days as there are.*

        ὅσος follows θαυμαστός and superlatives of quality. πλεῖστα ὅσα or
        ὅσα πλεῖστα, *quam plurima :* θαυμαστὸν ὅσον, *mirum quantum.*

        ὅσον οὐ (or ὁσονού), *all but.*

416. ὅτε, *when.* ὁτὲ μέν—ὁτὲ δέ ᵂ, *sometimes—sometimes.*

417. ὅτι, *that* (instead of Lat. acc. with *infin.*) ; 2) *because*, for διὰ τοῦτο ὅτι,
        i. e. διότι.

        ὅτι also strengthens superlatives, and is used to introduce a quotation
        in the very words of the speaker, where *we* use no conjunction (see 353, *f*).

        ὅτι μή, after negatives, *except.*

418. οὐ, *not :* in questions it requires the answer ' *yes.*'

        (ἡ) οὐ διάλυσις = *the non-destruction.*

        οὐ γὰρ ἀλλά is commonly used in the sense of '*for*' with increase of
        emphasis, *q. d.* '*for it is no otherwise, but.*' M.

        οὐ μή : see 287.

        οὐ μήν, *yet not, but not ;* 2) as a negative protestation. See ἦ μήν.

        οὐ μὴν ἀλλά (or οὐ μέντοι ἀλλά), properly, ' *yet not !—but ;*' it has
        generally the force of *yet, however ;* sometimes of *rather, much more.*

        οὐ πάνυ, *by no means.*

        οὔ φημι, *I say* (that) *not ; deny, refuse.*

419. οὐχ ὅτι ˣ—ἀλλὰ καί, *not only—but also.*

        οὐχ ὅτι—ἀλλ' οὐδέ, *not only—but not even.*

        οὐχ ὅπως—ἀλλὰ καί, *not only not—but also.*

        οὐχ ὅσον and οὐχ οἷον are also found for οὐχ ὅτι and οὐχ ὅπως
        respectively.

ᵛ ὃ δὲ πάντων δεινότατον (*but what is the most terrible thing of all*, is this).

ᵂ Whenever the forms τότε, ὅτε are used twice (sometimes only once) for ποτέ
—ποτέ, *sometimes—sometimes*, they are accented τοτέ—, ὁτέ—. B.

ˣ When μὴ ὅτι, μὴ ὅπως begin the sentence, ὑπολάβῃ τίς may be supplied ;
or they may be understood like the Latin *ne dicam*, and are thus stronger than the
preceding expressions, but both in a *negative* sense.

420. $\left\{ \begin{matrix} οὔτε, μήτε, \\ οὐδέ, μηδέ, \end{matrix} \right\}$ Both forms are *connecting* negatives, answering to *neque ;* 1) *nor, and not ;* 2) οὔτε or μήτε repeated are *neither—nor.*

The forms οὐδέ, μηδέ, have the further meaning of 1) *also not ;* 2) *not even,* which is always their meaning in the middle of a proposition. οὐδ' ὧς, *not even so.* See ὧς.

421. *οὖν, *therefore, then* [y]. It gives to relatives (ὁστισοῦν, &c.) the force of the Lat. *cunque (ever, soever).*

1) οὐκοῦν, properly an interrogative of inference, as οὐκοῦν εὔηθες τοῦτο ; ' *is* not *this,* then, *foolish ?* ' But, generally, the interrogative force, and with it the negation, vanishes, and οὐκοῦν is to be translated simply by ' *therefore,*' and begins a clause [z].

2) οὔκουν is a strengthened negative ; *not in the least.*—In the meaning ' *therefore not* ' without a question, it is better written οὐκ οὖν.

422. οὔπω, *never yet.*

οὐδέποτε, *never,* is used of both *past* and *future* time ; οὐδεπώποτε only of *past* time. (See πώ.)

Π.

423. *πέρ (enclit.), *quite :* used nearly like γέ, to strengthen a preceding word. It is frequently appended to *relatives,* and adverbs of *time, cause,* and *condition.* Thus ὥσπερ properly means ' *exactly as.*' It is derived, probably, from πέρι, in the sense of ' *very.*'

424. πῆ μέν—πῆ δέ (not πῇ μέν—πῇ δέ, Hermann), *partly—partly.*

425. πλήν, *except :* as conjunction, or preposition with *gen. :* πλὴν εἰ, *except if.*

426. πολλάκις, *often,* after εἰ, ἐάν, μή, has sometimes the meaning of (*forte*) *perhaps, perchance.*

427. *ποτέ (enclit.), *at any time.* With interrogatives it expresses surprise : τίς ποτε ; *who in the world?*

428. *πού (enclit.), *somewhere ;* 2) *perchance, perhaps ;* 3) *I imagine,* used in conversation when any thing is assumed in a half-questioning way, that the speaker may build something on the *assent* of the person appealed to.

429. πρός σε θεῶν, I adjure *you by the gods* (ἱκετεύω is generally omitted in this form of adjuration).

---

[y] οὖν is often used to *resume* a speech that has been interrupted by a parenthesis (= *I say*).

[z] οὐκοῦν, extra interrogationem, acerbam interdum habet ironiam. *Bremi,* Dem. p. 238.

K

430.   πρὸ τοῦ ᵃ (better προτοῦ), *before this* or *that time* (= πρὸ τούτου or
        ἐκείνου τοῦ χρόνου) ᵇ.

431.   *πώ (enclit.),⎫ *till now, hitherto :* but they are never joined to affirma-
        *πώποτε,   ⎭ tive propositions in this sense.

        οὔπω, μήπω ᶜ, *never yet, not yet.* πώποτε is seldom annexed to
        the simple οὐ, μή, but to οὐδέ, μηδέ. The form without πώ
        (οὐδέποτε, *never*) is commonly employed only *generally* or with
        respect to the *future.* Both πώ and πώποτε may be separated
        from the negative particle by other words between.

        These particles are also used with *relatives, interrogatives,* and *parti-
        ciples* used as equivalent to relative sentences. With these words
        there is no *negative* expressed, but the *notion* of a negative lies at
        the bottom of them all. τίς πω ;—ὅσα πώποτε ἠλπίσαμεν, &c.

432.   πώμαλα ᵈ, properly, *how so ? how then ?* hence, *by no means.*

T.

433.   τὰ μέν—τὰ δέ, *partly—partly* (adverbially).

434.   *τ' ἄρα or τ' ἄρ (poetical), ἄρα strengthened by τοί.

435.   *τέ (*que*). See καί.

        In the old language (as we find it in the Epic poets) τέ seems to
        impart to many pronouns and particles the *connecting* power,
        which they afterwards retained in themselves without the par-
        ticle.

        Thus we find μέν τε, δέ τε, γάρ τε, &c., and even καί τε.

        Especially the particle is found after all *relatives,* because these in
        the old language were merely forms of the *pronoun demonstrative,*
        which through this τέ obtained the connecting power (*and this*),
        and thus became the *relative* (*which*). As soon, however, as these
        forms were exclusively allotted to the relative signification, the
        particle τέ was dropt as superfluous. Hence we often find in

---

ᵃ ἐν γὰρ τῷ πρὸ τοῦ οὐδεμία βοήθειά πω τοῖς Μεγαρεῦσιν οὐδαμόθεν
ἐπῆλθεν. Thuc. iv. 120.

ᵇ It answers exactly to our ' *before this,*' ' *before that.*'

" Quando in serie orationis *præteritum tempus* memoratur, tunc de eo quod ante
illud etiam fuerit formula προτοῦ non videtur adhiberi posse, nisi simul insit *relatio
ad præsens tempus ;* hoc est, nisi diserte simul significare quis velit, *nunc non
amplius ita esse.*" Buttm. ad *Alcib.* I. 14.

ᶜ Not to be confounded with Homer's οὔπω, μήπω = οὔπως, μήπως, *in no way,
by no means.*

ᵈ For πῶς μάλα ; B. Others say for πῶ μάλα ;—πῶ being a rather uncommon
Doric form for πόθεν ;

Homer ὅς τε, ὅσον τε, &c. for ὅς, ὅσον, and the like. The particles ὥστε, ἅτε, and the expressions οἷός τε, ἐφ᾽ ᾧ τε are remains of the ancient usage.

436.   τῇ μὲν—τῇ δέ, *in one place and another; here—there; in one respect—but in another.*

437.   τί, *in some respect, in any respect, at all* [e].   τί μήν ; *why not ?*

438.   τὸ δέ often introduces a statement *opposed* to what has been said before, and may be translated by (*quum tamen* [f]) *whereas, but however,* or sometimes, *but rather.*   See *Heindorf,* Theæt. 37.

τὸ δέ with the *superlat.* often stand alone, with the omission of τοῦτό ἐστιν.   τ ὸ δ ὲ μ έ γ ι σ τ ο ν π άντα ταῦτα μόνος κατειργάσατο, *but the greatest thing is (this),* that, &c.   (See ὃ δέ—.)

439.   *τοί (enclit.), properly an old *dat.* for τῷ, meaning *therefore, certainly.* But these meanings have disappeared, and τοί has only a *strengthening* force [g]: it is frequently used with *personal* pronouns, and in *maxims, proverbs,* &c.

*τοίνυν, *therefore, then, now, so now.*   It is also used when a person proceeds with an argument; *now further, but now.*   Besides this, it is frequently used in *objections,* either in a continued narrative, or more commonly in replies: *why,* or *why then.*   [Very seldom as the first word of a clause.   P.]

τοίγαρ (*ergo*), *therefore.*

τοιγάρτοι and τοιγαροῦν, *therefore, even therefore and from no other cause, precisely for that reason.*

440.   τοτὲ μέν—τοτὲ δέ [h], *at one time—at another.*

441.   τούνεκα (Epic), *on that account ; therefore.*

442.   τοῦτο μέν—τοῦτο δέ, *on the one hand—on the other.*

443.   τῷ, *therefore.*

Ω.

444.   ὡς (relat. adv.), *as* (*as if, so as*) ; **2)** of time, *as, when ;* **3)** with numerals, *about ;* **4)** it strengthens superlatives, especially of *adverbs,* and some positives.

ὡς (prepos. = εἰς), *to,* with acc. : but only of *living* things.

---

[e] It is often added to πάνυ, σχεδόν, οὐδέν.

[f] τὸ δ᾽ οὐ δεῖ, ὡς, &c.—*quum tamen non oporteat.*

[g] According to Hartung, τοί has not a *strengthening* but a *restrictive* meaning, which, however, often comes to the same thing : *e. g.* ἔκτεινά τοι σ᾽ ἄν, *I would have killed you,* and nothing else = *I would* assuredly *have killed you.*   Nägelsbach thinks it the old *dat.* of the *pron.* σύ (τύ).

[h] See note on ὅτε.

ὡς (conjunc.), that ; 2) in order that, with subj., opt., or fut. indic. :
3) so that, with infin., more commonly ὥστε ; 4) since ; 5) quippe, for.

ὡς ἔνι [i] (= ὡς ἔνεστι, as it is possible) is used with superlatives : ὡς
ἔνι μάλιστα, as far as it is any way possible.

ὡς ἔπος εἰπεῖν, so to say.

ὡς συνελόντι (sc. λόγῳ) εἰπεῖν, to be short·; in a word.

[For which συνελόντι εἰπεῖν, and συνελόντι alone, are found.]

ὥς (with accent) = οὕτως, thus.   It is common in the poets, especially
the Ionians ; but in prose is found only in οὐδ' ὥς, καὶ ὥς.

---

*Table of the less obvious meanings of Prepositions in
Composition.*

ἀμφί, on both sides.

ἀντί, against, marking *opposition*.

ἀνά [k], up ; back again.

διά (dis) marks separation ; taking apart or aside.

ἐν, often into.

κατά [l], down ; it often implies completion, and hence 2) ruin, destruc-
tion (answering in both to per).

μετά (trans) marks transposition, change.

παρά sometimes signifies (like præter) missing or doing amiss.   παρα-
βαίνειν, to transgress, &c.

---

[i] When prepositions are employed instead of the compounds of εἶναι, or rather
when, this verb being omitted, they stand alone as *adverbs*, the accent is thrown
back on the first syllable. See ἄνα.

[k] With βαίνειν, &c. ἀνά, up, and κατά, down, mean respectively into the
interior, and down to the coast.

[l] Hence κατά is sometimes equivalent to up in English : καταφαγεῖν, to eat up.

TABLE

DIFFERENCES OF IDIOM,

&c.

ENGLISH.	GREEK.
1. (§ 1.) He who does.	The (person) doing (ὁ πράττων).
2. (§ 2.) Socrates.	*The* Socrates (*often*).
A woman.	*A certain* woman (γυνή τις).
	[When a *particular* person is *meant*, nough not *named.*]
3. (§ 3.) *My* slave.	*The* my slave.
Your slave, &c.	*The* your slave.
4. I have ⎱ a pain in my I am suffering from ⎰ head.	I am pained (*as to*) *the* head: acc. (ἀλγῶ).
5. He rejoiced (*or*, was vexed) *when the citizens were rich* (or, *that the citizens were rich*).	He rejoiced (*or*, was vexed) *at* (ἐπί) *rich the citizens.*
6. My friend and my brother's.	*The* my friend and *the of the* brother.
7. (§ 4.) The wisdom of the geometer.	(*Very often*) The of the geometer wisdom—*or*, the wisdom, *the* of the geometer.
8. The beautiful head.	As in English; or, 'the head the beautiful.'
9. The son of Philip.	*The* of Philip (*son*, υἱός, understood).
Into Philip's country.	Into *the* of Philip (*country*, χώραν, understood.)
10. The affairs of the state.	*The* (*neut. pl.*) of the state.
The people in the city.	*The* (οἱ) in the city.
Those with the king.	*The* (οἱ) with the king.
My *property*.	τὰ ἐμά.

ENGLISH.	GREEK.

11. (§ 5.) The men *of old.*
    ———————— *times.* }

The *long-ago* (men)—οἱ πάλαι.

    The men *of those days.* — The *then* (men).

    The *intermediate* time. — The *between* time.

    The *present* life. — The *now* life.

    The *upper* jaw. — The *up* jaw (ἡ ἄνω γνάθος).

12. (§ 6.) The rhinoceros has *a* very hard hide. — The rhinoceros has *the* (= its) hide very hard.

    They have strong claws. — They have *the* (= their) claws. strong.

13. The *beautiful;* beauty (in the *abstract*). — τὸ καλόν.

    Beautiful things.
    Whatever things are beautiful. } — τὰ καλά.
    What is beautiful.

14. Speaking. — The to-speak.
    Of speaking. — Of the to-speak.
    By speaking, &c. — By the to-speak, &c.

     — τὸ λαλεῖν: τοῦ λαλεῖν, &c.

15. Virtue. Gold. Eagles. — *The* virtue. *The* gold. *The* eagles (when the *class* is meant; or *eagles* generally).

16. To do kind offices. — εὖ ποιεῖν with *acc.* of person.
    — confer benefits on.
    — treat well.

17. To *prosecute on a charge* of murder. — To *pursue* of murder.
    To *be tried for* murder. — To *fly* of murder.

18. (§ 7.) *Some—others.* — { *The indeed—but the.* / οἱ μέν—οἱ δέ.

    But (*or* and) he (*or* it) . . . . — ὁ δέ . . . at the head of a clause.
    And he . . . — καὶ ὅς . . .

19. (§ 8.) The other party. — οἱ ἕτεροι.
    The *rest* of the country. — The *other* country.

20. The *whole* city; *all* the city. — πᾶσα ἡ πόλις.
    Every city. — πᾶσα πόλις.

21. (§ 9.) With *two* others. — Himself *the third* (pron. *last*).

22. To perform this service. — ὑπηρετεῖν τοῦτο (pers. *for whom* in *dat.*).
    To perform many services. — πολλὰ ὑπηρετεῖν.

23. His *own* } things. / One's *own* } — The things *of himself* (τὰ ἑαυτοῦ).

25. (§ 10.) *What comes from* the gods. — *The* (neut. pl.) of the gods.
    The *greater part* of . . . — ὁ πολύς } in agreement with the noun
    Half of . . . — ὁ ἥμισυς } governed by *of.*'

ENGLISH.	GREEK.

26. (§ 11.) *In my time.* In my father's time.

ἐπ' ἐμοῦ. ἐπὶ τοῦ πατρός.

In my power.

ἐπ' ἐμοί.

27. (§ 12.) To *be* so.

To *have* (themselves) so (οὕτως ἔχειν).

To be found guilty
——brought in—— } of . . &c.

To *be taken* or *caught* (ἀλῶναι with gen.).

28. (§ 13.) Not only—but also.

οὐχ ὅτι—ἀλλὰ καί. See note on 82.

To confer a great benefit on.

To benefit greatly (μέγα ὠφελεῖν).

To do a great injury to.

To hurt greatly (μέγα βλάπτειν).

OBS. τὰ μέγιστα to be used, if it is '*greatest*,' not '*great*.'

29. (§ 14.) I should *like* to behold.

I would gladly behold (ἡδέως ἂν θεασαίμην a).

————— extremely to behold.

ἥδιστ' ἂν θεασαίμην.

I would *rather* behold A than B.

ἥδιον ἂν θεασαίμην A ἢ B.

30. It is not *possible*.

It is not (οὐκ ἔστιν).

31. On *the plea* that I could then conquer, &c.

As so being-likely-to-conquer (ὡς οὕτως περιγενόμενος ἄν).

Though I *should have*, &c.

ἔχων ἄν.

32. (§ 15.) When you *have done*, you *will*, &c.

When you *shall have done* (ἄν with *subj.* 91*).

33. (§ 16.) What I please.

ἃ δοκεῖ (μοι). (If necessary, ἃ δόξειεν, or, ἃ ἂν δόξῃ).

34. (§ 17.) And you as much as any body. And you among the first. }

Having begun from you (100).

35. *Am slow* to do it (112).

Do it *by leisure* (σχολῇ).

36. CONDITIONAL PROPOSITIONS (79).

(1) If I have any thing, I *will* give it.

(1) If the *consequent* verb is in the *future*, the *conditional* verb is (generally) in the *subj.* with ἐάν b.

---

a θεᾶσθαι is '*to behold*' something that may be considered a *spectacle*. ἰδεῖν (ὁρᾶν, ὄψεσθαι) is simply *videre*, *to see*. Hence ἴδοιμι should be used in the phrase '*I should like to see*,' when the notion of a *spectacle* is quite out of place.

b Both verbs *may* be in the *future indicative* (the conditional verb with εἰ). The condition is then expressed in a more positive way, as a contemplated event: a construction which is often adopted when the condition expresses an event *hoped for* or *feared* (R.); as, εἴ τι πείσονται Μῆδοι, εἰς Πέρσας τὸ δεινὸν ἥξει.

ENGLISH.

If it has thundered, it has also lightened.

(2) If you *should* do so, I *should* laugh.
If you *were to* do so, I *should* laugh.
If you *would* do so, you *would* oblige me.

(3) If I *had* any thing, I *would* give it.
If I *had had* any thing, I *would have* given it.

37. (*That*) they *would* fetch.
(*That he*, &c.) *would* be able.
They *would* have died.
I *should* have died.

38. (§ 20.) We *should* (or *ought to*) set about the work.
The work *should be set-about.*
We *must set about* the work.
The work *must* be set about.

39. (§ 21.) I should have died *but for* the dog.

40. The *all but* present war.

41. (§ 22.) Having had his government taken away.
Having been entrusted *with* the arbitration.
Having had his eyes knocked out.

42. To conquer him *in* the battle of Marathon.

43. To flow with a full (*or* strong stream).

GREEK.

If the *consequent* verb is in any tense of the *ind.* but the future, or in the imperative, put the conditional verb in the *indic.* with εἰ.

(2) When both verbs have '*should*,' '*would*,' or the first '*were to*,' the second '*should*' or '*would*,' both are to be in the *optative* ; the *consequent* verb with ἄν.

(3) When the *consequent* verb has '*would*,' but the *conditional* verb not, both verbs are in a *past tense of the indicative* ; the *conditional* verb with εἰ, the *consequent* verb with ἄν.

εὑρεῖν ἄν.
δυνηθῆναι ἄν. } § 14.
Aor. with ἄν c (*imperf.* or *pluperf.* if necessary).

The work is *to-be-set-about* (verbal in τέος).

It is *to-be-set-about* (*neut.* of verbal in τέος) the work d.

I should have died, *if not through* the dog (εἰ μὴ διά, with *acc.*).

The *as-much-as not* (ὅσον οὐ) present war.

Having been taken away *his government.*

Having been entrusted *the arbitration.*

Having been knocked out *his eyes.*

To conquer him the battle at (ἐν) Marathon.

To flow much (πολύς *adj.*)

---

c As in the *consequence* of the fourth form of conditional propositions. 79, d.

d The '*work*' is to be in the case governed by the verb from which the verbal is derived.

ENGLISH.	GREEK.
To flow *with* milk.	To flow milk.
44. (§ 24.) Till late in the day.	Till *far-on* (πόῤῥω) of the day.
45. Willingly at least. Willingly.	To be willing (ἐκὼν εἶναι).
46. So to say. To speak generally.	As to say a word (ὡς ἔπος εἰπεῖν).
47. Sensible persons.	The sensible of persons (οἱ φρόνιμοι τῶν ἀνθρώπων, *sometimes;* but very often οἱ φρόνιμοι only).
48. To drink *some* wine.	To drink *of* wine.
(Not) to drink any wine.	(Not) to drink *of* wine.
49. My property, *wretched man that I am !*	My (property) *of* (me) *the wretched !* [τὰ ἐμὰ τοῦ κακοδαίμονος.]
50. What misery !	The misery (in the *gen.*).
51. (§ 25.) Who *in the world . . ?*	Who ever ? (τίς ποτε;)
52. To be nearly related to.	To be near to a person (*in respect*) of family.
53. (§ 26.) You shall not do it *with impunity.*	You shall not do it *rejoicing* (χαίρων).
54. I would not have done it *at all* (132).	I would not have done it *the beginning* (ἀρχήν or τὴν ἀρχήν).
55. (§ 28.) It is *the part of* a wise man.	It is of a wise man.
56. It is not a thing *that everybody can do.*	It is not every man's (παντός).
It is not every one that can do this.	It is not *every man's* to do this.
57. To be one's own master.	ἑαυτοῦ εἶναι.
58. (§ 29.) More powerful *than ever.*	More powerful *himself*[e] *than himself* (αὐτὸς αὑτοῦ).
59. Afflictions *too great for* tears.	Afflictions greater *than in-proportion-to* (ἢ κατὰ) tears.
Of superhuman size.	Greater *than according-to* man (ἢ κατ' ἄνθρωπον).
More than could have been expected from the small ʰumber of the killed.	More *than in-proportion-to* the dead (ἢ κατὰ τοὺς νεκρούς).
60. *Too young* to know, &c.	Younger *than so as to* know (ἢ ὥστε).
61. (§ 30.) With more haste than prudence. Hastily rather than prudently. More hastily than prudently.	More-hastily than more-prudently.

e Of course ' *themselves than themselves,*' when more than one are spoken of.

ENGLISH.	GREEK.

62. The greatest } *possible.*
   As great *as* }
   —— *as he could.*
   As many as he *possibly could.*

ὡς or ὅτι with superlat.

As-many as he could most (ὅσους ἠδύνατο πλείστους).

63. *If any other* man can do it, you can.

You, *if any other man* (εἴ τις καὶ ἄλλος), can do it.

If *any man* is temperate, *it is you.*

You, *if any other man,* are temperate.

64. I have injured you *more than any* other individual has.

I *one man* have injured you *the most* (πλεῖστα εἷς ἀνήρ σε ἔβλαψα).

65. (§ 31.) To charge a man *with a* crime.

To charge (ἐγκαλεῖν) a crime to a man.

66. (§ 35.) If it is agreeable to you. }
   If you are willing. }

If it is to *you wishing* it (εἴ σοι βουλομένῳ ἐστί).

67. And that too . . .

καί ταῦτα.

68. For the present at least.
   As far as *they* are concerned.

τό γε νῦν εἶναι.
τὸ ἐπὶ τούτοις εἶναι.

69. (§ 36.) I offer myself *to be interrogated.*

I offer myself *to interrogate.*

70. (§ 37.) It was done *that* robbers might not commit depredations, &c.

It was done τοῦ μὴ λῃστὰς κακουργεῖν, &c.

71. Nothing was done *because he* was not here.

Nothing was done διὰ τὸ ἐκεῖνον μὴ παρεῖναι.

72. He said that *he* was in a hurry.

He said to be in a hurry (*pron.* omitted).

73. (§ 40.) He is *evidently* hurt.
   I am conscious of thinking so. }
   —————— that I think so. }

He is evident (δῆλος) being hurt.
I am conscious (σύνοιδα) to myself *thinking so* (nom. *or* dat.).

74. I know }
   —remember } that I have done it.
   —rejoice }
   —am aware }

I know }
   —remember } having done it (*part.*).
   —rejoice }
   —am aware }

I am ashamed } of having done it.
I repent }

I am ashamed having done it.
It repenteth to-me having done it.

Know that you will be punished.
I perceived *that he thought,* &c.
He will not cease *to do* it.

Know about-to-give punishment.
I perceived him thinking, &c.
He will not cease *doing* it (*part.*).

75. He knew that the son he had begotten was mortal.

He knew having begotten a mortal son.

76. (§ 41.) I did it *unconsciously.* }
   —— *unknown to myself.* }

I was concealed-from (ἔλαθον) myself, doing it (*nom.*).

ENGLISH.	GREEK.
I did it *without being seen,* or *discovered; secretly.*	I was concealed (ἔλαθον) doing it. (or) I did it *being unobserved* (λαθών).
77. I arrived *first* (or *before them*).	I having arrived *anticipated* them (ἔφθην, or ἔφθην αὐτούς).
You cannot do it *too soon.*	Doing it, you will not anticipate (οὐκ ἂν φθάνοις).
Will you not do it *directly ?*	οὐκ ἂν φθάνοις ποιῶν ;
78. He held his tongue, *as supposing* that all knew.	He held his tongue, as (ὡς) all men knowing it (*acc.* or *gen.*).
79. (§ 43.) You act strangely *in giving* us, &c.	You do a strange thing, *who* give us, &c.
80. They pronounced her happy, &c. *in having such* children.	They pronounced her happy, &c. *what children she had.* (253, *b.*)
They have arms *to defend* themselves with.	They have arms *with which they will defend* themselves.
81. First of all (259).	First among the (ἐν τοῖς πρῶτος—πρώτη, πρῶτοι, &c.).
82. (§ 44.) From *some* of the cities.	From the cities *there is which.* ['which' in same case as 'cities.']
Somewhere.	There is where.
Sometimes.	There is when.
83. I feel thankful to you *for coming.*	I know you gratitude, *for what* (ἀνθ' ὧν) you came.
84. They destroyed *every* thing of value.	They destroyed *if* there was *anything* of value (εἴ τι, &c.).
85. (§ 45.) Such a man as you.	ὁ οἷος σὺ ἀνήρ.
(Of) such a man as you are.	οἵου σοῦ ἀνδρός, &c.
For men like us . . .	τοῖς οἵοις (or οἵοις περ) ἡμῖν.
To make *astonishing progress.*	To advance θαυμαστὸν ὅσον.
Surprisingly miserable.	θαυμασίως ὡς ἄθλιος.
86. (§ 46.) There was nobody whom he did not answer. } He answered every body.	*Nobody whom he did not* answer. ['nobody' under the government of 'answered:' ὅστις, who.]
87. Especially.	Both otherwise and also (ἄλλως τε καί).
As fast as they could.	As they had of speed.
88. (§ 47.) I am able.	οἷός τέ εἰμι.
It is possible.	οἷόν τέ ἐστι.
Are *adapted for* cutting.	Are *such* as to cut.
Am *of a character* to . . .	Am *such* as to . . .
89. Eighteen.	Twenty wanting two (280, *d*).
90. Far from it.	πολλοῦ δεῖν.
Am } Is } to be.	μέλλω } γενέσθαι (when 'am to be' = μέλλει } 'am *intended* to be').

ENGLISH.	GREEK.

91. (§ 48.) *Be sure to be* . . .   That (ὅπως) you shall be ['*see*' under-
                                     stood].

    Take care *to do* it.   Take care how (ὅπως) you shall do it.

92. (§ 49.) I fear that I shall.   I fear μή . . . (subj. *or* fut. indic.)

    ———————— not.   —— μὴ οὐ . . .

93. What prevents us from . . . ?   τί ἐμποδὼν μὴ οὐχὶ . .; with *inf.*

    To prevent them *from coming.*   To prevent them μὴ ἐλθεῖν.

94. (§ 50.) I had a narrow escape from   I came παρὰ μικρόν to die.
    death.

    I had a narrow escape.   I escaped by a little (παρ' ὀλίγον).

95. (§ 51.) Immediately on his arrival.   Immediately having arrived (εὐθὺς
                                           ἥκων).

    As soon as we are born. ⎫   Immediately being born (εὐθὺς γενό-
    From our very birth.   ⎭   μενοι).

96. (§ 52.) *What possesses you* to do   Having suffered what, do you do this?
    this?   (τί παθών ;)

    What induces you to do this?   Having learnt what, do you do this?
                                     (τί μαθών ;)

97. (319.) To be wholly wrapt up in   πρὸς τούτῳ ὅλος εἶναι.
    this?

98.   ⎧ To be consistent with.
  (1)⎨ —— like.
     ⎩ —— characteristic of.

  (2) To be on a man's side.   εἶναι πρός τινος.

     ⎧ To make for a man.
  (3)⎨ — be for a man's interest.
     ⎩ —— good for a man.

99. By what conduct.   Doing what.

    With what view.   Wishing what.

100. (§ 57.) He *went* and gave (when   He φέρων gave.
    used contemptuously or indig-
    nantly).

QUESTIONS ON THE SYNTAX.

[Words in SMALL CAPITALS are to be translated into Greek.]

§ 1.—1. What is the difference between the *imperf.* and the *aor.?* [The Aorist is used of *momentary* and *single* actions ; the Imperfect, of *continued* and *repeated* ones.] 2. What English tense does the *aor.* most nearly answer to? [Our *perfect indefinite* (the perf. formed by *inflexion*).] 3. Is the *aor.* ever used for the *perf.?* [Yes*, when the connexion of the past with the present is obvious from the context.] 4. Where is a governed *gen.* often placed? [Between an article and its noun.] 5. How do you construe οἱ πράττοντες? [*Those who do.*] 6. To what is the *artic.* with a *participle* equivalent? [To a personal or demonstrative pronoun with a relative sentence.]

§ 2.—7. Do proper names ever take the *art.?* [Yes.] 8. When? [When they are the names of persons *well known.*] 9. When is a proper name generally *without* the *art.?* [When it is followed by a *description* which has the article.] 10. Is there an indef. art. in Greek? [No.] 11. By what pron. may 'a' sometimes be translated? [By τίς.] 12. When? [When we might substitute '*a certain*' for '*a.*'] 13. Which generally *has* the art., the *subject* or the *predicate* (i. e. the *nom.* before or the nom. *after* the verb)? [The *subject.*]

§ 3.—14. YOUR SLAVE. [ὁ σὸς δοῦλος.] 15. Is the *art.* ever equivalent to a possessive pron.? [Yes, when it is quite obvious *whose* the thing in question is.] 16. When must the pronouns be used? [Whenever there is any opposition (as, when *mine* is opposed to *yours* or any other person's)]. 17. When an *adj. without the article* stands *before* the art. of the substantive, *from what* does it distinguish that substantive? [*From itself* under other circumstances.] 18. MY FRIEND AND MY FATHER'S. [ὁ ἐμὸς πατὴρ, καὶ ὁ τοῦ φίλου.]

§ 4.—19. THE SON OF PHILIP. [ὁ Φιλίππου: υἱός, *son*, understood.] 20. INTO PHILIP'S COUNTRY. [εἰς τὴν Φιλίππου: χώραν, *country*, understood.] 21. How does it happen that the article often stands alone? [In consequence of the omission of a *noun* or *participle.*]

§ 5.—22. What is often equivalent to an adjective? [An adverb with the article.] 23. THE MEN OF OLD. [οἱ πάλαι, the *long ago* men.]

---

* And even for the pluperfect.

§ 6.—24. How did the Greeks express ' she has *a* very beautiful head ?' [She
has *the* head very beautiful.] 25. Distinguish between τὸ καλόν and τὰ
καλά. [τὸ καλόν, is: ' *the beautiful,*' ' *the honorable,*' in the *abstract ;
beauty.* τὰ καλά, are : *beautiful* (or *honorable*) *things ; whatever things
are beautiful ; what is beautiful ;* or simply, *beautiful things.*] 26. How
is the first *pers. pl.* of the *subj.* often used ? [In exhortations.] 27. What
is ' *not* ' in an exhortation of this kind ? [μή.] 28. How may the *infin.*
become (virtually) a declinable substantive ? [By being used with the
article.] 29. Do *abstract nouns* and *names* of *materials* generally take the
art. ? [Yes.] 30. When does a noun (whether *sing.* or *plur.*) always
take the *art. ?* [When a *whole class,* or *any* individual of that class, is
meant.]

§ 7.—31. ὁ μέν—ὁ δέ : οἱ μέν—οἱ δέ. [(*this—that ; the one—the other*) (*these
—those ; some—others.*)] 32. How does ὁ δέ stand *once* in a narrative ?
[For *but* or *and he* or *it :* the article being here *a pronoun.*] 33. How
καὶ ὅς ? [For ' *and he :*' but only when the reference is to a *person.*]
34. When is αὐτός *self ?* [αὐτός is ' *self,*' when it stands in the *nom.
without a substantive,* or in *any case with one.*] 35. When is it *him, her,
it,* &c. ? [αὐτός is *him, her, it,* &c. in an oblique case without a substantive.] 36. When is αὐτός *same ?* [ὁ αὐτός is ' *the same.*'] 37.
Does αὐτός standing alone in an oblique case, ever mean *self ?* [Yes,
when it is *the first word* of the sentence.]

§ 8.—38. Does a noun with οὗτος, ὅδε, ἐκεῖνος, take the *art.* or not ? [Yes.]
39. Where does the *pron.* stand ? [Either *before* the article, or *after* the
noun.] 40. What does πᾶς *in the sing.* mean without the *art. ?*—[' *each,*'
' *every.*'] what with the *art. ?* [' *the whole ;*' ' *all* ']

§ 9.—41. In the reflexive pronouns (ἐμαυτοῦ, &c.) is the αὐτός emphatic ?
[No.] 42. How must *thyself* (in *acc.*) be translated when it is emphatic ? [αὐτός must precede the pronoun, αὐτὸν σέ, &c.] 43. How
do you translate ' *own* ' when it is emphatic ? [By the genitive of the
reflexive pronouns ἐμαυτοῦ, σεαυτοῦ, ἑαυτοῦ.]—how *his, theirs,*ʼ &c. ?
[By the gen. of αὐτός.] 44. Does ἑαυτοῦ ever stand in a dependent
sentence for the *nom.* of the principal one ? [Yes.] 45. What pronouns
are often used instead of a case of ἑαυτοῦ, to express, in a dependent
clause, the subject of the principal sentence ? [The simple αὐτόν, or
ἕ (οὗ, οἷ,—σφεῖς, σφᾶς, &c.] 46. Is οὗ ever *simply reflexive* in Attic
prose ? [No *.] 47. To what Attic prose-writer are the forms, οὗ, ἕ
confined ? [To Plato.]

---

* That is, οὗ, ἕ, &c. is not used by prose-writers in a principal sentence, to
express the subject of such sentence : its place is in a dependent or accessory clause,
to express the subject of the principal clause.

§ 10.—48. How is the *neut. plur.* of an adjective, standing without a noun, generally translated into English? [By the singular.] 49. How is the *neut. art.* with a *gen. case*, used? [To denote any thing that *relates to*, or *proceeds from*, the thing in question.] 50. How are *neut.* adjectives often used? [*Adverbially.*] 51. When is the *neut. singular* generally used *adverbially?* [When the adj. is of the *comparative* degree.] 52. When the *neut. plur.?* [When the adjective is of the superlative degree.] 53. Does a predicative adjective ever *not agree* in gender with the substantive it refers to? [Yes; when the assertion is made of a class or general notion; not of a particular thing.] 54. In what gender do πολύς (πλέων, πλεῖστος) and ἥμισυς stand, when followed by a *gen.?* [In the gender of the *gen.* that follows them.]

§ 11.—55. In what number does the verb generally stand, when the nom. is a *neut. plur.?* [In the *singular.*] 56. What exception is there? [When *persons* or *living creatures* are spoken of.] 57. Mention some predicates with which the *copula* is very often omitted?

(ἄξιος and χαλεπόν, θέμις, ὥρα, φροῦδος, ἀνάγκη,

ῥᾴδιον, and δυνατός (with its opposite word), and ἑτοῖμος.)

§ 12.—58. Do the moods of the *aor.* refer to *past time?* [No.] 59. How do the moods of the *aor.* differ from the moods of the *present?* [The moods of the aorist express *momentary* actions; those of the present, *continued* ones.] 60. Does the *part.* of the *aor.* refer to *past* time? [Yes.] 61. Are the moods of the *aor.* construed by the *pres.* in English? [Yes.] 62. When *μή forbids*, what moods does it take? [μή, when it *forbids*, takes the imperative of the present, the subjunctive of the aorist.] 63. What is the difference between μή with *imperat. pres.* and μή with the *subj. aor.?* [With the *subj. aor.* a *definite single act* is forbidden; with *imper. pres.* a *course of action.* The *imperat.*, therefore, often forbids a man to do *what he has already begun.*] 64. Of what tense is the *optative* the regular attendant? [*The* optative *is the regular attendant of the historical tenses* *.] 65. What mood is the *subj.* after a *pres.* or *fut.* turned into, when instead of the *pres.* or *fut.* an *historical* tense is used? [The *optative.*] 66. When do the particles and pronouns, which go with the *indicative* in *direct* narration, take the *optative?* [The particles and pronouns, which go with the indicative *in direct*, take the optative *in oblique narration* †.]

§ 13.—67. How is an assertion modified by the use of ἄν, or in *Epic* poetry

---

* *Or :* 'Historicum sequitur tempus modus optativus.'

† This is the *general* rule : but the indicative is frequently used in oblique narration.

κέ, κέν ? [ἄν gives an expression of *contingency* and *mere possibility* to the assertion.] 68. What is the principal use of ἄν ? [The *principal* use of ἄν is in the *conclusion* of a hypothetical sentence.] 69. When ἄν stands in a sentence which is not *hypothetical,* to what does it often refer ? [To an *implied condition.*] 70. What particles are formed by the addition of ἄν to εἰ, ὅτε, ἐπειδή ? [ἐάν, ἤν, ἄν,—ὅταν, ἐπειδάν.] 71. How is ἄν = εἰ ἄν distinguished from the simple ἄν ? [ἄν = ἐάν, εἰ ἄν, *regularly* begins the sentence.] 72. What are the *two* meanings of εἰ ? [εἰ is '*if :*' but like our '*if,*' it is often used for '*whether.*']

HYPOTHETICAL PROPOSITIONS.

73. (1) How is *possibility* without any expression of *uncertainty,* expressed ? [εἰ with *indic.* in both clauses *.]

74. (2) How is *uncertainty* with the prospect of *decision* expressed ? [By ἐάν with *subjunctive* in the conditional, and the *indic.* (generally the *future*) in the consequent clause *.]

75. (3) How is *uncertainty* expressed, when there is no such accessory notion (as the prospect of *decision*) ? [By εἰ with the *optative* in the conditional clause, and ἄν with the optative in the consequent clause.]

76. (4) How is *impossibility,* or belief that the thing *is not so,* expressed ? [εἰ with *imperfect* or *aorist indic.* in the conditional clause ; ἄν with *imperf.* or *aorist indic.* in the consequent clause.] 77. When is the *imperfect* used in this form of proposition ? [For *present* time, or when the time is quite *indefinite.*] 78. Can the *condition* refer to *past* time, the *consequence* to *present* ? [Yes.] 79. Which clause has ἄν, the *conditional* or the *consequent* clause ? [The consequent clause.]

§ 14.—80. To what is the *optat.* with ἄν equivalent ? [The optative with ἄν is equivalent to our *may, might, would, should,* &c.] 81. By what may the *optat.* with ἄν often be translated ? [The optative with ἄν is often translated by the *future.*] 82. What force does ἄν give to the *infin.* and *participle* ? [The same force that it gives to the *optative.*] 83. To what then is an infinitive with ἄν nearly equivalent ? [To an *infinitive future.*] 84. After what verbs is the future frequently so expressed ? [After verbs of *hoping, thinking, trusting, praying, knowing, confessing,* &c., when a *condition* is *expressed* or *implied.*]

§ 15.—85. What mood do the compounds of ἄν †, and *relatives* with ἄν *regularly* take ? [The *subjunctive.*] 86. What change takes place, if *any,* when

---

* The consequent clause may have the *Imperative.*

† That is, ἐάν, ὅταν, ἐπειδάν, &c.

these compounds or relatives with ἄν come into connexion with *past* time, or stand in *oblique* narration? [They either remain unchanged, or the simple words—εἰ, ὅτε, ἐπειδή: ὅς, ὅστις, ὅσος, &c.—take their place with the *optative*.] 87. To what Latin tense does the *aor. subjunct.* answer, when it stands with the *compounds of ἄν*, or with *relatives* and ἄν? [To the Latin *future perfect, futurum exactum.*]

§ 16.—88. How is what *often happened*, in *past* time, expressed *? [By the *optative.*] 89. What mood and particles would be used to express this sort of *indefinite frequency* for *pres.* or *fut.* time? [The relatives with ἄν and compounds of ἄν.] 90. What force does ἄν thus give to ὅς and other relatives? [The force of our —*ever*, —*soever.*]

§ 17.—91. What mood is used in *doubting* questions? [The subjunctive.] 92. After what verbs is it sometimes thus used? [After βούλει; θέλεις; οὐκ ἔχω or οἶδα, ἀπορῶ, ἐρωτῶ, ζητῶ.]

§ 18.—93. When conditional propositions depend on another verb, in what mood will the consequent clause stand? [In the *infinitive.*] 94. What will stand in a *dependent* consequent clause for ποιήσω? [ποιήσειν.]—for ποιοῖμ' ἄν, ἐποίουν ἄν? [ποιεῖν ἄν.]—for ποιήσαιμ' ἄν, ἐποίησα ἄν? [ποιῆσαι ἄν.]—for πεποιήκοιμ' ἄν, ἐπεποιήκειν ἄν? [πεποιη-κέναι ἄν.]

§ 19.—95. Does οὐ or μή deny independently and directly? [οὐ.] 96. When should *not* be translated by μή? [Μή is used in *prohibitions;* with *conditional* particles; and particles expressing *intention* or *purpose.*] 97. When do ὅτε, ὁπότε, take μή? [When ' *when* ' implies a condition.] 98. Is οὐ or μή used after ὅτι, ὡς, ἐπεί, ἐπειδή? [οὐ.] 99. Is οὐ or μή used (*generally*) to express the opinions of *another* person in oblique narration? [οὐ.] 100. How should you determine whether οὐδείς, οὐδέ, &c. are to be used, or μηδείς, μηδέ? [Wherever ' *not* ' would be translated by μή, we must use not οὐδείς, οὐδέ, &c., but μηδείς, μηδέ, &c.] 101. How must the *positive* adverbs and pronouns generally be translated into Greek in *negative* propositions? [By the corresponding *negative* forms †.]

§ 20.—102. Are the verbals in τέος *act.* or *pass.?* [*Passive.*] 103. What case of the *agent* do they govern? [The *dative.*] 104. What case of the

---

* Hermann properly observes, that the *optat.* does not itself *express* the repetition of the *act*, but only carries with it the notion of *indefiniteness*, the repetition being marked by the *other verb*, e. g. either a *frequentative* verb, or the *imperf.* or *pluperf.* tense (which both express *duration*), or by an aorist with πολλάκις, &c.

† Thus for *either—or; anywhere, at any time, any thing*, we must use *neither—nor; nowhere; never; nothing,* &c. Rule 111, as a general assertion, is absurd.

L

object? [The same case as the verbs from which they come.] 105. To
what are these verbals in τέος equivalent, when they stand in the *neut.*
with the agent, in the *dat.*, omitted? [To the participle in *dus* used in
the same way.] 106. When may they be used in *agreement* with the
object? [When formed from transitive verbs.] 107. Express "WE
SHOULD CULTIVATE VIRTUE," in two ways, with ἀσκητέος and ἀρετή.
[ἀσκητέον ἐστί σοι τὴν ἀρετήν, or ἀσκητέα ἐστί σοι ἡ ἀρετή.] 108. What
peculiarities are there in Attic Greek with respect to the use of these
verbals? [The *neut. plur.* is used as well as the *neut. sing.* The *agent*
is sometimes put in the accus. as well as the object.] 109. Construe
πειστέον ἐστὶν αὐτῷ, and πειστέον ἐστὶν αὐτόν. [πειστέον ἐστὶν
αὐτόν, *we must persuade him.* πειστέον ἐστὶν αὐτῷ, *we must obey him.*]

§ 21.—110. What verbs govern twò accusatives? [Verbs of *taking away from,*
teaching, concealing, asking, putting on or *off,* take two accusatives.]

§ 22.—111. What case does the *acc. after* the *active* verb become, when the *act.*
verb is turned into the *passive?* [The *nom.*] 112. When the *act.* verb
governs two *accusatives,* may either of them (and if so, which?) remain
after the *pass.* verb? [The acc. of the *person* becomes the *nom.;* that of the
thing continues to be the object of the passive verb, as in Latin.] 113.
May the *dat.* of the *act.* become the *nom.* of the *passive?* [Yes; sometimes.] 114. Will the *acc.* after the *act.* then remain as the *acc.* after the
passive? [Yes.] 115. Construe (ἐγὼ) πεπίστευμαι τοῦτο. [I am
entrusted *with* this: or, I have had this entrusted to me.] 116. Do
intrans. verbs ever take an *acc.?* and, if so, when? [Intransitive verbs
take an *acc.* of a noun of *kindred meaning;* and sometimes of one that
restricts the general notion of the verb to a particular instance.]

§ 23.—117. Does the *acc.* ever follow an *adj.?* [Yes.] 118. What *prepos.*
might be *supposed* omitted? [κατά, *as to.*] 119. What *acc.* is sometimes
found with verbs that do not properly govern the *acc.?* [The accus. of
a *neut. pronoun.*] 120. How is the *duration of time* expressed? [By the
accusative.] 121. How is the *distance* of one place from another expressed? [By the accusative.]

§ 24—122. What case do *partitives,* &c. govern? [Partitives, numerals, superlatives, &c. govern the genitive.] 123. What case do adverbs of *time*
and *place* govern? [The genitive.] 124. What case expresses the
material out of which a thing is made, and such other *properties, circumstances,* &c. as *we* should *express* by '*of*'? [The genitive.] 125. Can
'*once a day*' be translated literally? [No: it must be, '*once the* day.']
126. How does the *gen.* stand after *possessive* pronouns? [In a kind of
apposition to the personal pronoun implied.] 127. How does the *gen.*
stand *alone,* or after *interjections?* [The gen. is used alone, or after
interjections, as an *exclamation.*]

§ 25.—128. What case do verbal adjectives, in ικος, &c., with a *trans.* meaning
govern? [The genitive.] 129. What case do verbs relating to *plenty,
want, value,* &c., govern? [The genitive.] 130. What case do verbs
relating to the *senses* govern? [The genitive.] 131. What exception
is there? [Verbs that denote *sight,* which take the acc.] 132. By what
prepos., understood, might the *gen.* sometimes be supposed governed?
[By ἕνεκα, *on account of.*] 133. After what verbs does the gen. frequently stand in this way? [After words compounded with a *privative.*]
§ 26.—134. Mention two large classes of verbs that govern the gen. [Most
verbs that express such notions as *freeing from, keeping off from, ceasing
from, deviating* or *departing from,* &c. govern the *gen.* Most verbs that
express *remembering* or *forgetting ; caring for* or *despising ; sparing ;
aiming at* or *desiring ; ruling over* or *excelling ; accusing of* or *condemning,*
&c. govern the *genitive ;* but not without many exceptions.]
§ 27.—135. What case does καταγιγνώσκω (*condemn*) take of the *charge* or
punishment? and what case of the *person?* [καταγιγνώσκω has *accus.*
of the *charge* or *punishment ; gen.* of *person.*] 136. May we say, τοῦτο
κατηγορεῖται αὐτοῦ, this is laid to his charge? [Yes.]
§ 28.—137. In what case does the *price* or *value* stand? [The *price* or *value*
is put in the *genitive.*] 138. In what case is the thing *for which* we
exchange another, put? [The thing *for which* we exchange another is
put in the *genitive.*] 139. What case of a noun of *time* answers to *when?*
and what to *since* or *within* what time? [The gen.] 140. In what case
is the part *by which* a person is *led, got hold of,* &c., put? [The *gen.*
expresses the part *by which* a person *leads, takes,* or *gets hold of* any
thing.]
§ 29.—141. In what case is the thing *with which another is compared,* put when
ἤ, *than,* is omitted? [In the genitive.] 142. How is '*greater than
ever*' expressed? [By using αὐτός before the *gen.* of the reflexive
pronoun.] 143. How is '*too great*' expressed? [*Too great,* &c. is expressed by the *comparative* with ἤ κατά before a *substantive ;* ἤ ὥστε
before a *verb* in the *infinitive.*] 144. STILL GREATER: MUCH GREATER?
[ἔτι μείζων : πολλῷ μείζων.]
§ 30.—145. How are two comparatives, joined together by ἤ, to be translated?
[By *more than,* or *rather than,* with the *positive.*] 146. By what
words are superlatives strengthened? [By ὡς, ὅτι, ὅπως, ἤ, &c.]
147. What force have εἴ τις καὶ ἄλλος, si quis alius, and εἷς ἀνήρ, unus
omnium maxime? [The force of superlatives.] 148. What case do
περιττός, and adjectives in -πλάσιος, govern? [The genitive]
§ 31.—149. What does the *dat.* express? [The person *to* or *for* whom a thing
is done.] 150. What words does it follow? [Words that express *union*
or *coming together,* and those that express *likeness* or *identity.*] 151. In

what case is the *instrument*, &c. put? [The *instrument*, the *manner*, and the *cause*, are put in the *dative*.] 152. In what case is the *definite time-when* put? [In the dative.] 153. Does the *dat.* ever express the *agent?* [Yes.] 154. After what words is this most common? [After the *perfect pass.* and *verbals* in τέος, τός.] 155. What case do verbs of *reproaching* take besides a *dat.* of the *person?* [Verbs of *reproaching*, &c. take *acc.* of the *thing*, as well as dat. of person, especially when it is a *neut. pronoun.*]

§ 32.—156. What does the *middle* voice denote? [That the agent does the action *upon himself;* or *for his own advantage;* or that he *gets* it *done* for his own advantage.] 157. What are the tenses that have the *middle* meaning when the verb has it at all? [*Pres., imperf., perf.,* and *pluperf.* of the *passive form;* and the futures and aorists mid.] 158. Has the *aor.* 1. of the *pass.* form ever a *mid.* meaning? [Yes.]

§ 33.—159. What verbs of the middle form must be considered simply as deponents? [Middle forms, of which there is *no active.*] 160. Mention some *aor.* 1. *pass.* with *mid.* meaning. [κατεκλίθην (ἴ). ἀπηλλάγην, ἐπεραιώθην, ἐφοβήθην, ἐκοιμήθην, ἠσκήθην.] 161. Mention some fut. 1. *mid.* with *pass.* meaning. [ὠφελήσομαι, ὁμολογήσομαι, φυλάξομαι, θρέψομαι.] 162. How is ' *by*,' to express the *agent* after the *pass. verb*, translated? [By ὑπό with *gen.;* also by παρά and πρός with *gen.*]

§ 34.—163. What signification does the *perf.* 2. (commonly called *perf. mid.*) prefer? [The *intrans.* signif.] 164. Has it ever the *pure reflexive* meaning of the middle? [No.]

§ 35.—165. What does the *fut.* 3. express? [A *future* action *continuing* in its *effects.*] 166. What notions does it express *besides* that of a *future action continuing in its effects?* [The *speedy completion* of an action, or the *certainty of its completion.*] 167. What verbs have the *fut.* 3. for their regular future? [Those perfects that are equivalent to a *present* with a new meaning: *e. g.* μέμνημαι, κέκτημαι.] 168. What answers to the *fut.* 3. in the *active* voice? [ἔσομαι with *perf. participle.*] 169. What is *generally* preferred to the *opt.* and *subj.* of the *perf.?* [The *perf. part.* with εἴην or ὦ.] 170. In what verbs is the *imperat. perf.* principally used? [In those verbs whose perfects have the meaning of a present: μέμνησο, &c.] 171. What does the 3 *pers. imperat.* of the *perf. pass.* express? [It is a strong expression for *let it be done*, &c.] 172. How is a *wish* expressed in Greek? [εἴθε with the optative—the optative alone—or ὤφελον †, ες, ε, alone, or with εἴθε, εἰ γάρ or ὡς, and followed by the infinitive.] 173. What *mood* and *tense* are used with

† *Debuit.*

εἴθε, if the wish *has not been*, and now *cannot be, realized?* [The *indic.* of *aorist* or *imperf.*, according as the time to which the wish refers is *past* or *present.*]

§ 36.—174. Mention a use of the infinitive that the Greek and English *have*, but the Latin has *not*. [It is used to express the *purpose.*] 175. What does the particle ὥστε express? [A *consequence.*] 176. How is *so—as to* expressed? [*So—as to;* ὥστε with *infinitive.*] 177. How is *so—that* expressed? [*So—that;* ὥστε with *infinitive* or *indicative.*]

§ 37.—178. What does the infin. with the *article* in *gen.* express? [The infinitive with the article in the *gen.* sometimes denotes a *motive* or *purpose.*] 179. When the *infin.* has a *subject* of its own, in what case does it *regularly* stand? [In the accusative.] 180. What *prepos.* with the *infin.* is equivalent to a sentence introduced by *because?* [διά.] 181. When is the subject of the infinitive generally not expressed? [When the subject of the infinitive belongs to, and is expressed with, the former verb.] 182. When the subject of the *infin.* is omitted, because expressed with the former verb, in what case is the noun *after* the *infin.* generally put? [In the same case that the subject of the infinitive stands in *in the other clause.*] 183. What is this construction called? [*Attraction.*]

§ 38.—184. May *attraction* take place when the infin. is introduced by the *art.* or ὥστε? [Yes.]

§ 39.—185. What kind of sentences may be translated into Greek by a *participle?* [Relative sentences, and sentences introduced by *when, after, if, since, because, although,* &c.] 186. How may the English *participial substantive*, under the government of a preposition, often be translated? [By a participle in agreement.] 187. How may *the first* of two verbs connected by *and*, often be translated into *Greek?* [By a participle.]

§ 40.—188. What participle often expresses a *purpose?* [The participle of the *future* often expresses a *purpose.*] 189. Mention some verbs that take the participle where *we* should use the *infin.*, a *participial substantive*, or '*that.*' [Many verbs that signify *emotions, perception by the senses, knowledge, recollection, cessation* or *continuance*, &c., take the participle, where *we* should use the *infinitive* mood, the *participial substantive*, or '*that.*']

§ 41.—190. By what are φθάνω, *come*, or *get before*, and λανθάνω, *am concealed*, generally construed? [By adverbs.] 191. Mention the adverbs and phrases by which λανθάνω may be construed. [*Without knowing it; unconsciously, unknown to myself: without being observed; secretly; without being seen* or *discovered.*] 192. How may λαθών be construed? [By *secretly, without being observed, seen,* &c.] 193. How φθάσας or ἀνύσας? [*Quickly; at once, immediately.*] 194. When φθάνω and λανθάνω are translated by adverbs, how must the participles with which they are connected, be translated? [By verbs.]

(*Genitive Absolute, &c.*)

§ 42.—195. Which case is put *absolutely* in Greek? [The genitive.] 196. What
does the participle, put *absolutely*, express? [The *time*, or generally any
such relation to the principal sentence, as *we* should express by *when,
after, since, as, because, though, if*, &c.] 197. In what *case* do the participles of impersonal verbs stand *absolutely*? [In the *nominative* ;
of course without a noun, and in the neuter gender.] 198. When the
time relates to a *person*, what construction is used instead of the *gen.*
absolute? [ἐπί is then generally expressed.] 199. How is a *motive*,
which is attributed to *another* person, generally expressed? [By the
particle ὡς with the *gen.* or *acc.* absolute.]

(*The Relative.*)

§ 43.—200. What does the relative often introduce? [A *cause, ground, motive,*
or *design* of what is stated.] 201. What use of the relative is less common
in Greek than Latin? [That of merely *connecting* a sentence with the
one before it.] 202. In which clause is the *antecedent* often expressed?
[In the relative clause.] 203. Where does the relat. clause often stand,
when this is the case? [Before the principal clause.] 204. With what
does the relative often agree in case? [With the antecedent in the
principal clause.] 205. What is this called? [*Attraction of the Relative.*]
206. When the relative is *attracted*, where is the antecedent often placed?
[In the relative clause, but in the case in which it would stand in the
principal clause.]

§ 44.—207. In such a sentence as "the fear, *which* we call *bashfulness*," should
which agree with *fear* or with *bashfulness*? [With *bashfulness*.]
208. Explain ἔστιν οἵ. [It is equivalent to ἔνιοι, some, and may be
declined throughout.] 209. What is the Greek for *sometimes?* [ἔστιν
ὅτε.]—*somewhere?* [ἔστιν ὅπου.] 210. What is the English of ἐφ' ᾧ
or ἐφ' ᾧτε? [*On* condition that.]—of ἀνθ' ὧν? [*Because, for.*]—of εἴ
τις?—[*Whosoever* ; εἴ τι, whatsoever.] 211. By what parts of the verb
is ἐφ' ᾧ or ᾧτε followed? [By the *future indic.* or the *infin.*]

---

§ 45.—212. Give the English of τοῦ οἵου σοῦ ἀνδρός. [*Of such a man as
you.*] 213. How may this construction be explained? [ἀνδρὸς τοιούτου, οἷος σὺ εἶ.] 214. What words does ὅσος follow, when it has the
meaning of *very?* [Such words as θαυμαστός, πλεῖστος, ἄφθονος, &c.]
§ 46.—215. What is the construction of οὐδεὶς ὅστις οὐ? [The declinable
words are put under the immediate government of the verb.]

§ 47.—216. What tenses follow μέλλω in the *infin.?* [The *future, present,* or *aorist.*] 217. Which infin. is the *most common* after μέλλω, and which the least? [The *future infin.* is the *most,* the aorist the *least* common.]

§ 48.—218. What *mood* or *tense* follows ὅπως, when it relates to the future? [The *subj.* or the *future indic.*] 219. May it retain them in connexion with past time? [Yes.] 220. Is the verb on which ὅπως, &c. depends, ever omitted? [Yes : the construction is equivalent to an *energetic imperative :*—ὅρα or ὁρᾶτε may be supplied.] 221. With what *mood* or *tense* is οὐ μή used? [With the *fut. indic.* or *aor. subj.*] 222. In what sense? [As an emphatic *prohibition* or *denial.*] 223. According to Dawes, what *aorists* were *not* used in the *subj.* with ὅπως and οὐ μή? [The subjunctive of the aor. 1. act. and *mid.*] 224. Is this rule correct? [No.] 225. What is Buttmann's opinion? [That the *subj.* of the *aor. 2.* was employed with a *kind of predilection,* and that, when the verb had no such tense, the *fut. indic.* was used in preference to the *subj.* of the *aor. 1.*]

§ 49.—226. How is μή used after expressions of *fear,* &c.? [With the *subjunctive* or *indic.*] 227. When is the *indic.* with μή used in expressions of *fear ?* [When the speaker wishes to intimate his conviction that the *thing feared,* &c. *has* or *will really* come to pass.] 228. How does it happen that μὴ οὐ sometimes stands with a verb in the subjunctive, but *without* a preceding verb? [The notion of *fear* is often omitted before μὴ οὐ, the verb being then generally in the *subj.*] 229. After what kind of expressions is μὴ οὐ used with the infin.? [After many negative expressions *.] 230. Is it ever used with the participle or infin.? and, if so, when? [μὴ οὐ is sometimes used with the participle and with ὥστε and *infin.*, after negative expressions.]

§ 50.—231. When is μή used with *relative* sentences, *participles, adjectives,* &c.? [Whenever the negative does not *directly* and *simply* deny an assertion with respect to some *particular mentioned* person or thing.] 232. Does the *infin.* generally take μή or οὐ? [μή.] 233. When does it take οὐ? [When opinions or assertions of *another* person are stated *in sermone obliquo.*] 234. When should μή follow ὥστε? and when οὐ? [With ὥστε, the infinitive takes μή, the indicative οὐ.]

§ 51.—235. What case do some adverbs govern? [The same case as the adjectives from which they are derived.] 236. How is ὡς sometimes used? [As a preposition = πρός.] 237. When only can ὡς be used as a *prepos.?* [It is only joined to *persons.*] 238. What mood do ἄχρι, μέχρι, ἕως, ἔστε take? [The *subj.* or *opt.* when there is any *uncertainty ;*

---

* See 293. (1,) (2,) (3.)

the *indic.* when not.] 239. Does πρὶν ἂν ἔλθω relate to the *past* or the *future ?* [To the future.] 240. How is '*before I came*' expressed? [πρὶν ἢ ἐλθεῖν ἐμέ : πρὶν ἐλθεῖν ἐμέ : or πρὶν ἦλθον ἐγώ.] 241. Is ἤ ever omitted before the infin. after πρίν? [Yes; in Attic Greek nearly always.]

§ 52.—242. In what kind of questions is ἆρα generally used? [In questions that imply something of *uncertainty, doubt,* or *surprise.*] 243. What interrog. particles expect the answer '*Yes ?*' [The answer '*Yes*' is expected by,—ἆρ' οὐ ; ἢ γάρ ; οὐ ; οὔκουν ; ἄλλο τι ἤ ;] 244. What expect the answer '*No*'? [The answer '*No*' is expected by,—ἆρα μή ; ἢ που; *num forte ?* μή or μῶν ;] 245. What particles give an *ironical* force to οὐ? [δή, δή που.] 246. Does οὐ expect '*yes*' or '*no*' for answer? [οὐ expects *yes;* μή, *no.*] 247. In what kind of questions are εἶτα, ἔπειτα used? [Such as express *astonishment* and *displeasure.*] 248. What words are used as a simple *interrog.* particle? [ἄλλο τι ἤ.] 249. Construe τί παθών ;—τί μαθών ; [τί παθών ; *what possesses you to . . .* &c. ?—τί μαθών ; *what induces you to . . .* &c.?

§ 53.—250. What are the proper forms of pronouns and adverbs for indirect questions ? [Those which are formed from the direct interrogatives by the prefixed *relative* syllable ὁ—.] 251. Are the simple *interrogatives* ever used in indirect questions? [Yes.] 252. Are the *relatives* ever so used? [Yes ; but very seldom.] 253. When the person addressed repeats the question, what forms does he use? [The forms beginning with ὁ—.] 254. When a pron. or noun is the *acc.* after one verb, and the *nom.* before the next, which case is generally omitted? [The *nominative.*]

§ 54.—255. By what particles are *direct* double questions asked? [By πότερον, or πότερα,—ἤ, less commonly by ἆρα—ἤ.] 256. By what particles are *indirect* double questions asked? [εἴτε—εἴτε, εἰ—ἤ, πότερον—ἤ.]

§ 55.—257. After what verbs is εἰ used for ὅτι, *that?* [After θαυμάζω, and some other verbs expressive of *feelings.*] 258. After what verbs has εἰ the force of *whether?* [After verbs of *seeing, knowing, considering, asking, saying, trying,* &c.] 259. When is ἐάν used in this way? [When the question relates to an *expected case that remains to be proved.*]

§ 56.—260. How can an interrogative sentence be *condensed* in Greek? [By attaching the interrogative to a *participle,* or using it in an *oblique* case.] 261. What clause may thus be got rid of? [A relative clause attached to an interrogative one.]

§ 57.—262. What is ἢ μήν ? [A solemn form of asseveration.] 263. When is the prepos. σύν omitted? [Before αὐτῷ, αὐτῇ, &c. which then = *together with, with.*] 264. How is ἀμφότερον used? [ἀμφότερον is

used *adverbially*, or *elliptically*, by the poets, for *both; as well—as*, &c.]
—265. How ἀμφότερα? [In reference to *two words*, without being made
to conform to them in case.]—266. What force has καί, when it refers to
ἄλλος? [The force of *especially, in particular.*] 267. Explain the use
of the *part. fut.* with ἔρχεσθαι, &c. [ἔρχεσθαι, ἰέναι, with *part. fut.*,
is, *to be going to*, or *on the point of.*] 268. How is ἔχω sometimes used
with a *past partic.*? [As an emphatic circumlocution.] 269. How is it
used with ληρεῖν, &c.? [ἔχω with the *second pers.* of ληρεῖν, παίζειν,
φλυαρεῖν, &c. is used to make a good-humoured observation.] 270. How
is φέρων used in some expressions? [φέρων appears redundant in some
expressions, but denotes a *vehemence of purpose, not altogether free from
blame.*]

§ 58.—271. To what is δίκαιός εἰμι equivalent? [Τὸ δίκαιόν ἐστιν, ἐμὲ &c.]
—272. How is ὅσον used? [ὅσον is used elliptically with the *infin.*]
273. What words are followed by ἤ? [Words that *imply* a comparison :
e. g. φθάνειν, διαφέρειν, ἐναντίος, διπλάσιος, ἴδιος, ὕπερθεν, πρίν.]
274. After what phrases is a tense of ποιεῖν omitted? [After οὐδὲν
ἄλλο ἤ—, ἄλλο τι ἤ— ; τί ἄλλο ἤ— ; &c.] 275. By what are a person's *quoted* words introduced? [By ὅτι.] 276. How is the *aor.* used
with τί οὐ? [For the *present.*]

INDEX I.

☞ Obs. Look under '*am*' for adjectives, phrases, &c. with *to be*.

F. M. = future middle.

(?) implies, that the pupil is to ask himself how the word is conjugated or declined.

A.

A, = *a certain*, τίς, 13.
About (of *time*), ὑπό (*acc.*), 326.
—- (after to *fear*, to *be at ease*, &c.), περί (*dat.*), 282.
—- (after *talk, fear, contend*), περί (*dat.*), sometimes ἀμφί (*dat.*), 282.
—- (after *to be employed*), περί, or ἀμφί, with *acc.*, 282.
Abrocomas, 229, q. Ἀβροκόμας, G. α.
Abstain from, ἀπέχομαι (*gen.*), 138.
———- : we must—, ἀφεκτέον ἐστι, with *gen.*
According to reason, κατὰ λόγον, 274.
Accuse, κατηγορεῖν † (properly, *speak against*) τινός, or τινός τι, 156.— ἐγκαλεῖν (properly, *cite* a person; *call* him *into* court) τινί and τινί τι, 183. Both are *judicial* words, but used with the same latitude as our '*accuse*.' Of the two, ἐγκαλεῖν should probably be preferred, if the charge relates to private matters. V.
Accustom, ἐθίζω, 52.
(Am accustomed, εἴθισμαι or εἴωθα, 52.)
Acquire, κτάομαι, 87.
Act, ποιέω, 60.
—- insolently towards, ὑβρίζειν εἰς τινα, 138.

Act strangely, θαυμαστὸν ποιεῖν, 259.
—- unjustly (= *injure*), ἀδικεῖν τινα and τι (also εἰς, πρός, περί τινα), 138.
Admire, θαυμάζω, F. M. generally, 8.
Adopt a resolution, βουλεύεσθαι, 190.
Adorn, κοσμέω, 206.
Advance, προχωρέω, 274.
Affair, πρᾶγμα, *n.* 8.
Affliction, πάθος, *n.* 150.
Afford, παρέχω, 214.
After, μετά (*acc.*), 293.
—- a long time, διὰ πολλοῦ χρόνου, 269.
—- some time, διαλιπὼν χρόνον, 235.
——— διὰ χρόνου, 269.
—- our former tears, ἐκ τῶν πρόσθεν δακρύων, 232.
—- the manner of a dog, κυνὸς δίκην, 250.
Again, αὖθις, 100.
Against (after to *march*), ἐπί, *acc.* 24.
εἰς, 259.
—- (= in violation of), παρά, 299.
—- (after *commit an injury*), εἰς or περί, with *acc.* 138.
—- πρός (*acc.*), 319.
—- (after verbs of *speaking*, &c.), κατά, *gen.* 274.
Age (a person's), ἡλικία, 144.
Agreeable, ἡδύς, 214.

† The constructions of κατηγορεῖν are very numerous : κατηγορῶ σοῦ τινός and τι; or σέ τινος and τι; or σοῦ (*and* σέ) περί τινος; and κατηγορῶ κατά σου.

156 INDEX I.

Agreeable : if it is—, εἰ σοι βουλομένῳ
ἐστί, 206.
Agricultural population, οἱ ἀμφὶ γῆν
ἔχοντες, 278.
Aid, ἐπικουρέω, dat., also acc. of the
thing, 239.
Aim at, στοχάζομαι, gen. 156.
Alas, φεῦ,—οἴμοι, 144.
Alexander, ᾿Αλέξανδρος, 24.
All, ὁ πᾶς, or πᾶς ὁ —. Pl. πάντες.
See note on 45. 46.
— but (as-much-as not), ὅσον οὐ, 125.
— day, ἀνὰ πᾶσαν τὴν ἡμέραν, 259.
Alliance. See Form.
Allow to taste, γεύω, 150.
——- to be done with impunity, περι-
ορᾷν (-ιδεῖν, -όψεσθαι), with inf. of
thing to be prevented ; the partic. of
a wrong to be revenged, 331. See
note º.
Almost, ὀλίγου δεῖν, or ὀλίγου only,
282.
Already, ἤδη, 65.
Also, καί, 92.
Although, καίπερ, 175.

(a.)

Am able, δύναμαι (possum), 87.—οἷός
τέ εἰμι † (queo), 280. See Can.
— (an) actual murderer, αὐτόχειρ εἰμί,
299.
— adapted for, οἷός εἰμι, 280.
— angry with, ὀργίζομαι, dat. 183.
δι᾿ ὀργῆς ἔχειν, 269*.
— ashamed, αἰσχύνομαι, 239.
— at a loss, ἀπορέω, 100. [See 98,
99.]
— at dinner, δειπνέω, 288.
— at enmity with, δι᾿ ἔχθρας γίγνεσθαί τινι, 269*.
— at leisure, σχολάζω, 112.
— at liberty. See 245, b.
— awake, ἐγρήγορα, 193.
— aware, μανθάνω (?), 239.

(b.)

Am banished, φεύγειν, 269*.
— broken, κατέᾱγα, 193.
— by nature, πέφῡκα, ἔφυν, 214.

(c.)

Am come, ἥκω, with meaning of perf.
206.
— commander, στρατηγέω, 52.

Am confident, πέποιθα, 193.
— congealed, πέπηγα, 193.
— conscious, σύνοιδα ἐμαυτῷ, 239.
— contemporary with, κατὰ τὸν αὐτὸν
χρόνον γενέσθαι, 183.
— contented with, ἀγαπάω, with acc.
or dat. 52.

(d.)

Am dishonoured by, ἀτιμάζομαι πρός
τινος, 319.
— distant from, ἀπέχω, 138.
— doing well, εὖ πράττω, 8.
———— ill, κακῶς πράττω, 8.

(e.)

Am evidently, &c. See 239.

(f.)

Am far from, πολλοῦ δέω, 282.
— fixed, πέπηγα, 193.
— fond of, ἀγαπάω, 52.
— fortunate, εὐτυχέω, 92.

(g.)

Am general, στρατηγέω, 52.
— glad, ἥδομαι, dat. 20.
— going (to), μέλλω (augm. ?), 282.
— gone, οἴχομαι(?), perf meaning, 206.
— grateful for, χάριν οἶδα (gen. of
thing, dat. of pers.), 222. [For οἶδα,
see 73.]

(h.)

Am here, πάρειμι, 52.

(i.)

Am I ... ? (in doubtful questions) 134,
note e.
— ill (of a disease), κάμνω (laboro) ;
καμοῦμαι, κέκμηκα, ἔκαμον, 183.
— in my right mind, σωφρονέω, 125.
— in a passion or rage, χαλεπαίνω,
dat. 183.
— in safety, ἐν τῷ ἀσφαλεῖ εἰμι, 299.
— in the habit of performing, πρακτικός (εἰμι), with gen. See 146.
— indignant, ἀγανακτέω, 337.
— informed of, αἰσθάνομαι(?), 190.

(l.)

Am likely, μέλλω (?), 282.
— lost, στεροῦμαι, 168, r.

† Or οἷόςτε (οἷόστ').

(m.)

Am mad, μαίνομαι (?), 125.
—- my own master, ἐμαυτοῦ εἰμι, 158*, i.

(n.)

Am named after, ὄνομα ἔχω ἐπί τινος, 288.
—- near, ὀλίγου δέω, or ὀλίγου only, 282.
—- next to, ἔχομαι, gen. 146, d. .
—- not a man to, 280, b.
——— afraid of, θαρρέω (acc.), 138.

(o.)

Am of opinion, νομίζω, 52.
—- service to, ὠφελέω (acc.), 82.
—- a character (to), εἰμὶ οἷος, 280, b.
—- off, οἴχομαι (?), perf. meaning, 206.
—- on my guard, φυλάττεσθαι, acc. 190.
—- on his side, εἰμὶ πρός (gen.), 319.
—- on an equal footing with, ὅμοιός εἰμι, 226, b.

(p.)

Am pained at, ἀλγέω, 20.
—- persuaded, πέποιθα, 193.
—- pleased with, ἥδομαι, dat. 20.
—- present, πάρειμι, 52.
—- produced. See 214.
—- prosperous, εὐτυχέω, 92.
—- punished, δίκην διδόναι, or δοῦναι: gen. of thing ; dat. of person by whom, 228.

(s.)

Am safe, ἐν τῷ ἀσφαλεῖ εἰμι.
—- slow to, &c., σχολῇ (by leisure), with a verb, 112.
—- suffering (from a disease). See ' am ill of.'
—- surprised at, θαυμάζω (F. M.), 8.

(t.)

Am thankful for, χάριν οἶδα, gen. of thing, 222. For οἶδα see 73. note 1.
—- the slave of, δουλεύω, dat. 359.
—- there, πάρειμι, 92.
—- to, μέλλω (?), 282.

(u.)

Am undone, ὄλωλα, ἀπόλωλα, 193.
—- unseen by, λανθάνω (?), acc. 154.

(v.)

Am vexed, ἄχθομαι (?) (dat. but ἐπί in construction explained in 17, c), 20.

(w.)

Am wholly wrapt in, πρὸς τούτῳ ὅλος εἰμί, 319.
—- wise (= prudent), σωφρονέω, 125.
—- with you, πάρειμι, 92.
—- within a little, ὀλίγου δέω, 282.
—- without fear of, θαρρέω, acc. 138.

Ambassador, πρέσβυς, 259.
Ambitious, φιλότιμος, 214.
Among the first, translated by ἀρξάμενος (having begun). See 100.
And that too, καὶ ταῦτα, 206.
—— yet, εἶτα, ἔπειτα, 316.
—— nevertheless, εἶτα, ἔπειτα, 316.
Ancestor, πρόγονος, 156.
Animal, ζῶον, 65.
Annoy, λυπέω, 41.
Answer, ἀποκρίνομαι (?), 278.
Apart, χωρίς, 309.
Apollo, Ἀπόλλων (?), 341.
Appear (with part.), φαίνομαι, 239.
Apt to do, or perform, πρακτικός (gen.), 150.
—— govern, ἀρχικός (gen.), 150.
Arbitration, δίαιτα, 132.
Are there any whom . . ? 262, d.
Arise, ἐγείρομαι (pass.), 193.
Arms, ὅπλα, 168*.
Army, στράτευμα, n. 24.
Arouse, ἐγείρω (perf. with Attic redupl.), 193
Arrange, τάσσω (later Attic τάττω), 96.
—κοσμέω, διακοσμέω (to arrange, with a view to a pleasing appearance of elegance, symmetry, apt arrangement, &c.), 206.
Arrive, ἀφικνέομαι (?), 144.
——— first, φθῆναι (?) ἀφικόμενος, 240, d.
———————, but only, &c., 353, b.
Art, τέχνη, 214.
As he was, 351.
— his custom was. See Custom.
— many as, ὅσοι, 175.
——————— possible, ὅσοι πλεῖστοι, 170, c.
— silently as possible, σιγῇ ὡς ἀνυστόν, 170, b.
— far as they are concerned, τὸ ἐπὶ τούτοις εἶναι, 206.
— far at least as this is concerned, τούτου γε ἕνεκα, 250.

As far as depends on this, τούτου γε
ἔνεκα, 250.
— much as any body. See 100.
— the saying is, τὸ λεγόμενον, 184, d.
— possible (after superlatives), ὡς, ὅτι,
172.
— he possibly could, 170, c.
— fast as they could, ὡς τάχους εἶχον,
278.
— soon as he was born, εὐθὺς γενόμενος, 309.
— long as, ἔστε, 306.
— to, ὥστε with inf., 212.
— (before partic.), ἅτε, ἅτε δή, 240, a.
Ask, ἠρόμην, aor. 2 : ἐρωτάω used for
the other tenses, 73.
—- for, αἰτέω (two accusatives), 87.
Assist in the defence of, βοηθέω, dat.
121.
Assistance.   See Fly or Run.
Associate with, ὁμῑλέω, dat. 183.
Assuredly (in protestations), ἦ μήν, 344.
————— (will not), οὐ μή, 284.
Astonished (to be), θαυμάζω (F. M.).
At, 319.
— all, ἀρχήν, or τὴν ἀρχήν, 92, 132.
—.   Not at all (οὐδέν τι).
— a little distance, δι' ὀλίγου, 269*.
— a great distance, διὰ πολλοῦ, 269*.
— any time, ποτέ.
— ease about, θαῤῥεῖν περί, 282.
— first, ἀρχόμενος. 235.
— home, ἔνδον, 125
— last, τὸ τελευταῖον, 31 ; τελευτῶν,
235.
— least, γέ, 73.
— once, ἤδη, 65 —How to translate it
by the partic. φθάσας, or by οὐκ ἂν
φθάνοις ; see 240, e. f.
— the beginning, ἀρχόμενος. 235.
— the suggestion of others, ἀπ' ἀνδρῶν
ἑτέρων, 243.
Athens, 'Αθῆναι, 15.
(O) Athenians, ὦ ἄνδρες 'Αθηναῖοι,
337.
Attach great importance to, πρὸ πολλοῦ
ποιεῖσθαι, 243.—περὶ πολλοῦ ποιεῖσθαι or ἡγεῖσθαι, 282.
Attempt, πειράομαι, 121.—(= dare)
τολμάω, 239.
Attend to, τὸν νοῦν προσέχειν, 331.
————— a master, εἰς διδασκάλου φοιτᾷν,
259.
Avoid = fly from, φεύγειν, 35.

B.

Bad, κακός, 20.
Banished (to be), φεύγειν, 269.
Banishment, φυγή, 156.
Barbarian, βάρβαρος, 132.
Bare, ψῑλός, 235.
Bathe, λούομαι. 188 (1).
Battle, μάχη, 73.
Base, αἰσχρός, 35.
Bear, φέρειν (?), 60.—ἀνέχομαι (= en-
dure) refers to our power of enduring
(labours, insults, &c.), 214.—τολμάω
(= sustinere), to bear to do what re-
quires courage, 239, y.
Beautiful, καλός, 20.
Beauty, κάλλος, n. 8.
Because (διὰ τό, &c.), 216, b. ἀνθ' ὧν,
268.
Become, γίγνομαι (?), 15.
Before †, πρίν or πρίν ἤ, 308.
————— (= in preference to), πρό (gen.),
243 : ἀντί, gen. 208, e.
Beget, γεννάω, 239.
Begin, ἄρχομαι, 100.
Beginning, ἀρχή. 132.
Behave ill to, κακῶς ποιεῖν, acc. 35.
Behold, θεάομαι, 87.
Belong to, gen. with εἶναι.
Belly, γαστήρ, f. (?), 235.
Benefit, ὠφελέω (acc.), 82.
Beseech, δέομαι, 150, (gen. 146, b.) δε-
ήσομαι, ἐδεήθην.
Besides, ἐπί (dat.),288. παρά(acc.),299.
Best,   } see Good, 35.
Better, }
Bethink myself, φροντίζω, 288.
Between, μεταξύ, 28.
Beyond, παρά (acc.), 299.
Bid, κελεύω, 112.
Bird, ὄρνις. See 15, note g.
————— : young—, νεοσσός, 214.
Birth, γένος, n. 150.
Black, μέλας, 20.
Blame, μέμφομαι, dat., ἐγκαλέω, dat.
183.
Body, σῶμα, 138.
Boldly, θαῤῥῶν. part. 331.
Both, ἄμφω, ἀμφότερος. See 28.
Both—and, καί—καί, or τέ—καί, 112.
Both in other respects—and also, ἄλλως
τε καί, 278.
Boy, παῖς, 15.

————————————————————

† How to translate ' before ' by φθάνω, see 240, d.

Brave, ἀνδρεῖος, 175.
——- a danger, κινδυνεύειν κίνδυνον, 127, d.
Bread, ἄρτος, 299.
Break, ἄγνυμι, κατάγνυμι (?), 193.
—— (a law), παραβαίνω, 228.
Breast, στέρνον, 193.
Bring, ἄγω, 341.
——- assistance to, ἐπικουρέω, dat. also acc. of the thing, 239.
——- forth, τίκτω (?), 15.
——- up, τρέφω, 190.—παιδεύω, 214.
τρέφω relates to physical, παιδεύω to moral education : i. e. τρέφω to the body, παιδεύω to the mind.
——- bad news, νεώτερόν τι ἀγγέλλειν, 311, g.
Brother, ἀδελφός, 20.
Burn out, ἐκκαίω, 341, καύσω, &c.—ἐκαύθην.
But, δέ—(a μέν should be in the former clause), 38, h.
——- for, εἰ μὴ διά, with acc. 125.
Buy, ἀγοράζω, 163.
By { ὑπό, with gen. of agent, 326.
{ πρός, after to be praised or blamed by.
— (= close by), πρός, 319.
— (= cause), ὑπό, gen. and after passive verb, 326.
— Jupiter, &c., νὴ Δία, νὴ τὸν Δία, 341.
— the hands of, ὑπό, gen. 326.
— the father's side, πρὸς πατρός, 319.
— fives, &c, ἀνὰ πέντε, 259.
— what conduct ? τί ἂν ποιοῦντες; 339, a.
— compulsion, ὑπ' ἀνάγκης, 326.

C.

Calculate, λογίζεσθαι πρὸς ἑαυτόν, 319.
Calumniously : to speak—of, λοιδορέομαι, dat. 183.
Can, δύναμαι (possum), 87.—οἷος τέ εἰμι (queo), 280. The former relates to power, the latter to condition or qualification. Aug. of δύναμαι?
Can; that can be taught, } διδακτός.
Capable of being taught, }
Care for, κήδομαι (gen.), 156.
Carefully provide for, ἔχεσθαι, gen. 146, d.
Cares, φροντίδες, 150.
Carry a man over, περαιοῦν, 188 (1).

Catch (in commission of a crime), ἁλίσκομαι (?), 74, s.
Cause, αἴτιον, 100.
——- to be set before me, παρατίθεμαι, 188.
Cavalry, ἱππεῖς (pl. of ἱππεύς), 96.
Cease, παύομαι of what may be only a temporary, λήγω of a final cessation, at least for the time. λήγω terminates the action ; παύομαι breaks its continuity, but may, or may not, terminate it. They govern gen., 154. 188 (1).—παύομαι with partic. 239.
Certain (a), τίς, 13, d.
Character : of a—to, εἶναι οἷος (inf.), 280.
Charge (enemy), ἐλαύνειν εἰς, sometimes ἐπί, 96.
——- with, ἐγκαλέω, dat. of pers., acc. of thing, 183.
——- κατηγορέω †, gen. 156.
——- : prosecute on a—, διώκειν, gen. of crime, 35.
——- : am tried on a—, φεύγειν, gen. of crime, 35.
Chase, θήρα, 154.
Chastise, κολάζω, F. M., 121.
Chatter, λαλέω, 288.
Child, παιδίον, 150.
Childless, ἄπαις, 150.
Choose, αἱρέομαι (?), 190, a.
——- : what I choose to do, ἃ δοκεῖ (μοι), 96. See Diff 33.
Citizen, πολίτης (ῑ). 8.
City, πόλις, f. 8.—ἄστυ, n. 24. Ἄστυ refers to the site or buildings : πόλις to the citizens. Hence ἄστυ never means ' state,' as πόλις so often does. The ἄστυ was often an old or sacred part of a πόλις.
Clever, σοφός, 20. δεινός, 214.
Cleverness, σοφία, 24.
Cling to, ἔχεσθαι, gen. 146, d.
Close by, ἐπί, dat. 288. πρός, 319.
Collect, ἀθροίζω, 175.
Combat a disorder, ἐπικουρεῖν νόσῳ, 239.
Come, ἔρχομαι (?), 112, h.
——- : am—, ἥκω, perf. meaning, 206.
——- (= be present to assist), παρεῖναι, 92.
——- for this (to effect it), ἐλθεῖν ἐπὶ τούτῳ.
——— (to fetch it), ἐλθεῖν ἐπὶ τοῦτο.
——- off, ἀπαλλάττω (ἐκ or ἀπό), 154.

† See note on Accuse.

Come on *or* up, πρόσειμι, 175.
―――- next to, ἔχεσθαι, *gen.*
―――: said that he would―, ἔφη ἥξειν,
    89, *b, or* εἶπεν ὅτι ἥξοι, 195, *e.*
Command (an army), στρατηγέω, 52.
Commence a war, ἄρασθαι πόλεμον
    πρός, *acc.* 188.
Commit, ἐπιτρέπω, *dat.* 132.
―――― a sin, ἁμαρτάνω (?) (εἰς *or*
    περί, with *acc.*), 154.
―――― an injury, ἀδικεῖν ἀδικίαν, 138.
Company, ὁμιλία, 112.
―――: keep―, ὁμιλέω, *dat.*
Complaint (a), ἀσθένεια (= a *weakness,*
    an *infirmity*), 319.
Concerned, as far as this is,⎫ τούτου γε
―――― - as far at least ⎬ ἕνεκα, 249.
    as this is,   ⎭
Condemn, καταγιγνώσκω (?), 156, obs.
Condition : on―, ἐφ' ᾧ *or* ᾧτε, 267.
Confer benefits on, εὖ ποιεῖν, *acc.* 35.
Confess, ὁμολογέω, 190.
Confide to, ἐπιτρέπω, 132.
Conquer, νικάω (*vincere ;* gain a victory
    over *enemies*) ; περιγίγνεσθαι (?),
    overcome (*gen.*). ☞ ' Iu' *omitted after*
    conquer *when it stands before* ' battle,'
    217, *e.*
Consider, σκοπέω (of carefully *examin-
    ing* and reflecting on a point', 100.―
    φροντίζω (of *anxious* consideration),
    288. ― with oneself, παρ' ἑαυτὸν
    (σκοπεῖν *or* σκέπτεσθαι), 319.
Considerable, συχνός, 163.
Consideration, ἀξίωμα, 144.
Constitution, πολιτεία, 206.
Consult, βουλεύειν, 190.
―――― together, βουλεύεσθαι, 190.
Consume, ἀναλίσκω (?), 235.
Contemporary with, to be. See 183.
    177, *a.*
Contend with, ἐρίζω, *dat.* 183.
Contention, ἔρις, ιδος, 183.
Continuous, συχνός, 163.
Contrary to, παρά (*acc.*), 299.
Contrivance, τέχνη, 214.
Corn, σῖτος, 259.
Corpse, νεκρός, 150.
Country, χώρα (a country), 24.―πα-
    τρίς (native country *or* native city),
    228.
Crocodile, κροκόδειλος, 28.
Cross (a river), περαιοῦσθαι, with *aor.
    pass.* 188 (1).
Crowded, δασύς, 150.
Crown, στέφανος, 144.
Cry, κλαίω (?), 150. δακρύω, 282.
Cultivate, ἀσκέω, 121. Aor. mid.?
    p. 63, *d.*

Custom: according to―, ⎱ κατὰ τὸ
―――: as his―was, ⎰ εἰωθός, 52.
Cut, τέμνω (?), 46.
―――- out, ἐκκόπτω, 132.
―――- to pieces, κατακόπτω, 132.
Cyrus, Κῦρος, 24.

D.

Damage : to inflict the most―, πλεῖστα
    κακουργεῖν (*acc.*).
Damsel, κόρη, 15.
Dance, χορεύω, 168*.
Danger, κίνδυνος, 132.
―――― (to brave, incur, expose oneself
    to, a), κινδυνεύειν κίνδυνον.
Dare,.τολμάω, 239.
Daughter, θυγάτηρ (?), 20.
Dead, νεκρός, 150.
Death, θάνατος, 41.
Deceive, ἀπατάω, ἐξαπατάω, 41.
Decide, κρίνω (?), 92.
Defend, ἀμύνειν with *dat.* only, 222.
Deliberate, βουλεύεσθαι περί, *gen.* 190.
Delight, τέρπω, 41.
Deny, ἀρνέομαι, 293.
Depends on you, ἐν σοὶ ἔστι, 259.
Deprive of, ἀποστερέω, 125. στερέω,
    168*.
Desire, ἐπιθυμέω, *gen.* ἐπιθυμία, 156.
Desist from, λήγω, *gen.* 154.
Despicable, φαῦλος, 144.
Despise, ὀλιγωρέω, *gen.* καταφρονέω,
    gen. 156.
Destroy, διαφθείρω (?), 92. ἀπόλλυμι(?),
    193.
Determined (when *or* though we have,
    &c.), δόξαν ἡμῖν, 245, *c.*
Die, θνήσκω, ἀποθνήσκω (?), 125.
Differ, διαφέρω (?), *gen.* 154.
Difficult, χαλεπός, 65, 214.
Dine, δειπνέω, 288.
Dining-room, ἀνώγεων, *n.* 96.
Directly, εὐθύς, 309.
―――――, *by* φθάνω, 240.
―――――- to, εὐθύ (*gen.*), 309.
Disappear : to make to―, ἀφανίζω,
    306.
Disappeared, φροῦδος, 65.
Disbelieve, ἀπιστέω, *dat.* 132.
Disease, νόσος, *f.* 154.
Disgraceful, αἰσχρός, 35.
Dishonour, ἀτιμάζω, 319.
Disobey, ἀπιστέω, *dat.* 132.
Disposition, ἦθος, *n.* 138. τρόπος, 150.
Dispute with, ἐρίζω, *dat.* 183.
Do, 8, πράττειν (= *agere* and *gerere*)
    denotes generally the exertion of

power upon an object: to *do;* to *employ oneself about something already existing;* hence, to *manage* or *administer* any thing; to *conduct a business.* Hence used with *general* notions, as οὐδέν, μηδέν, and with *adverbs,* εὖ, &c.—ποιεῖν (*facere*), to *make,* to *prepare,* &c.: also 'do' generally, when the object is a neuter pronoun, as in '*what must I do?*'—πράττειν denotes *activity* generally; ποιεῖν, *productive* activity.

Do the greatest injury, τὰ μέγιστα βλάπτειν (*acc.*).

—: to *be doing well* or *ill,* εὖ or κακῶς πράττειν.

— any thing whatever for the sake of gain, ἀπὸ παντὸς κερδαίνειν, 280.

— evil towards, κακουργέω, 222.

— good to, εὖ ποιεῖν, *acc.* 35.

— harm to, κακουργέω, 222.

— injustice to, ἀδικέω, 138.

— kind offices to, εὖ ποιεῖν, *acc.* 35.

— nothing but, οὐδὲν ἄλλο ἤ (ποιεῖν *often omitted*), 357, *e.*

— service to, ὠφελέω, 82.

— with (a thing), χράομαι, *dat.* (*contraction?*) 138.

Dog, κύων (?), 41.

Doors : in—, ἔνδον, 125.

Down, κάτω, 28.

—- from, κατά (*gen.*), 274.

Downwards, κάτω, 28.

Drachma, δραχμή, 163.

Draw up (of an army), τάσσω, 96.

——- = arrange, κοσμέω, 206.

Drawn up four deep, ἐπὶ τεττάρων τετάχθαι, 288.

Drink, πίνω (?), 144.

During the disease, κατὰ τὴν νόσον, 274.

Dwell, οἰκέω, 273.

E.

Each, πᾶς, 46.

Eagle, ἀετός, 36.

Ear, οὖς, ὠτός, *n.* 20.

Early in the morning, πρωΐ, 193.

Easy, ῥάδιος. See 65.

Eat, ἐσθίω (?), 144.

Educate, παιδεύω, 214.

Egg, ὠόν, 15.

Elect = *choose,* αἱρεῖσθαι (?) (ἀντί), 190, *a.*

Elephant, ἐλέφας, ντος, *m.* 35.

Empty, μάταιος, 206.

Enact laws : when θεῖναι νόμους? when θέσθαι? See 188.

Endeavour, πειράομαι, 121, 206.

Endure, ἀνέχομαι (?), 214.

Enemy (the), οἱ πολέμιοι, 46.

Engage in a war, ἄρασθαι πόλεμον πρός, *acc.* 188.

Enjoy, ἀπολαύω (*gen.*), 259.

Enough : to be —, ἀρκεῖν, 175.

——: more than enough, περιττὰ τῶν ἀρκούντων, 170, f.

—— τὰ ἀρκοῦντα (i. e. things that suffice).

Entrust, ἐπιτρέπω, πιστεύω, 132.

—— to, ἐπιτρέπω (lays more stress on the *entire giving up* of the thing in question, so that it is now quite in the other person's hands). — πιστεύω (gives more prominence to the fact that I put *sufficient confidence* in the other person to entrust the thing in question to him), 132.

Envy, φθόνος: (v.) φθονέω, *dat.* 183.

Equestrian exercises, τὰ ἱππικά, 163.

Equivalent to, ἀντί, *adv.*

Err, ἁμαρτάνω (?), 154.

Escape from, φεύγω, *acc.* 87.

Especially, ἄλλως τε καί, 278.

——: and—, καί, *referring to* ἄλλος, 347.

Even, καί, 82.

Ever, ποτέ, 87. ἀρχήν or τὴν ἀρχήν, 132.

Every, πᾶς, 46.

—— body, πᾶς τις, 52. (οὐδεὶς ὅστις οὐ, 276.)

—— day, ἀνὰ πᾶσαν ἡμέραν, 259.

—— five years, διὰ πέντε ἐτῶν, 269.

Evidently. See 239.

Evil-doer, κακοῦργος, 222.

Evils (= *bad things*), κακά, 20.

Exact (payment), πράττεσθαι, 163.

Examine (a question, &c.), σκοπέω, 100.

Except, πλήν (*gen.*).

—— if, πλὴν εἰ, 309.

Excessive, ὁ ἀγᾶν (*adv.* with *art.*), 228.

Excessively, ἀγᾶν, 228.

Exclude from, εἴργω, 154.

Exercise, ἀσκέω, 121.

Existing things, τὰ ὄντα, 65.

Expediency, τὸ συμφέρον, 228.

Expedient, 228. vide *It is.*

Expedition (to go on an), στρατεύω, 65.

Expose myself to a danger, κινδυνεύειν κίνδυνον, 132.

External (things),·τὰ ἔξω, 125.

Extremely (like). See 87.

Eye, ὀφθαλμός, 132.

F.

Faith, πίστις, *f.* 132.

Faithful, πιστός, 87.

Fall, πίπτω (?), 293.

—— in with, ἐντυγχάνω (?), *dat.* 183.

M

162 INDEX I.

Fall into a person's power, γίγνεσθαι
ἐπί τινι, 293.
Family, γένος, n. 150.
Far, far on, πόρρω: = much, πολύ, 144.
—- from it, πολλοῦ δεῖν, 282.
Fast, ταχύς, 35.
Father, πατήρ (?), 20.
Fault: to find—with, ἐπιτιμάω,dat. 183.
Fear, φοβέομαι (fut. mid. and pass.:
aor. pass.), 41.—δείδω (of a lasting
apprehension or dread), 293*.
— (subst.) φόβος.
— δέος, n. 326.
Feasible, ἀνυστός, 175.
Feel grateful or thankful, χάριν εἰδέναι†,
gen. of thing, 222.
— pain, ἀλγέω, 20.
— sure, πέποιθα (πείθω), 120.
Fetch (of things sold), εὑρίσκω (?), 87.
Fight, μάχομαι (?), 73.
—- against, πρός τινα, 319.
—- on horseback, ἀφ' ἵππων, 243.
—- with, μάχομαι‡, dat. 183.
Find, εὑρίσκω, 87 ; to be found guilty,
ἁλῶναι with gen. 73.
— a man at home, ἔνδον καταλαβεῖν,
125.
— fault with, ἐπιτιμάω, dat. 183.
— out, εὑρίσκειν (?).
Fire, πῦρ, n. 41.
First (the—of all), ἐν τοῖς πρῶτος. See
259.
Fit to govern, ἀρχικός, gen.
Five-and-five, ἀνὰ πέντε.
Fix, πήγνυμι, 193.
—: am fixed, πέπηγα, perf. 2.
Flatter, κολακεύω, 87.
Flatterer, κόλαξ, 87.
Flesh, κρέας, n. (G. αος, ως,) 144.
Flog, μαστιγόω, 235.
Flow, ῥέω (?), 132.
— with a full or strong stream. See 132.
Fly from, φεύγω, 35.
—- for refuge, καταφεύγω, 41.
—- to the assistance of, βοηθέω, dat. 121.
Follow, ἕπομαι, dat. 183.
Folly, μωρία, 156.
Fond of honour, φιλότιμος, 214.
— gain, φιλοκερδής, 319.
Food (for man), σῖτος, 259.
Foot, πούς, ποδός, m. 20.
For (= in behalf of), πρό, 243.
For, γάρ, 41 ; for one's interest, 319.
—- such a man as me at least, οἵῳ γε
ἐμοί, 279, z.
—- the sake of, ἕνεκα gen. 214. χάριν
gen. 250.

For my sake, χάριν ἐμήν, 250.
—- praise, ἐπ' ἐπαίνῳ, 288.
—- the present at least, τό γε νῦν εἶναι,
206.
—- this cause or reason, ἐκ ταύτης τῆς
αἰτίας, ἐκ τούτου, 224.
—- your years, πρὸς τὰ ἔτη, 175.
—- a long time, gen. χρόνου συχνοῦ,
πολλῶν ἡμερῶν; 158*, e.
Force, κράτος, n. 41.
Forefather, πρόγονος, 156.
Foresee, προγιγνώσκειν. See 235.
Forget, ἐπιλανθάνομαι (?), gen. 156.
Form an alliance, σύμμαχον ποιεῖσθαί
τινα, 188 (2).
Former, ὁ πρίν, 156 (27).
Formerly, πάλαι, 28.
Forth from, ἐκ, ἐξ, gen.
Fortify, τειχίζω, 222.
Fortune, τύχη, 92.
Forwardness, τὸ πρόθῡμον, adj. 60.
Fountain, πηγή, 132.
Fourth, τέταρτος, 52.
Fowl. See 15, note 8.
Free, ἐλεύθερος, 150.
— from, ἀπαλλάττω, gen. 154.
Freedom, ἐλευθερία, 150.
Frequently, πολλάκις, 8.
Friend, φίλος, 20.
From (after receive, learn, bring, come),
παρά, 299. ὑπό (gen.), 326.
— (after hear), πρός (gen.), 319.
— our very birth, εὐθὺς γενόμενοι,
309.
— fear, ὑπὸ δέους, 326.
— (of cause), sign of dat.
Front, ὁ πρόσθεν, 282.
Full of, μεστός, 150.
Full speed (at), ἀνὰ κράτος, 41.
Future (the), τὸ μέλλον, 235.

G.

Gain, κερδαίνω. κέρδος, n. 282.
Gate, πύλη, 193.
General, στρατηγός, 52.
Gentle, πρᾶος (?), 138.
Geometer, γεωμέτρης, ου, 24.
Get, κτάομαι (of what will be retained
as a possession), 87.—τυγχάνειν with
gen. (of what is obtained accidentally,
by good luck, &c.) 183, b.—εὑρίσκεσ-
θαι (to get possession of an object
sought for).
—- τυγχάνω, gen. 183, b. εὑρίσκομαι,
188.
—- hold of, κρατέω, 163.
—- off, ἀπαλλάττω ἐκ or ἀπό, 154.

† For conjug. of εἰδέναι, see p. 21, note 9.
‡ For conjug. see 73.

Get (teeth, &c.), φύω, 214.
—- taught, διδάσκομαι, 188.
—- the better of, περιγίγνομαι (gen.),
87. περίειμι (gen.), 156.
Gift, δῶρον, 175.
Give, δίδωμι, 41.
—— one trouble; πόνον or πράγματα
παρέχειν, 214.
—— orders, ἐπιτάττω, 359.
—— a share of, μεταδίδωμι, 175.
—— some of, μεταδίδωμι, 175.
—— a taste of, γεύειν, acc. of pers.,
gen. of thing.
—— to taste, γεύω (gen. of thing), 150.
Given : to be—, δοτέος, 144.
Gladly, ἡδέως.
Go, ἔρχομαι (?), 112.
— away, ἄπειμι (= will go away. See
note 65, g).—ἀπέρχομαι, 112.
— in to, εἰσέρχομαι παρά, 107, d.
— into, εἰσέρχομαι, 112.
— on an expedition, στρατεύω, 65.
— and do a thing, 343 (h), 350.
God, Θεός.
Gold, χρυσός, m. as a sum of gold
money, χρυσίον, 35.
Golden, χρύσεος, οῦς, 144.
Good, ἀγαθός—ἀμείνων, ἄριστος, 35.
Govern, ἄρχω (gen.), 150.
Government, ἀρχή, 132.
Gratify, χαρίζομαι, 273.
Great, μέγας (?).
Greater, greatest, μείζων, μέγιστος, 46.
Greatly (with injure, benefit, &c.), μέγα.
=far, πολύ, 156.
Greece, Ἑλλάς, άδος, f. 144.
Greek, Ἕλλην, ηνος, 144.
Grudge, φθονέω, gen. of object, dat. of
pers., 183.
Guard, φυλάττω, 190, e.
——— against, φυλάττεσθαι, acc. 190.
Guard, }
Guardian, } φύλαξ (κ).

H.

Habit : in the—of performing, πρακ-
τικός, gen. 146, a.
Hair, θρίξ, τριχός, f. 175.
Half, ἥμισυς. See 59.
Hand, χείρ, f. (?) 20.
Hang oneself, ἀπάγχομαι, 188 (1).
Happen, τυγχάνω †, 240, b.
Happened : what had—, τὸ γεγονός.
Happy, εὐδαίμων, ονος, 20.
Harass, πόνον or πράγματα παρέχειν,
214.
Hard, χαλεπός, 65, 214.
Hare, λαγώς. See 15.

Harm : come to some—, παθεῖν τι (suffer
something).
Haste, σπουδή, 183.
Have, ἔχω. See 15, note i.
—— a child taught, διδάσκομαι, 125, t.
—— an opportunity : when or though
you have, &c., παρόν, 250.
—— a narrow escape, παρὰ μικρὸν
ἐλθεῖν, 299.
———————————— παρ' ὀλίγον
διαφεύγειν, 299.
—— any regard for, κήδομαι, gen. 156.
—— confidence in, πέποιθα, 193.
—— done supper, ἀπὸ δείπνου γενέσθαι, 243.
—— in one's hand, διὰ χειρὸς ἔχειν, 269.
—— lost, στερέω, 168*.
—— no fear of, θαῤῥέω, acc. 138.
—— slain a man with one's own hand,
αὐτόχειρ εἶναι, 299.
—— the tooth-ache (= suffer pain in
my teeth), ἀλγῶ τοὺς ὀδόντας. See
17, b.
Head, κεφαλή, 20.
Hear, ἀκούω, F. M. 92.—on its government, see 148.
Hearing: there is nothing like—, οὐδὲν
οἷον ἀκοῦσαι, 278.
Heavy, βαρύς, 183.
Heavy-armed soldier, ὁπλίτης, 154.
Hen, ὄρνις. See 15, note g.
Henceforth, τὸ ἀπὸ τοῦδε, 30, f.
Hercules, Ἡρακλῆς, 183.
Here, ἐνθάδε, 28.
Hide, δορά, 35.
———, κρύπτω, ἀποκρύπτω, 125.
Hill, λόφος, 288.
Hinder, κωλύω, ἀποκωλύω, 293.
Hire, μισθοῦμαι, 158.
Hit (a mark), τυγχάνω, 183 (note) †.
Hold a magistracy or office, ἄρχειν
ἀρχήν, 132.
—— cheap, ὀλιγωρέω (gen.), 156.
—— my tongue about, σιωπάω, F. M. 87.
———————— (without acc.), σιγάω,
F. M. 269*.
Home : at—, ἔνδον, 125.
———, to find a man at—, ἔνδον κατα-
λαβεῖν, 125.
Honey, μέλι, ιτος, n. 132.
Honorable, καλός, 32.
Honour, τιμή, 150.
Hope, ἐλπίζω, 87.
Hoplite, ὁπλίτης, 154.
Horn, κέρας, n. (?) 35.
Horse, ἵππος, 15.
——- soldier, ἱππεύς, 96.
House, οἶκος, 41.

† For conjug. of τυγχάνω, see 183.

How much, πόσον, 87.
Hunting, θήρα, 154.
Hurt, βλάπτω, 82.

I.

I at least, ἔγωγε, 156.
I for my part, ἔγωγε, 156.
Idle, ἀργός, 299.
If any body has ... it is you, εἴ τις
καὶ ἄλλος (ἔχεις, &c.), 170, d.
— it is agreeable to you, εἴ σοι βουλο-
μένῳ ἐστί, 206
— it should appear that I ... ἐὰν φαίνωμαι, &c. with partic. 239, c.
— you are willing, εἴ σοι βουλομένῳ
ἐστί, 206.
Ill, κακῶς, 8.
— (adj. = weak), ἀσθενής, 319.
Imitate, μιμέομαι.
Immediately, εὐθύς, 309.—how to translate it by φθάσας, &c., see 240, f.
——— on his arrival, εὐθὺς ἥκων,
309.
Immortal, ἀθάνατος, 125.
Impiety, ἀσέβεια, 156.
Impious, ἀνόσιος, 299. ἀσεβής, 156.
Impossible, ἀδύνατος, 65.
Impudence, ἀναίδεια, 87.
Impunity : with—, χαίρων (rejoicing).
In addition to, ἐπί (dat.), 288. πρὸς
τούτοις, 319.
— (in answer to where?) ἐν, dat. 259.
— (a man's) power, ἐπί with dat. of the
person, 65.
— (after to conquer), omitted, 127, e.
— all respects, πάντα, 134. κατὰ πάντα, 274.
— an uncommon degree, διαφερόντως,
235.
— behalf of, πρό, 243.
— comparison of, πρός, 319.
— (= in doors), ἔνδον, 125.
— preference to, ἀντί, 214.
— proportion to, κατά (acc.), 274.
— reality, τῷ ὄντι, 65.
— reference to, εἰς, 259. πρός, acc. 319.
— (space or time), ἀνά, 259.
— the time of, ἐπί with gen. 65.
——- habit of doing, πρακτικός, 150.
——- world, who? τίς ποτε, 150.
Incur a danger, κινδυνεύειν κίνδυνον,
132.
——— danger, κινδυνεύειν, 132.
Indeed, μέν, 38, h.
Infinitely many, μυρίοι, 228.
Infirmity, ἀσθένεια, 319.
Inflict damage on, κακουργέω, 222.
Injure = hurt, βλάπτω, 82. ἀδικέω, 138.
Injury : do an—to, βλάπτω.

Injury : to commit an—, ἀδικεῖν ἀδι-
κίαν, 138.
Injustice, ἀδικία, 82. to do—to, ἀδικέω,
138.
Insolence, ὕβρις, 138, f.
Insolent person, ὑβριστής.
Instead of, ἀντί, 214.
Insult, ὑβρίζω, acc. ὕβρις, f. 138.
Interest, for a man's—to be translated
by πρός, with the gen. of person, 319.
Intermediate, μεταξύ, 26.
Into, εἰς, acc.
Intoxication, μέθη, 326.
Is a good thing for, ⎫
— advantageous to, ⎪ ἔστι πρός
— characteristic of, ⎬ (τινος), 319.
— consistent with, ⎪
— like, ⎭
— enough, or sufficient for, ἀρκεῖ, 175.
— to be, μέλλει ἔσεσθαι, 280, h.
— of a character to, ἐστὶν οἷος, 280, b.
It being disgraceful, αἰσχρὸν ὄν, 250.
— being evident, δῆλον ὄν, 250.
— being fit, προσῆκον, 250.
— being impossible, ἀδύνατον ὄν, 250.
— being incumbent, προσῆκον, 250.
— being plain, δῆλον ὄν, 250.
— being possible, δυνατὸν ὄν, 250.
— depends on you, ἐν σοὶ ἔστι, 259.
— is allowed (licet), ἔξεστι, 112.
— is expedient, συμφέρει, dat. 228.
— is necessary, ἀνάγκη (omitting the
verb), 65.
— is not a thing that every body can do,
οὐ παντός ἐστι, 158.
— is not every body that can, 163, 280.
— is possible, οἷον τέ ἐστι, 282.
— is profitable, συμφέρει, dat. 228.
— is right, ὀρθῶς ἔχει, 222.
— is right that, δίκαιόν ἐστι, 353, a.
— is the nature of, πέφυκα, ἔφυν, 214.
— is the part of, ἔστι (gen.), 158*, h.

J.

Jaw, γνάθος, f. 26.
Journey (v.), πορεύομαι, 24. στέλλο-
μαι (?), 188 (1).
Judge, κριτής (general term), 8.—δι-
καστής (only of a judge in the strict
sense), 239, x : (verb) κρίνω, 92.
Jupiter, Ζεύς, Διός, &c. voc. Ζεῦ, 193.
Just, δίκαιος, 87.
Just as he was, ᾗπερ or ὥσπερ εἶχεν, 351.

K.

Keep company with, ὁμιλέω, dat. 183.
——— (for one's self), αἱρεῖσθαι, 188.
Kill, ἀποκτείνω (?), 82.
King, βασιλεύς, 24.

Knee, γόνυ, γόνατ, n. 20.
Knock out, ἐκκόπτω (aor. 2 pass.), 132.
Know, οἶδα (of positive *knowledge*), 73.
—γιγνώσκω (seek to become acquainted with), aor. ἔγνων, know (from *acquaintance* with it): (with *partic.*, 229.)
—— (γιγνώσκω), 235.
—— how, ἐπίσταμαι (?), 293.
——: I don't—, οὐκ ἔχω, or οὐκ οἶδα, 67.

L.

Labour, πόνος, (v. πονέω,) 154.
Laid myself down, κατεκλίθην, 190.
Lamb, ἀμνός, 41.
Large, μέγας.
(At) last, τὸ τελευταῖον, 30, f.
Laugh, γελάω, ἄσομαι, 222. }
—— at, καταγελάω, 278. } F. M.
Laughter, γέλως, ωτος, 278.
Law, νόμος, 132.
Lawful, θέμις (= *fas*), 65. ὅσιος, δίκαιος, 293.
Lay down, κατατίθημι, 163.
—- eggs, τίκτω (?), 15.
—- to the charge of, κατηγορέω, 156.
—- waste, τέμνω (?), 46.
Lazy, ἀργός, 299.
Lead, ἄγω, 341.
Lead (of a *road*), φέρω, 73.
Leaf, φύλλον, 214.
Leap, ἅλλομαι, 273.
Learn, (with *partic.*) μανθάνω (?), 239.
Leather bottle, ἀσκός, 15.
Leave off, λήγω, gen., 154. παύομαι, 188 (1).
Leisure, σχολή, 112.
Let for hire, μισθόω, 188.
Liberty, ἐλευθερία, 150.
Lie down, κατακλίνομαι (κατεκλίθην), 190.
Life, βίος, 28. by *infin.*, τὸ ζῆν, 150.
Lift up, αἴρειν, 188 (2).
Like a dog, κυνὸς δίκην, 250.
—— ὅμοιος, (*dat.*) 183.
—— ἀγαπάω, 52.
—— to do it = *do it gladly* (ἡδέως).
——, should like to ... ἡδέως ἄν, 87.
——, should extremely like to.. ἥδιστ' ἄν, 87.
Likely, εἰκός (*neut. part.*), 331.
Lily, κρίνον (?), 144.
Little (a little), ὀλίγῳ, 168*.
Live, ζάω, 127, d. b.
—— (= spend one's life), διατελέω, 60.
—— about the same time, κατὰ τὸν αὐτὸν χρόνον γενέσθαι, 183.
Long (of *time*), συχνός, 163. μακρός, 214.

Long ago, πάλαι, 28.
Loss: to be at a—, ἀπορέω, 99.
Love, φιλέω (of *love* arising from regard, and the perception of good and amiable qualities), 20. — ἀγαπάω (stronger ; implying affection arising from the *heart*, &c.), 52.—ἐράω † (of the *passion* of love), 274.
Lover of self, φίλαυτος, 222.
Lower, ὁ κάτω (*art.* with *adv.*).

M.

Madness, μανία, 24.
Magistracy, ἀρχή, 132.
Maiden, κόρη, 15.
Maintain, τρέφω (?), 190.
Make to cease, παύω, gen. of that from which, 154.
—— to disappear, ἀφανίζω, 206.
—— a great point of, περὶ πολλοῦ ποιεῖσθαι or ἡγεῖσθαι, 282.
—— progress, προχωρέω, 274.
—— immense (or astonishing) progress, θαυμαστὸν ὅσον προχωρεῖν, 271, c.
—— self-interest the object of one's life, πρὸς τὸ συμφέρον ζῆν, 228.
—— for one's interest, εἶναι πρός (gen.), 319.
Male, ἄρρην, 150.
Man, 46. (*Obs.*)
——: am not a man to, 280, note a.
Manage, πράττω, 8.
Many, πολύς, 46. the many, οἱ πολλοί, 46.
—— times as many or much, πολλαπλάσιοι (αι, α), 175.
——— numerous, πολλαπλάσιοι, 175.
March, ἐλαύνω (?), πορεύομαι, 24.
—- of a single soldier, εἶμι (?), 96.
Mare, ἵππος, f. 15.
Mark, σκοπός, 183, b.
Market-place, ἀγορά, 154.
Master, δεσπότης, 222.
—— διδάσκαλος (= *teacher*), 168.
—— (v.) κρατέω, (gen.) 156.
May (one—), ἔξεστι, 222.
—— (*though* or *when* I may), παρόν, 250.
Meet, ἐντυγχάνω, dat. 183.
Might (one—), ἐξῆν, 222.
—— (*when* or *though I*, &c. might), παρόν, 250.
Mild, πρᾷος (?), 138.
Milk, γάλα, γαλακτ, n. 132.
Mina, μνᾶ, 82.
Mind (as the seat of the passions), θῡμός, 121.
Mine, ἐμός, 20.
Minerva, Ἀθηνᾶ, 341.

---

† Aor. generally of sensual love, but ἔρασθαι τυραννίδος common.   *Pape.*

† καμοῦμαι, κέκμηκα.

Superhuman (of—size), μείζων ἢ κατ᾽
ἄνθρωπον, 165, d.
Superintend, ἐπισκοπέω, 206.
Supply to, παρέχω, 214.
Surpass, περίειμι (gen.), 156.
Surprised (am), θαυμάζω, F.M., 8.
Surprising, θαυμαστός, 259.
Surprisingly, θαυμασίως ὡς, 271, d.
Suspect, ὑποπτεύω, acc. of pers., 293*.
Swallow, χελιδών, ὄνος (?), 341.
Swear by, ὄμνυμι, acc. (?) 351.
Sweet, ἡδύς, 214.

T.

Table, τράπεζα, 188.
Take, λαμβάνω (?), 92. αἱρεῖν, 190.
—— away from, ἀφαιρέω, 125.
—— place. See Happen.
—— care, φροντίζω, 288.
—— hold of, λαβέσθαι, 163.
—— in hand, ἐπιχειρέω, dat. 121.
—— myself off, ἀπαλλάττομαι, 154.
Aor. 190, d.
—— off, ἐκδύω, 125.
—— pleasure in, ἥδομαι, dat. 20.
—— up, αἴρειν, 188 (2).
Talent, τάλαντον, 82.
Talk, λαλέω, 35.
Task, ἔργον, 121.
Taste : give to—, allow to—, γεύω (acc.
of person, gen. of thing).
Tasted, one who has never, ἄγευστος,
with gen. 150.
——, to have never, = to be ἄγευ-
στος (with gen.).
Taught, that can be—, διδακτός, 293*.
Teach, διδάσκω (?), 125.
Teacher, διδάσκαλος, 168*.
Tear, δάκρυον, 168*.
——, shed —, δακρύω, 282.
Temper, θυμός, 121.
Temperance, σωφροσύνη, 125, u.
Temperate, σώφρων, 125, u.
Temple, ναός (νεώς, Att.), 41.
Ten thousand, μύριοι, 228.
Terrible, δεινός, 214.
Thales, Θαλῆς (?), 183.
Than any other single person, εἷς ἀνήρ,
170, e. εἷς γε ἀνὴρ ὤν, 173.
—— ever, αὐτός with gen. of reciprocal
pronoun, 167.
Thankful, to be or feel, χάριν εἰδέναι †,
gen. of thing, 222.
Thanks, to return, χάριν εἰδέναι †, gen.
of thing, 222.
That, ἐκεῖνος, 46.
——, in order that, ἵνα, 73.
—— (after verbs of telling), ὅτι, 73.

The—the (with compar.), ὅσῳ—τοσ-
ούτῳ, 168*.
The one—the other, ὁ μέν—ὁ δέ, 38.
The morrow (the next day), ἡ αὔριον, 26.˙
Thebans, Θηβαῖοι, 125.
Theft, κλοπή, 73.
Then (time), τότε, 92.
—— (of inference), οὖν, 100.
—— in questions, εἶτα, 311, h. ἔπειτα,
311, i. (See 316.)
There, ἐκεῖ, 28.
—— (am), πάρειμι, 92.
—— being an opportunity, παρόν, 250.
——, to be, πάρειμι. See 89, b.
Therefore, ἐκ ταύτης τῆς αἰτίας, ἐκ
τούτου, 222.
Thick, δασύς, 150.
Thickly planted with trees, δασὺς δέν-
δρων, 150.
Thine, σός, 20.
Thing, πρᾶγμα, 8.
Things that are ; existing things, τὰ
ὄντα, 65.
Think, νομίζω, 52. οἴομαι (2 sing. οἴει),
87.
—— happy, εὐδαιμονίζω, 150.
Third, τρίτος, 52.
This, οὗτος, ὅδε, 46.
—— being determined, δόξαν ταῦτα,
245, c. See note º.
—— being the case, ἐκ τούτου, 224.
Three, τρεῖς, τρία, 15.
Through (of space, time, and means), διὰ
(τοῦ), 269.—(cause), διὰ (τόν), 326.
ὑπό, gen.
—— (the whole country), ἀνὰ πᾶ-
σαν τὴν γῆν, 259.
Throw, ῥίπτω, 235.
Thy, σός, 20.
Till late in the day, μέχρι πόρρω τῆς
ἡμέρας, 144.
Time, χρόνος, 28.
——, it is, ὥρα, 65.
——, in my, &c., ἐπ᾽ ἐμοῦ, 65.
To, 288, 319.
To Sardis, Chios, &c., ἐπὶ Σάρδεων,
ἐπὶ τῆς Χίου, 288.
To speak generally, ὡς ἔπος εἰπεῖν, 144.
Together with, σύν (omitted before
αὐτῷ, αὐτῇ, &c.), 345.
Toil, πόνος, 154.
To-morrow, αὔριον, 28.
Too (and that —), καὶ ταῦτα, 206.
—— great for, &c., comparative with ἢ
κατά before a subst., ἢ ὥστε before
infin., 168.
—— soon (after cannot), 240, c.
Tooth, ὀδούς, G. ὀδόντος, m. 20.

† For εἰδέναι, see p. 21, note q.

Touch, ἅπτομαι, 150.
Towards, after '*to act insolently,*' εἰς, 319.
———— πρός, 319. εἰς, 259.
———— home, ἐπ' οἶκον, 288.
Town, ἄστυ, *n.* 96.
Transact, πράττω, 8.
Transgress, παραβαίνω, 228.
Treat ill, κακῶς ποιεῖν, *acc.* 35.
———— well, εὖ ποιεῖν, *acc.* 35.
Treaty, σπονδαί, *pl.* 228.
Tree, δένδρον (?), 144.
Trick, τέχνη, 214.
Trouble, πόνος, 154.
True, ἀληθής, 274.
———— happiness, ἡ ὡς ἀληθῶς εὐδαιμονία, 274.
Trust (I) (= am confident), πέποιθα, 120, i; 193.
———— (have confidence in), πιστεύω with *dat.* only, 132.
Truth (the), τὸ ἀληθές, 274.
————, ἀλήθεια, 274.
Try (for murder), διώκειν φόνου, 35 ; (*am tried,*) φεύγειν, *gen.*
——-, πειράομαι (governs *gen.*)ₗ 121.
Tunic, χιτών, 125.
Turn, τρέπω, 73.
Turned (am—into), γίγνομαι (?), 15.
Twice as many, διπλάσιοι, 175.
Two by two, κατὰ δύο, 274.

U.

Uncommon degree (in an), διαφερόντως, 235.
Unconsciously, 240, *c* (1).
Uncovered, ψῖλός, 235.
Under, ὑπό, 326.
Undergo, ὑπομένω, 214.
Understanding, on an, ἐπὶ τῷ εἶναι, &c. 226, b.
Undertake an expedition, πορεύομαι, 24.
Unexpected, ἀπροσδόκητος, 224.
Unexpectedly, ἐξ ἀπροσδοκήτου, 224.
Unfortunate, κακοδαίμων, 144.
Unjust, ἄδικος, 138.
Unknown to myself, 240, *c.*
Unless, εἰ μή, 112.
Until, ἄχρι, μέχρι, ἕως, ἔστε, 306.
Up (*adv.*), ἄνω, 28. ἀνά (*prep.*), *acc.* 259.
Upper, ὁ ἄνω, 28.
Upper-chamber, ὑπερῷον, 96.
Upwards, ἄνω, 28.
Use, χράομαι, *dat.* (*contr.?*) 138.
Used to, *imperf.*, 94, t.
Useless, μάταιος, 206.
Utility, τὸ συμφέρον, 228.

V.

Vain, μάταιος, 206.
Value, τιμάομαι, 163.

Value very highly, πρὸ πολλοῦ ποιεῖσθαι, 243. περὶ πολλοῦ ποιεῖσθαι or ἡγεῖσθαι, 282.
Vanished, φροῦδος, 65.
(A) vast number, μυρίοι, 228.
Very, πάνυ, 214. περ, 78.
———— highly, πλεῖστον, 158*, b.
———— many, μυρίοι, 228.
———— well, ἄριστα.
Vexed, am—at, ἄχθομαι (?), *dat.* 20.
Victory, νίκη, 132.
Villages, in—, κατὰ κώμας, 274.
Villain, κακοῦργος, 222.
Villainy, κακουργία, 222.
Violet, ἴον, 144.
Virtue, ἀρετή, 8.
Voluntarily, ἐθελοντής, οὖ, 299.
Volunteer (as a), ἐθελοντής, 299.

W.

Wall, *v.* τειχίζω, (*subst.*) τεῖχος, *n.* 222.
Want, δέομαι, 150.
Wanted, if I am, &c., ἐάν τι δέῃ, or εἴ τι δέοι, 89, *a. b.*
War, πόλεμος.
Ward off, ἀμύνειν τί τινι, 222.
———— from myself, ἀμύνομαι, *acc.* 222.
Was near (=almost), ὀλίγου δεῖν, 280, *c.*
Wash, λούειν, 188 (1).
Watch over, ἐγρηγορέναι περί, *gen.* 193.
Water, ὕδωρ, *n.* 15.
Way, ὁδός, *f.* 154.
Weak, ἀσθενής, 319.
Weakness, ἀσθένεια, 319.
Wealthy, πλούσιος, 20.
Weep for, κατακλαίειν (?), 188 (2), 278.
Weigh anchor, αἴρειν (*anchor,* subaud.), 188.
Well, εὖ, 8.
———— to be, καλῶς ἔχειν.
What ? τί ;
———— kind of ? ποῖος ;
———— is, τὰ ὄντα, 65.
———— comes from (the gods), τὰ τῶν θεῶν, 54.
———— comes next (to), τὰ ἐχομένα, *gen.* 146, *d.*
———— induces you to ..? τί μαθών; 318.
———— possesses you to ..? τί παθών; 318.
———— , to—place, ποῖ, ὅποι, 144, 67, l.
———— we ought, ἃ χρή, 89, *c.*—τὰ δέοντα, 206.
Whatsoever, ὅστις, 92. εἴ τις, 269.
When, ὅτε, ἐπειδή, ἐπειδάν, 92.
——-? πότε ; 92.
——- you, he, &c. {may, {might, } {πάρον, } 250.
——- you ought, &c., δέον, 250.

INDEX II.

[List of PHRASES and WORDS explained †.]

A.

(ὁ) ἀγᾶν φόβος, 228.
ἀγαπᾶν τοῖς παροῦσι or τὰ παρόντα, 73.
ἄγων (= with), 235.
αἰσχύνομαι { ποιεῖν / ποιῶν } p. 73, note b.
αἰτεῖσθαι (mid.), not with two accusatives, 123, note.
Ἀλέξανδρος ὁ Φιλίππου, 22.
ἄλλο τι ἤ—; ἄλλοτι; 317.
ἄλλως τε καί, 278.
ἀλῶναι κλοπῆς, 73.
ἀμφότερον (-α), 346.
ἀνθ' ὧν, 268.
ἄνω, 8.
ἀπὸ σοῦ ἀρξάμενος, 100.
—- δείπνου γενέσθαι, 243.
—- τοῦ προφανοῦς, 243.
ἀποδιδράσκειν τινά, 138.
ἀρχήν or τὴν ἀρχήν, 132.
ἀρχόμενος, 235.
αὐτοῖς ἀνδράσιν, 343.
αὐτός, 40.   αὐτὸς αὐτοῦ, 165.
ἀφ' ἑαυτῶν, 243.

B.

βίου εὖ ἥκειν, 206.

Δ.

δεδογμένον, 245, n.
δεινότατος σαυτοῦ ἦσθα, 165, l.
δέον, 245, a.
δῆλός εἰμι, 239.
διαλιπὼν χρόνον, 235.
δι' ὀργῆς ἔχειν, &c., 269*.
δίκαιός εἰμι, 353.
δίκην διδόναι (gen.), 228.
διώκειν φόνου, 35.
δοκοῦν, 245, l.
δόξαν (δόξαν ταῦτα, &c.), 245, c.
δορὶ ἑλεῖν, 193, h.
δυνατώτεροι αὐτοὶ αὑτῶν, 165, e.
δυοῖν δέοντα (not δεόντοιν), 280.

E.

ἑαυτοῦ εἶναι, 158*, i.
ἐγκαλεῖν τί τινι, 183.
εἰ σοι βουλομένῳ ἐστίν, 206.

εἰ μέλλει γενέσθαι, 280.
εἰ μὴ διά, 125.
— τις, 269.
——- καὶ ἄλλος, 170, d.
εἴθ' ὤφελον (ες, ε), 206.
εἴργω, εἴργω, 154, b.
εἰρημένον, 250.
εἰς ἀνήρ, 170, e.
εἰς διδασκάλου (πέμπειν, φοιτᾶν), 259.
— τὴν Φιλίππου, 22.
εἰσὶν οἱ λέγοντες } 264, g.
——- οἳ λέγουσι }
ἐκινδύνευσεν ἂν διαφθαρῆναι, 359.
ἑκὼν εἶναι, 144.
ἐμποδὼν εἶναι, 293*
ἐν τοῖς πρῶτος, 259.
ἕνεκα τῶν ἑτέρων, 250.
ἔνδον καταλαβεῖν, 125.
ἐξ ἀπροσδοκήτου, 224.
ἐξόν, 245, b.
ἐπ' ἐμοί, 65.
ἐπ' ἐμοῦ, 65.
ἐπὶ τῷ εἶναι, 226, b.
ἐπικουρεῖν νόσῳ, 239.
ἐστιν οἵ (= ἔνιοι), 264.
—— οὕστινας . . . ; 262, d.
εὐθὺ τῆς πόλεως, 309.
εὐθὺς ἥκων, 309.
ἐφ' ᾧ or ᾧτε, 267.
ἔχεσθαί τινος, 146, d.
ἔχων (= with), 235.

H.

ἡ αὔριον, 26.
ἢ κατά, with acc. 165, d.
— ὥστε, with infin. 165, e.
ἡ πολλὴ τῆς χώρας (not τὸ πολύ), 59.
ἡδέως ἂν θεασαίμην, 84.
ἥπερ εἶχεν, 351.

Θ.

θαυμάσας ἔχω, 343.
θαυμασίως ὡς, 271, d.
θαυμαστὸν ὅσον, 271, c.
θεῖναι } νόμους, 188 (3).
θέσθαι }

K.

καὶ ὅς, 37, c.
— ταῦτα, 206.

---

† Phrases not found here may be looked for in their Alphabetical place in the *last* section.

INDEX III.

[List of Words that have some irregularity of Declension or Conjugation.]

Λ.

λαμβάνω, 92.
λανθάνω, 154.
λύω, 190.

Μ.

μαίνομαι, 125.
μάχομαι, 73.
μήτηρ, 20.

Ν.

ναῦς, 125.

Ο.

ὀδούς, 20.
ὄζω, 150.
οἶδα, 73, q.
οἴκαδε, 331.
οἴομαι, 87.
ὄϊς, 41, l.
οἴχομαι, 206, a.
ὄλλυμι, 193.
ὄμνυμι, 343, a.
ὁράω, 73.
ὄρνις, 15.
οὖς, 20.
ὀφείλω, 206.

Π.

παίζω, 343, c.
πάσχω, 168*.
πεινάω, 127, b.
πήγνυμι, 193.
πίνω, 144.

πίπτω, 293*.
πλέω, 188.
πορεύομαι, 24.
Ποσειδῶν, 341.
ποῦς, 20.
πρᾷος, 138.

Σ.

σιγάω, F.M., 269*.
σῖτος, 259, m.
σκοπῶ, 333, b.
στεροῦμαι, 168*.
Σωκράτης, 15.

Τ.

τέμνω, 46, q.
τίκτω, 15.
τιτρώσκω, 269*.
τρέχω, 65.
τυγχάνω, 183.

Υ.

ὕδωρ, 15.

Φ.

φέρω, 60.
φθάνω, 241.

Χ.

χείρ, 20.
χελιδών, 341.
χράομαι, 127, b.
χρή, 89, i.

THE END.

For EU product safety concerns, contact us at Calle de José Abascal, 56–1°, 28003 Madrid, Spain or eugpsr@cambridge.org.

www.ingramcontent.com/pod-product-compliance
Ingram Content Group UK Ltd.
Pitfield, Milton Keynes, MK11 3LW, UK
UKHW012343130625
459647UK00009B/492